D0810478

Victor D. Rappoport is an attorney who has specialized in entertainment law for the past eight years, and has been house counsel to various recording companies including MGM and ABC Records. In addition, Mr. Rappoport has been a member of several recording groups, is a musician and songwriter, and has managed recording artists.

VICTOR D. RAPPOPORT

A SPECTRUM BOOK

Prentice-Hall, Inc., Englewood Cliffs, N.J. 07632

Library of Congress Cataloging in Publication Data

Rappoport, Victor D.
  Making it in music.

  (A Spectrum Book)
  "Chapters 1 through 4 first published as The singer's and songwriter's sur-
vival kit . . . © 1974."
  Includes index.
  1. Music, Popular (Songs, etc.)–Writing and publishing. 2. Music trade–United
States. I. Title.
MT67.R29 1979   789.9 '1 '028   78-21620
ISBN 0-13-547612-7
ISBN 0 13-547604-6 pbk.

Chapters 1 through 4 first published as
*The Singer's and Songwriter's Survival
Kit* by Victor D. Rappoport,
© 1974 by Victor D. Rappoport, world rights reserved.
This expanded edition © 1979
by Prentice-Hall, Inc., Englewood Cliffs, New Jersey 07632

All rights reserved. No part of this book
may be reproduced in any form or
by any means without permission in writing
from the publisher.

A SPECTRUM BOOK

Printed in the United States of America

10   9   8   7   6   5   4   3   2   1

*Dedicated to my friend and wife, Nora-thea,
who is always full of ideas.*

Editorial/production supervision and interior design by Maria Carella
Manufacturing buyer: Cathie Lenard

PRENTICE-HALL INTERNATIONAL, INC., *London*
PRENTICE-HALL OF AUSTRALIA PTY., LIMITED, *Sydney*
PRENTICE-HALL OF CANADA, LTD., *Toronto*
PRENTICE-HALL OF INDIA PRIVATE, LIMITED, *New Delhi*
PRENTICE-HALL OF JAPAN, INC., *Tokyo*
PRENTICE-HALL OF SOUTHEAST ASIA PTE., LTD., *Singapore*
WHITEHALL BOOKS, LIMITED, *Wellington, New Zealand*

Contents

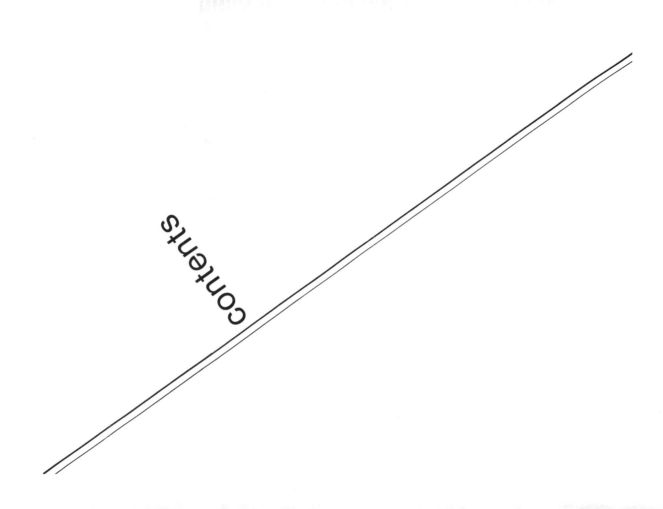

appendices *71*

index   *307*

introduction

Many people think of the record business only as a "glamour" industry containing exciting and creative people. While the above is true, you must remember that the record business is a business, and you should treat it as such. You should learn as much as possible about the record business so that you will be better equipped to protect yourself from the "rip-off artists" as well as being aware of the ways by which you can retain more of those cold hard dollars for yourself.

Although this book cannot begin to encompass all matters relating to the music business, I sincerely hope that the information it contains has enlightened you a bit and will assist you in your dealings with others during the course of your career as a singer or songwriter.

From the 1950s to date, the music industry has grown from a multi-million to a multi-billion dollar-per-year business. It is still possible for a person with talent to become successful as a songwriter and/or recording artist. There are literally millions of individuals who are involved in the music field, many of whom attempt to break into the music business by submitting their songs and recorded performances to third parties in hopes of receiving an offer to sign with a recording or publishing company or to have their songs recorded by a major recording artist.

It was not too many years ago when I as a teen-ager with a burning desire to become a recording star, formed a singing group with three other young men called "The Quarternotes." I wrote a few rock songs, and we sang these songs along with other popular songs in various night-spots in the Los Angeles area. During our free evenings we practiced our routines at home. It was hard work, but we were determined, and during the two-year period that we were together, we dreamed of the day when we each would become rich and famous as recording stars. Many people encouraged us and liked our style. Although we made a few demos, spent a lot of our own money, and even had a record released, nothing of any great moment ever resulted from our efforts, and our singing group eventually broke up.

I believe that our group could have made it if we would have known of the ways and means by which we could have exploited our product to the fullest extent while at the same time protecting ourselves from unscrupulous operators. I recall one demo session our group held.

We had just met a "well known" record producer whom I will refer to as Producer X. Producer X assured us that he would produce a professional demonstration record of two original songs I had written. He said that he would take care of everything including the rental fee for the recording studio and the payments to the musicians for the sum of $500. About two weeks later, after the four of us had scraped the $500 together, I telephoned Producer X and advised him that I had the money. He told me to give him a few days to arrange for the session.

A few days later, I called him and he asked me to bring the group and the money and meet him at 11:00 P.M. the following evening at a certain recording studio in Hollywood. The next night we went to the studio, and after Producer X took the $500 we proceeded to record the demo. The arrangements were "head arrangements" (arrangements done on the spot) by Producer X and after spending a total of not more than 30 minutes which covered our singing the songs a few times with the accompaniment of the three musicians, our demo tape was ready. The engineer played back the tape for us through the large studio speakers which would make the worst performance sound like a symphony, and all of the musicians and Producer X congratulated us on our "hit" record. Shortly thereafter, Producer X mailed me two copies of the demo. To my utter disappointment and anger, I became aware of what had occurred. The demo was terrible. The arrangement was poor; the mix was atrocious; the voices were barely audible in contrast to the music. It was apparent when the record was played on a conventional record player through small speakers. (Following the completion of a demo, always have the engineer play the tape through a small standard speaker in the studio to get an idea of how the song would sound coming through the speaker in a car radio.) I called Producer X and informed him of the poor quality of the demo. He advised me that he would be glad to do another demo for an additional $500. I told him that he had already cheated us and that I didn't want to do any business with him in the future. He just laughed and hung up on me.

A few weeks later, Tom, one of the members of our group signed a combined recording and songwriting contract with a small record company. The contract was for one year plus four one-year options with no advance payable to Tom except for $50 per selection for the "single" the company agreed to record during each year of the term of the contract. In addition, Tom agreed to assign the copyrights in all of the songs he composed to a publishing company which was a subsidiary of the record company. The "general manager" of the record company made a lot of unwritten promises to Tom. Tom was superstar material, and Tom's record would be promoted throughout the United States, etc., but the promises were a lot of hot air without any substance. Oh, yes; during the first contract year, the company had Tom record one single record called "Teachin' and Reachin'," which was even released—if you can call the distribution of about 100 records to noninfluential people a legitimate record release. Nothing happened with the record. (Who has ever heard of "Teachin' and Reachin'?") When Tom discovered that the record company to which he was signed was a fly-by-night operation, he approached the "general manager" and told him that he wanted a release. Tom was told he would be given a release from his contract for $1,000, which was ostensibly to reimburse the record company for its costs in recording and releasing "Teachin' and Reachin'," but Tom was further advised that notwithstanding any such release, the songwriter's contract would continue in full force. At this point, Tom sought legal advice. Tom was extremely fortunate because, being a minor (Tom was 19 years old and at that time persons under 21 years old were able to disaffirm certain agreements they entered into), he had the right to disaffirm the recording and songwriting contract which he did. A few days later, Tom received a nasty telephone call from the "general manager" who told Tom that he was a no-good bum. This telephone call was the last time Tom ever heard from anyone at the record company.

During the years I have been involved with the legal aspects of the recording industry, I have heard countless stories of woe from prospective recording artists and songwriters. For example, I heard how one songwriter from the Midwest spent over $10,000 during a two-month period to record five of his songs. He was told by a certain "songwriter's search" company to whom he had submitted his songs for a determination of the commercial potential of such songs that out of all the songs submitted to the company by persons from all over the country, his five songs were chosen as showing the most promise as potential hits, but that the songs had to be recorded properly so that they could be presented as a "package" to a well-known publishing company. The writer was advised that although he would have to pay for the recording of the songs, the songwriter's search company would attempt to recoup for the writer any sums spent by the writer to record the songs from amounts which the publishing company might advance in a deal relating to the five songs.

Over a two-month period, the songwriter mailed checks to the songwriter's search company following receipt by him of bills which were supposed to represent recording costs to record his songs. As you may have expected, the songs were never accepted by the publishing company, and the songwriter was $10,000 poorer. Also as you may have expected, the songwriter's search company had gone out of business long before the songwriter had become suspicious and attempted to recover his money. As it turned out, the recordings were rough demos; the cost to record *all five* of the songs should not have exceeded $1,000.

Another singer-songwriter responded to an advertisement by

a certain company calling for the submission of new songs to be recorded by "top recording stars." He read the ad and submitted two of his original songs to the company. A few months later, he heard one of his songs being played over the radio. He purchased the album containing the song and discovered that his other song was also on the album, but nowhere did the album refer to him. A stranger was listed as the composer of both songs. He demanded an explanation from the company, which responded by denying that they had ever heard of him. Even though the songs would be protected upon creation under the new federal copyright law, the songwriter would have to prove in a lawsuit that the songs were his original works and that the company had misappropriated the songs without his consent. To bring such a lawsuit would involve an expenditure of many hundreds of dollars in legal fees. In order to have some evidence of the date on which the songs were written, the songwriter should have used the simple and inexpensive procedure of mailing a lead sheet of the songs to himself, as explained below.

Perhaps some of you have had experiences similar to those described above. I have written this book in an attempt to give the prospective singer-songwriter the benefits of my experiences in the record industry, and although it takes many years to become familiar with all areas of the record business, a person should be aware of certain fundamental facts before he spends excessive amounts of time and money attempting to break into the record business.

While it is true that there are some unscrupulous operators in the music business, most of the individuals and companies connected with the music business with whom I have had contact have been honest and legitimate. It is important, however, for you to apprise yourself of the reputations of the people with whom you intend to deal. Some methods by which you can find out the music-business track record of a person will be discussed later.

For your convenience, I have divided this book into an introduction and various general areas, plus appendixes. Although you will find this book helpful and informative, it is not intended to replace a lawyer or accountant.

2

so you
have written
a song—
now
what?

THE PROBLEM

Suppose that you have written what you believe to be the next monster hit. You want to let others hear your song, but you are not certain how you can protect yourself. The simple answer is that the instant you have created the musical composition, you are protected under the federal copyright law. No one may make commercial use of your musical composition without your consent.

While in most cases you are safely able to permit others to hear the song or to record the song or to distribute lead sheets (the written lyrics and music of a song) to others without placing your ownership of the song in jeopardy, someone might claim that he wrote the song before you did. Therefore, if you do not plan to have your song published or recorded in the foreseeable future, and you do not wish to go through the procedure of filling out forms and registering the song for copyright with the Copyright Office, you can complete the following procedure which will protect you to a certain extent. Prepare a "lead sheet" of the song yourself or have one prepared. After your lead sheet has been prepared, date it, sign it, have it witnessed, and if possible, notarized. Then place the lead sheet in an envelope, seal it, and mail the envelope to yourself by registered mail, return receipt requested. After you receive the envelope, keep it in a safe place and do not open it. In the event that someone makes unauthorized use of your song, the fact that you mailed the song to yourself on the date indicated on the registration would be considered evidence in establishing the date on which you wrote the song.

AFTER YOUR MUSICAL COMPOSITION
HAS BEEN PUBLISHED

The publication of a musical composition generally means the sale, placing on sale, or public distribution of copies. Many times it is difficult to determine whether the distribution of copies of a musical composition has been a "publication" or is simply a preliminary distribution and not a publication. Therefore you may want to affix notice of copyright to copies that are to be circulated beyond your control to avoid the danger of inadvertent publication of the musical composition without the proper notice of copyright. You do not lose your copyright, but your rights could be affected if too many copies were distributed without the copyright notice and you did not register the composition for copyright within five years after publication without notice.

Assuming that your previously unpublished musical composition has been "published," you must now follow certain important procedures in order to preserve your copyright rights in the now-published musical composition.

Produce Copies with Copyright Notice

Produce the musical composition in copies by printing or by other methods of reproduction, and be certain that each and every copy contains a copyright notice in the correct form and position. Such a copyright notice must contain the following three elements:

a. The word "Copyright" or the abbreviation "Copr." or the symbol ©. The use of the symbol © may secure copyright protection in some countries outside of the United States under provisions of the Universal Copyright Convention. Therefore, it may be wise to utilize the © instead of using "Copyright" or "Copr."

b. *The year date of publication.* The date is usually the year in which the copies of the work were first placed on sale, sold, or publicly distributed by the copyright proprietor. If the work is a compilation or derivative work, the year date of the first publication of the compilation or derivative work is sufficient.

c. *The name of the copyright owner or owners.* The above three elements of the copyright notice must appear together in such manner and location as to give reasonable notice of the claim of copyright, for example: © 1978. Richard Roe. Further, all copies of the published musical composition should contain the required copyright notice in order to ensure protection under the copyright act.

Publish the Work With Copyright Notice

Cause the copies to be placed on sale, sold, or publicly distributed with the proper copyright notice.

Register the Copyright Claim.

You must register your published musical composition for copyright with the Copyright Office and deposit the appropriate copies of the published musical composition in the Copyright Office before you can bring an action for copyright infringement against someone who has made unauthorized use of your published musical composition. It is important to register your published musical composition for copyright without much delay; although registration is not absolutely essential, it gives notice of ownership to others and is a condition to the recording of copyright transfers. Such registration should be made promptly following publication and in connection with such registration the following material is to be sent to the Register of Copyrights, Library of Congress, Washington D. C. 20540.

a. *A Completed Registration Application.*

b. *Copies.* Submit two complete copies of the best edition of the musical composition as first published. Note that "lead sheets" may be deposited for the registration for copyright of a published musical composition if such lead sheets represent complete copies of the best edition as first published.

c. *Registration Fee.* The fee to register a published musical composition is $10. Make your check or money order payable to the Register of Copyrights. Please note that currency is sent at the risk of the sender.

After your published musical composition has been registered for copyright, the Copyright Office will issue you a certificate along with a copyright number. The duration of the copyright in the musical composition as well as for copyrights in sound recordings are set forth below:

Post-1978 Works. The general rule for a work created on or after January 1, 1978, whether or not published, is that copyright lasts for the author's (or surviving joint author's) lifetime plus 50 years after the author's death. But a "work made for hire" or an anonymous or pseudonymous work is protected for 75 years from publication or 100 years from creation, whichever is shorter.

Pre-1978 Works Not Copyrighted Under Federal Copyright Law. An unpublished work created before 1978, if it was protected by the now-superseded principles of state common-law copyright, is now federally protected as if it had been a post-1978 work, and it also has a guaranteed term of federal copyright of at least 25 years after 1978 plus an additional term of 25 years thereafter if the work is published during the first 25 year period. A special rule applies to sound recordings created before February 15, 1972, which still are not protected by federal copyright, but which may be protected under state laws against piracy occurring until February 19, 2047 (75 years after sound recordings became copyrightable). All works published or copyrighted before September 19, 1906, and many published since then but not copyrighted or renewed, are permanently in the public domain.

Pre-1978 Works Copyrighted Under Federal Copyright Law. A work federally copyrighted before 1978 is protected for an initial term of 28 years from first publication or from registration as an unpublished work, with possible renewal (which must be expressly exercised) for an additional term of 47 years (a total of 75 years). Beginning January 1, 1978, all copyrights expire on the last day of the calendar year of the applicable term, and then anyone is free to copy or otherwise use the work forever, although new matter in a revised version may still be copyrighted, and copyright protection for derivative works may continue.

Notice of Intention to Obtain Compulsory License Requirement. Once a musical composition has been registered for copyright, it becomes subject to the so-called "compulsory license" provisions of the copyright law. Under these provisions, once the copyright owner has himself recorded the musical composition or has permitted it to be recorded, any other person is entitled to make recordings of that musical composition under the conditions specified in the "compulsory license" provisions of the copyright law.

Such a person may either negotiate a license with the copyright owner of a musical composition which has been previously recorded by the copyright owner or which the copyright owner has permitted to have been recorded, and record such musical composition under the terms of such license or such a person may utilize the compulsory license provisions of the copyright law which provisions do not require him to get permission from the copyright owner to use the song but such provisions do require him to pay fixed royalty fees at specific times.

Compilations and Derivative Works. A new version of a musical composition in the public domain, or a new version of a copyrighted musical composition that has been produced by the copyright owner or with his consent is copyrightable as a compilation or derivative work. Copyrightable compilation and derivative works include abridgments, adaptations, arrangements, dramatizations, translations, and works republished with new literary, dramatic, or musical material. However, the copyright in a new version covers only the additions, changes, or other new material appearing for the first time in the musical composition. There is no way to restore copyright protection for a work in the public domain, such as by including it in a new version.

To be copyrightable, a new version of a musical composition must either be so different in substance from the original as to be regarded as a new work or it must contain an appreciable amount of new material. This new material must be original and copyrightable in itself. If only a few slight variations or minor additions of no substance have been made, or when the revisions or added material consist solely of uncopyrightable elements (such as short phrases, titles, etc.), registration is not possible.

If the musical composition is an entirely new version, it may be permissible to use an entirely new notice of copyright containing the later year date of publication and the name of the owner of copyright in the new version.

If the musical composition contains material which was originally registered for copyright in unpublished form and is now published for the first time, the proper notice depends upon whether or not the *original* musical composition has been changed. If the published musical composition is essentially the same as the unpublished version, the notice should contain the year date of original copyright.

common
sense
prior to, during,
& after
you record
a demo

3

WHY A DEMO

Each year record companies are bombarded by thousands of demonstration records in the form of tapes and disc records submitted by people who want to become successful recording artists and songwriters. Unfortunately, a good number of these demos, some of which contain good material, are rejected by record companies. Some record companies reject unsolicited demos by sending them back to the senders unopened unless the person who submitted such a demo has signed an appropriate release form to avoid the possibility of such person claiming at a later date that the record company utilized his song without his consent. The A&R (artist and repertoire) personnel at some record companies will go through the motions of listening to the demos submitted but will reject most of them either on the basis that the demo was not "commercial" enough or that the record company is at present not in the market for the type of material contained in the demo.

Therefore, prior to submitting your demo to a record company, it would be wise for you to purchase a current copy of *Cashbox,* *Billboard,* or *Record World,* and look at the hit record charts in these publications to determine the general areas of music upon which particular record companies are currently concentrating. If your demo is in the rhythm-and-blues vein you would want to submit a copy of your demo to a record company that has R&B hit records on the charts. After you have chosen a particular record company (or companies), either call or write to the A&R department to determine if that particular company is presently reviewing demos and to whom you should send a copy for such review. If possible, talk directly to the person in the A&R department who is in charge of reviewing new material to at least familiarize him with your name prior to submitting your demo. This sort of preparation may give you an edge.

Also, when you send your demo to a record company for review, it may be helpful to write a friendly personal letter to the individual who will be reviewing your demo instead of sending the same form letter to all of the record companies to which you send copies of your demo.

Notwithstanding the difficulties you may be confronted with in arousing the interest of a record company in your song, the demo is almost always the only vehicle connecting you and such record company. Therefore, to arouse such interest, your demo should be of *good quality*. It is important to keep in mind that since an A&R man listens to *many, many* demos each year, your chances of arousing a record company's interest in your song will not be too great unless your demo is more or less professionally done, or, in the rare case, unless it contains material that is exceptionally unique and commercial. Also, if your demo embodies an original song, then, in addition to submitting it to record companies you may wish to submit it to a music-publishing company or to an established recording artist in hopes that the publishing company or artist will become interested in recording your song or have it recorded or (in the case of the publishing company) sign you as a songwriter.

There is nothing wrong with making your own demo. Although many demos are recorded at home on small tape recorders or by other nonprofessional methods, it would be wise for you to record your demo at a recording studio. There are usually several small recording studios in most medium-sized towns, and in larger towns and cities you will probably be able to choose from among dozens of recording studios. You should be able to record your demo at any of these small recording studios for approximately $25–$50 per hour, including an engineer. The tape upon which your song is recorded will be an additional expense to you of $10–$40, depending upon how many songs you wish to record. If you do not have background singers or musicians to accompany you, you may nevertheless want to have your voice recorded on an 8- or 16-track tape to which the accompaniment can later be recorded on the unused tracks.

The American Federation of Musicians (AFM) requires that applicable union-scale payments be paid to each member musician when the musician performs at a recording session whether the session is to record a master recording or a demo. (There are a few exceptions, mentioned later.) Therefore, if you hire a musician to accompany you on your demo and pay him less than union scale and your demo is purchased by a record company, the AFM will require that the record company pay the musician applicable union scale if your recording is released commercially.

The same rule regarding union-scale payments applies to any singers you may hire to accompany you on your demo who are members of the American Federation of Television and Radio Artists (AFTRA). The point: a good demo can be purchased by a record company as a master recording, and almost all record companies who purchase masters require a representation and warranty by the seller of the master that all applicable union-scale payments to the vocalists and musicians who performed on the recording were paid by the seller. If you sign an agreement with such a clause, you will have violated the agreement if you failed to pay the vocalists and musicians who accompanied you applicable union scale. If you refuse to sign an agreement with such a clause, the record company might very well back off and not want to purchase your recording. Therefore, if possible, you should comply with the rules of the AFM and AFTRA when you hire musicians and vocalists to accompany you. Upon your request, the office of the AFM or AFTRA near you will furnish you with the amounts of scale payments. Some local offices of the AFM allow special reduced rates for musicians who perform on a demo. Check with your local office of the AFM to see if such reduced rates apply in your area. Also, there is a special reduced rate allowed by AFTRA for the recording of demos; however, there are certain conditions imposed by AFTRA on the person who hires the singers to perform on the demo, so check with your local office of AFTRA for details.

When you choose a recording studio in which to record your demo, try to choose one where the engineer is also able to arrange and produce. If you are fortunate enough to find such a recording studio (there are a few such studios in Los Angeles), the engineer will be able to organize and coordinate the musicians and background singers who accompany you so that the finished demo will be of professional quality. Your performance will thus be greatly enhanced.

After the demo has been completed, insist upon having it played over a small speaker so you can hear how your song will sound coming through the speaker of a small radio, such as a car radio. Finally, in addition to the tape and/or disc copies of your demo, request that the original multi-track tape embodying your song be sold to you by the recording studio. Although the multi-track tape is very wide and will most likely have been recorded at 15 inches per second, so that it cannot be played on a conventional tape recorder, if your song generates any interest, a record company might want to have the multi-track tape.

GUARDING YOURSELF

If you are approached by someone who offers to record your song for you, carefully analyze all of the details contained in such an offer. For example, if the person offers to pay the recording costs of your demo but conditions such payment on your signing a management and/or recording (or recording-songwriter's) contract with him, you must consider a variety of things. Be certain that such a person is reputable. This can be done in a number of ways. Has anyone ever heard of him or his company? What is the track record of this person insofar as the record business is concerned—has he ever had any hits? Are any recording artists of stature signed to him or to his company? Is he mentioned in the trade papers? What is the financial position of this person? (This may be checked through local credit bureaus or through Dun and Bradstreet.) Further, ask yourself if it is worth the price of a demo or two for you to be contractually bound to such a person for an extended period of time.

Sometimes the person offering to record and pay for your demo will ask you to assign to him the copyright rights to the song being recorded and/or other of your songs in consideration for his paying for the recording of your demo. In this case, as in the previous cases, be certain whether it is worthwhile to deal with the person at all. If this person has a music publishing company, is it a successful operation or is it a company in name only into which the person will place your song along with songs written by others hoping to sell all of the rights in this "catalog" of songs to a large publishing company. The sale may never occur. As a general rule, anyone who offers to record your demo and pay for it will request that you sign some type of agreement with him. For a discussion of various types of agreements relating to the record business, please see Chapter 5.

Assuming that you have analyzed the proposed agreement and signed it, you should now be certain that the costs incurred in recording your demo (as well as all future recording costs) are legitimate because it is customary for such costs to be recouped from your royalties. Your agreement will probably provide for such recoupment. Here are questions you should ask:

1.   Is the recording studio where you are recording charging you the going rate, or are you being charged an excessive rate?

2.   Is the person to whom you are "signed" a signatory to the AFM and AFTRA agreements, and is he paying the musicians and vocalists who accompany you applicable union scale pursuant to the rules and regulations of the AFM and AFTRA?

3.   Have all invoices and statements relating to your recording costs been shown to you, and are you satisfied that you are only being charged for the costs indicated by such invoices and statements.

4.   Does your agreement state that the costs of the demo are recoupable only from your royalties or are they recoupable from

all sums including advances payable to you? (The person with whom you have contracted should not have the right to recoup recording costs from advances.)

Since record-company executives are especially interested in signing an individual who possesses talents as a singer *and* songwriter, your demo should include four or five different *original* tunes.

Rarely, if ever, will a record company be interested in an unknown singer who sounds like a major recording artist or who submits a demo containing only nonoriginal material unless the person has a truly unique voice or style. Therefore, your chances to arouse the interest of a record company executive will be enhanced if your demo contains original material.

A list of various recording studios throughout the country can be found in the Appendix.

RECORD PRODUCERS

As a great chef combines various ingredients in the proper proportions to make a delicious dish, a record producer combines the elements of the recording in the right proportions to create the "right" sound. The producer supervises the entire recording process. He uses certain combinations of musical instruments. He has the duty of editing and mixing the various sounds until he feels the mix is right for the final master recording from which records are manufactured. Many times, the difference between a hit record and an unsuccessful record is the producer. As is the case with some individuals who call themselves "managers" or say they have a "production company" when in reality they are simply middlemen who know little or nothing about the music business and only want to have you sign a contract with them so they can deal you off to someone else or tie you up legally for years, there are some people who call themselves record producers yet know nothing about producing records. These individuals might ask you to sign a contract with them. If you sign, it is likely that you will not receive a fair shake even if the "producer" sells your services to a record company, because the record company would pay the "producer" and the "producer" would pay you. Since most agreements between these "producers" and unknown artists do not provide for an advance to the artist and offer a very low royalty rate, the "producer" would keep the "gravy" he receives from the record company and would give you the leftovers unless your agreement provided otherwise. It cannot be emphasized enough that before signing a contract with someone calling himself a record producer, an unknown artist should check out the track record and reputation of the producer.

4

copyright
in sound
recordings

IN GENERAL

It is now possible to secure copyrights in certain recordings by virtue of a federal statute which became effective in late 1971. Prior to the enactment of this law, sound recordings were not copyrightable, therefore, so-called "record pirates" would obtain a copy of a hit record, rerecord the performance on their own labels, and distribute copies of these records containing the stolen performances, thereby reaping tremendous profits. The annual volume of such record piracy exceeded $100 *Million!* Now the "free ride" is over for the pirates. Copyright protection in sound recordings may now be secured provided that the sound recording was "fixed" and first published with the statutory copyright notice on or after February 15, 1972. Once a sound recording is copyrighted, anyone who duplicates it without the consent of the copyright proprietor is subject to severe civil and criminal penalties.

As mentioned earlier, statutory copyright in sound recordings created on and after January 1, 1978, endures for the life of the author plus 50 years. The requirements for securing copyright in a sound recording are set forth below. Even though the ownership of a copyright in a sound recording is not nearly as valuable a right as the ownership of the copyright in a musical composition, no one can predict what benefits may accrue to the sound recording copyright owner in the future. If you intend to release any records on your own label either now or in the future, the following is the procedure for you to follow to retain ownership in the sound recordings in such records.

Sound Recording—A Definition

A sound recording is a work resulting from the fixation of a series of musical, spoken or other sounds. Common examples incluse recordings of music, drama, narration, or other sounds embodied in phonograph discs, open-reel tapes, cartridges, cassettes, player-piano rolls or similar material objects in which sounds are fixed and can be perceived, reproduced or otherwise communicated either directly or with the aid of a machine or device. A sound recording within the meaning of the new law does not include a sound track when it is an integrated part of a motion picture or other audiovisual works.

Fixation—A Definition

A work is "fixed" in a tangible medium of expression when its embodiment in a copy or phonorecord, by or under the authority of the author, is sufficiently permanent or stable to permit it to be perceived, reproduced or otherwise communicated for a period of more than transitory duration. A work consisting of sounds, images or both that are being transmitted is "fixed" if a fixation of the work is being made simultaneously with its transmission.

SOUND RECORDINGS THAT CANNOT BE STATUTORILY COPYRIGHTED

The law provides statutory copyright only for published sound recordings fixed on or after February 15, 1972. The statute specifies that this provision is not to "be construed as affecting in any way rights with respect to sound recordings fixed before that date." Therefore, sound recordings fixed prior to February 15, 1972 are not copyrightable.

SECURING STATUTORY COPYRIGHT IN
YOUR SOUND RECORDING

a. When you create your sound recording, you are protected under the federal copyright law. No one can copy your sound recording without your consent.

b. *Publish the Sound Recording with Copyright Notice.* Publication generally means the sale, placing on sale, or public distribution of copies of the sound recording. Performance of a sound recording by playing it, even in public or on radio or on television, ordinarily does not constitute publication in the copyright sense.

c. *Register the Claim to Copyright.* Promptly after publication, mail to the register of Copyrights, Library of Congress, Washington, D.C. 20540, two complete copies of the best edition of the sound recording, together with an application on Form PA duly completed and signed and a fee of $10. You may obtain free copies of Form PA by writing to the Register of Copyrights at the above address.

THE COPYRIGHT NOTICE FOR SOUND
RECORDINGS.

The copyright notice on a sound recording should appear on the surface of the copies of the recording or on the label of the container, in such a manner and location as to give reasonable notice of the claim of copyright. The copyright notice for sound recordings consists of the symbol℗, the year date of first publication of the sound recording, and the name of the copyright owner of the sound recording. Example:℗1978 Richard Roe Records.

Make sure that you use the legal name of the copyright owner and group the elements of the notice together as in the example given above. The law provides an alternative; that the notice for sound recordings may consist of the symbol℗, the year date of first publication and an abbreviation by which the name of the copyright owner can be recognized or a generally known alternative designation of the owner. Also, the law states that if the producer of the sound recording is named on the labels of containers of the copies of the sound recording, and if no other name appears in conjunction with the notice, his name shall be considered a part of the notice. If you are not certain whether it is correct to use one of these variant forms of the notice, you should seek professional legal advice first.

REGISTRATION OF COPYRIGHT IN A SOUND RECORDING

Registration of a claim to copyright in a sound recording should be made by mailing to The Register of Copyrights, Library of Congress, Washington, D.C. 20540, two complete copies of the best edition of the sound recording, an application on Form PA duly completed and signed, and a fee of $10. After registration, the Copyright Office will issue you a certificate showing that the statements set forth therein have been made a part of the records of the Copyright Office.

Complete Copies of the Best Edition

The statute calls for the deposit of two complete copies of the best edition of the sound recording as first published. A complete copy means the actual sound recording, together with any sleeve, jacket, or other container in which it was first published, as well as any liner notes or other accompanying material.

Where the sound recording was first published in several physical forms, the "best edition" ordinarily means a vinyl disc rather than tape; or when only tape is involved, open-reel tape, the cartridge, or the cassette in descending order of preference. Usually a stereo recording is considered the "best edition" as against a mono recording. Please remember that all the editions should bear the prescribed notice of copyright in order to secure and maintain copyright protection.

When to Register

The law states that after a sound recording is published with the notice of copyright; registration can be made at any time during the life of the copyright.

Application for Registration

As stated earlier, Application Form PA is for sound recording and is provided by the Copyright Office free upon request. Care should be taken to see that it is properly completed and signed.

Fee

The registration fee is $10. Make the check or money order payable to the Register of Copyrights. Cash is sent at your own risk.

Mailing Instructions

Processing of the material will be more prompt if the application, copies, and fee are all mailed together in the same package. Special attention should be given to the preparation of the containers for the shipment of sound recordings in order to prevent damage in transit. The Copyright Office will not accept for registration sound recordings damaged in shipment.

New Versions

Under the copyright law, a new version of a work in the public domain, or a new version of copyrighted work that has been produced by the copyright owner or with his consent, is copyrightable as a "new work."

Sound recordings that are copyrightable as "new works" include compilations, recordings reissued with substantial editorial revisions or abridgments of the recorded material, and recordings republished with new recorded material.

COPYRIGHT IN NEW VERSION COVERS ONLY THE NEW MATTER

The copyright in a new version covers only the additions, changes, or other newly recorded sounds appearing in the new sound recording. There is no way to restore or create statutory copyright protection for a sound recording that is in the public domain or for a recording that was fixed before February 15, 1972. Similarly, protection for a sound recording under an existing statutory copyright cannot be lengthened by republishing the work with new matter.

WORKS REISSUED WITHOUT SUBSTANTIAL NEWLY RECORDED MATERIAL.

To be copyrightable as a new version, a sound recording must either be so different in substance from the original recording as to be regarded as a "new work," or it must contain a substantial amount of new recorded material. When only a few slight variations or minor additions of no substance have been made, registration is not possible. For example, if the only change is to reissue the recording on tape that had previously been published on a disc, no new registration would ordinarily be in order. Likewise, if the only change is to mechanically rechannel the same series of sounds, a new registration would generally not be appropriate. Further, there may be changes in features appearing on the label, jacket, or other material accompanying the recording which are either uncopyrightable, or would be subject of copyright in some category other than sound recording. Examples of uncopyrightable elements are titles, short phrases, or format. Elements that may be the subject of copyright in one of the classes other than sound recordings include new literary or musical expression in legible form or new pictorial material.

Copyright Notice for New Versions of Sound Recordings and Works Reissued Without New Recorded Material

For the copyright in a sound recording to remain in force, it is necessary that all published copies contain the prescribed copyright notice for sound recordings. If a sound recording is reissued without either substantial revisions or new recorded material, the original copyright notice should be retained. If the copyright has been assigned to a new owner, the name of the original copyright owner should be used in the notice unless the assignment has been recorded in the Copyright Office. The new owner of a copyright may substitute his name in the notice *but this substitution must not be made until after the assignment has been recorded.* If the work is a new version, it may be permissible to use an entirely new notice of copyright, containing the name of the owner of the copyright in the new version.

OTHER TYPES OF SOUND RECORDINGS

Although most of the sound recordings to be copyrighted will most likely embody the performances of music, dramas or narrative works, the subject of what is recorded may sometimes be sounds such as birdcalls, sounds of locomotives, etc. Such recordings may also be copyrightable and subject to registration if the amount of original recorded material is substantial. This would become important if you had recorded sound effects and you wanted to sell the records.

SOUND RECORDINGS FIRST PUBLISHED AS A UNIT ALONG WITH OTHER COPYRIGHTABLE MATERIAL

Sometimes sound recordings are first published with other copyrightable materials as a unit. Some examples of this are disc records published in jackets containing substantial original textual or pictorial matter, and which bear a copyright notice appropriate for the material; recordings for learning a foreign language which are published in a box with manuals; and disc records, published in a container which contains exercise books, filmstrips, textbooks, etc. A combination or collection of various other materials that has been published as a unit may qualify for registration as a "book" when *both* of the following conditions are met:

a. The work contains a copyright notice consisting of the word "Copyright," the abbreviation "Copr.," or the symbol ©, accompanied by the name of the copyright owner and the year date of first publication. Example: © Richard Roe, Inc. 1978.

b. The notice is placed on the copies in such manner and location as to give reasonable notice of the claim of copyright.

As an alternative to registering one claim for a published combination of various materials, you may make separate registrations for the different parts, provided that they bore their own copyright notices from the time of first publication.

basic
agreements
relating to the
recording
industry

Although the music business is concerned with musical compositions, recorded performances, and the like—all basically intangible—it is often the case that these intangibles will generate millions of dollars in record and sheet-music sales. The person who is unsophisticated or unwary may find his song a hit on the "charts", but because he has signed a one-sided agreement against himself, he may never reap the rewards of his efforts. You would not want to purchase a car if you did not know what the terms of the deal were—i.e., how much the total cost would be including interest; what would happen if you missed one payment—could you make it up next month, or could the finance company or dealer repossess it immediately, etc., nor would you want to buy a bag of groceries unless you knew what was inside the bag. Similarly, as a songwriter or singer you should not sign an agreement with someone unless you first understand what you are signing. The best way to protect yourself is to seek legal advice from an attorney who is skilled in the legal aspects of the record business.

Sometimes it is difficult to find such an attorney when you need one. Until you are able to contact an expert record lawyer, it is important for you to know something about the agreement which you may be asked to sign. The following information is designed to assist you in understanding the economics of the record business and to give you a basic "feel" for the "deal points" which are found in certain agreements relating to the record business.

As discussed earlier, you may be approached by someone who will agree to pay for the recording of your demo if you will sign an agreement with him, or you may be asked to sign an agreement relating to the record business for other reasons, for example, with someone who likes your style and who wants to help you break into the record business, etc. You will most likely be asked to sign a management agreement, an exclusive songwriter's agreement, an exclusive recording agreement, or any combination of the agreements.

MANAGEMENT AGREEMENTS

In California an artist's manager or agent is the person who will usually be hired by the artist to book engagements for the artist (such as tours, concerts, etc.), as well as negotiate the terms and conditions of agreements between the artist and third parties relating to the recording and/or entertainment industry in general. Such artist's manager or agent must be licensed by the state and such prospective licensee must meet certain qualifications and must comply with the terms and provisions of the Labor Commission. One of these conditions is that the amount of commission that the licensed artist's manager or agent is entitled to receive is limited.

On the other hand, the unlicensed personal manager may charge as much commission as he can get from the artist (although the standard commission of the personal manager is 20–25 percent of the gross earnings of the artist). The main function of the personal manager is to advise and counsel the artist in connection with the artist's professional development. Some personal managers will travel with the artist and will take care of the day-to-day needs of the artist while the artist is performing. Although a personal manager need not be licensed by the state, he must take care not to perform the functions of an agent or artist's manager which require a license, such as procuring contracts or employment for the artist, for if this occurs, the unlicensed personal manager may find that the artist can terminate his agreement with the manager and in some cases the artist may be entitled to the past earnings that the manager has received from the artist.

The standard personal management agreement will most probably state that the manager's function is strictly limited to advising and counseling the artist. In the event of a lawsuit between the artist and manager, the court will determine what the manager in fact did, and not what the contract provides to make its determination as to whether the personal manager was functioning as an artist's manager or agent without the proper license. If you are asked to sign a personal management agreement, examine it to see if its terms and conditions are slanted in favor of the manager. If so, question those terms and conditions and attempt to have the agreement constructed so it is fair to both you and the manager. Some of the basic terms and conditions customarily found in personal management contracts are as follows:

Term

The standard management contract usually provides for an initial period of one year plus four or five additional one-year options exercisable by the manager. If this provision is found in your agreement, you may wish to have the agreement modified to provide that *you* can terminate the term of the agreement after a certain period of time has elapsed if you have not been earning at least a specified minimum amount of money (to be determined by you and the manager and stated in the agreement) each week as a result of the efforts of the manager. You may also wish to provide in your agreement that unless one of your records is on the "Top Hits" charts of *Billboard, Cashbox,* or *Record World* during a particular period of your management agreement, that the manager cannot exercise the next option provided for in the agreement.

Since the personal manager's main function is to advise and counsel you in all areas of your career as an entertainer, it follows, in theory at least, that your career should be enhanced by the services rendered to you by the manager. Therefore, it is reasonable for you to request these modifications.

Payment to the Manager

The standard management contract usually provides for the payment to the manager of a commission equal to 20–25 percent of your gross earnings, which is to be paid by you in consideration for the services to be rendered to you by the manager. You should provide in your agreement that the manager will be entitled to participate only in your earnings relating to the entertainment industry and not from any nonentertainment related endeavor of yours or from any investment of yours, etc. Nor should the manager be entitled to participate in any earnings of yours from events which occurred prior to the date of execution of the personal management agreement. Also, if you have signed a recording and/or songwriter's agreement with the manager or with a company affiliated or related to the manager, you should question whether the manager should be entitled to his full commission under the management contract and also be entitled to additional sums arising out of the recording or songwriter's contract—this would in effect give him a double commission.

Power of Attorney

Some personal management contracts provide that the artist irrevocably appoints the manager as his attorney-in-fact to (among other things) collect all monies and sign any agreements or amendments to agreements between the artist and third parties. To grant a manager the right to execute an agreement on your behalf and/or to collect all monies payable to you resulting from your services as an entertainer is an extremely broad grant of rights, and unless you are certain of the reputation and competence of the manager, question whether you would want him to have such broad powers.

Manager's Prior Approval of Your Future Agreements

Standard management contracts provide that the artist will not enter into any agreements or arrangements relating to his career as an entertainer without the prior approval of the manager. If you find such a provision in your agreement, you may want to modify it to provide that you will consult with the manager with respect to such agreements or arrangements, but in the event of any disagreement, your decision would be *final.*

Manager's Services Are Usually Nonexclusive

Almost all standard personal management contracts provide that although the artist cannot utilize the services of another manager, the manager has the right to perform the same services as he is performing under his contract with the artist for other artists. Since the manager may be entitled to a substantial sum under your agreement with him, he should devote a reasonable amount of his time to the development of your career. If he must delegate his authority of advising and counseling you to someone else because of other responsibilities, you may wish to provide in your agreement that you shall have the right of approval of such other person and in the event you do not approve of such person (or other persons up to a maximum of replacements to be determined by you and the manager and set forth in the contract), then you would have the right to terminate the agreement. As stated earlier, before you sign a management agreement, determine what the person's track record in the record business has been. The problem is that most successful managers and agents do not want to represent an unknown artist unless the artist has a record deal in the offing or unless the artist is exceptionally good. This is because it is difficult for the manager or agent to exploit the talent of the unknown artist. One way for the unknown artist to be heard and seen by managers, agents and record company executives is to perform on "talent" nights at local clubs. This can be done by calling at the club and stating that you are interested in showcasing your material. Make certain you are prepared when you perform because it is possible that your performance could be seen and heard by someone who could give you the break you need. If you live far from music centers, you can send a demo of your material directly to personal managers and agencies. A list of various booking agents and contacts and personal managers can be found in the Appendix.

RECORDING ARTIST'S AGREEMENTS

As stated earlier, you may be requested to sign an exclusive recording agreement as a vocalist and musician with a person or company. Again, it must be stressed that prior to signing such an agreement you should check out such person or company thoroughly since you could be on the hook for an extended period of time with little or no benefit to you if you happen to sign with the wrong person or company.

Some of the major "deal points" relating to the standard exclusive recording artist's agreement of which you should be aware are as follows (the term "record company" or "company" as used below will mean the party you are contracting with whether an individual or company):

Term of Agreement

Most recording agreements provide for an initial contract period of one year, and the record company will usually have four additional options to extend the term of the agreement for four additional years. Therefore, unless there are conditions imposed which restrict the right of the record company to exercise its options, you could be bound to a record company that you grew to hate for five years, with no right to record for anyone else. Accordingly, it is important for you as a recording artist to be able to say to the record company: "Unless record company has done so and so during the current year of the agreement, record company shall not have the right to exercise the next option and I will be free to go elsewhere and record." If you decide to sign an agreement with an individual or a small company that plans to "deal off" your contract to a large record company, you may want to include a clause in your agreement that gives you the absolute right to terminate the term of all contracts between you and that individual or small company if the agreement between the individual or company and the large record company relating to your services as a recording artist has not been concluded within a given period of time from the date you first signed with such individual or small company. This would enable you to walk away after the expiration of whatever time period you have agreed upon if the one with whom you have signed had not been successful in placing you.

Advances

One method of protecting yourself from the record company's simply exercising its options year after year with little or no benefit to you is to insist upon the payment by the record company to you of a sum of money in the form of a nonreturnable advance upon the exercise of each option, with an increase in the amount of the advance during each subsequent year. For example, the agreement could provide for an advance of $5,000 payable by the record company to you upon the exercise of the first option; $10,000 payable upon the exercise of the second option, and so forth. Such a clause would tend to induce the record company to actively promote your records during the current period of your agreement; if there was no "action," then the company might wish to drop you after the first year instead of paying you the advance, and you would be able to go elsewhere.

Record and Release
Requirement

Another way to prevent the record company from exercising its options without first doing something of benefit to you is to contractually require the record company to record and commercially release in the United States a certain number of your records each year. Since the first year of the contract will be the trial year for you inasmuch as you will probably be an unknown at the time you entered into the contract, you should not expect the record company to agree to record and release more than one or two single records during the first year. The record company should, however, be obligated to record and release a greater number of your recordings during each option year as a condition to its exercise of the next option. To contractually require a record company to record and release one LP album in the first option year, two LP albums in the second option year, and three LP albums during each of the remaining option years is a reasonable request on your part. The other side of the coin is to provide for a maximum number of master recordings containing your performances that the record company can compel you to record in any one year without your consent. If you become a "hot" artist, you would not want the record company to have the unlimited right to record as many masters of your performances as it desired. For you to request a clause in your agreement providing for a maximum of three LP albums per year without your consent is not unreasonable.

Guaranteed Payment on a Minimum Number of Record Sales

Still another method to protect yourself from the indiscriminate exercise of an option by the record company is to provide in the contract that the record company cannot exercise its next option unless you have been paid an amount equal to the royalties that would have been paid to you if a certain number of your records had been sold during the current year. For example, if the record company agreed to pay you a sum equal to the royalties you would receive if 50,000 full-priced LP albums of yours were sold, and only 10,000 LP albums were sold, the record company could not exercise its next option unless it first paid you a royalty equal to the sale of 50,000 full-priced LP albums.

Guaranteed Number of Records Sold

A variation of the preceding condition is that the record company could not exercise its next option unless a minimum agreed-upon number of your records had been sold during the then current period. This type of condition would not permit the record company to pay you if the minimum number of records had not been sold. Either your records would enjoy sales of a certain minimum number or the contract would end.

"Pay or Play" Clause

Some recording contracts contain a provision which permits the record company to pay the artist union scale in lieu of recording the agreed-upon number of masters in a given year. In the event this provision is in your agreement, it may be advisable to have it deleted because its existence could defeat the whole idea of requiring the record company to comply with the above "record and release" provision as a condition to the exercise of each option.

By now you have realized that the whole idea of conditioning the record company's right to exercise its options on some type of performance by the company is that a record company that is satisfied with your performance during a particular contract year will want to exercise its next option even with the conditions you have imposed attached to such exercise. Further, you can always agree at a later date to the elimination of an existing condition to the company's right to exercise an option.

Recording Costs

As stated earlier, you should have the right to examine all statements relating to recording costs of your recordings because these costs will most likely be recouped from your royalties. This can most easily be handled by an audit clause, which will be discussed later. Sometimes a record company which owns a recording studio will absorb a certain amount of costs incurred in the recording of masters by a recording artist, but in most cases such an artist will be well known and will have strong bargaining power. Since you are most probably as yet (but hopefully only temporarily) an unknown artist, the recouping of recording costs from your royalties by the record company will most likely be a foregone conclusion.

However, the record company should not have the right to recoup costs that are not ordinarily recoupable items from your royalties. Such costs as transportation and room and board for recording sessions held at the recording company's request in a distant place, promotion expenses, advertising expenses, and producer's advances and royalties should not be recoupable from your royalties. To the extent that your agreement provides for recoupment by the company from your royalties of these types of extraordinary costs you may want to have the agreement modified to exclude them.

Top-Line Label of Company

Examine your contract to determine whether the record company has the right to release your records on any label it chooses. If this is the case, your record could be released on a second or third-line label—not nearly as desirable as a first-line label. Therefore, you may wish to have a clause added to your contract providing for the initial release of your records to be on a top-line label of the record company.

After the initial release of a record, the company might want to sell such record as a budget-line record—which means that your royalties on such sales would be substantially reduced compared to the regular royalties payable on full priced sales. Also, if a budget-line record is released too soon after the release of the same record on a top-line label it may appear to the public that the record company is dumping the artist. The time may come when it may benefit you to allow the record company to sell your records as budget line, but the company should be contractually obligated to wait about eighteen months after the initial release of a particular record before it sells such a record as budget line. Also, the royalty payable to you on such budget line sales should preferably be 75 percent of the full royalty rate, but should not be less than 50% of the full royalty rate.

Decisions Relating to the Creative Aspects of Your Records

The standard recording contract will usually provide that the record company will have the right to make most if not all of the creative decisions regarding the recording and packaging of the artist's records. If your contract states that the company has the right to choose the selections to be recorded, the individual producer to be utilized to produce your recording, the recording studio to be used and the control over the type and format of the art work for album covers, etc., consider requesting that the contract be revised to give you the right to make such creative decisions—or at least that you and company should mutually approve the creative elements making up both your recordings and the art work for the album covers. The creative decisions are very important—for if the record company has the sole right to make all such creative decisions, you could be stuck with a producer whom you dislike without having the right to replace him; or all of the songs in any record of yours could be chosen for you without any right on your part to object. Further, the record company could release any LP album of yours with a cover you loathed, and you would have no right to have the art work changed.

Coupling and Repackaging

The standard recording contract permits the record company to combine the recordings of one artist with the recordings of another artist on the same record. This is referred to as "coupling" in the record business. Such standard recording agreement also permits the record company to rerelease records under completely different album covers. This is referred to as "repackaging."

If you become successful as a recording artist, would you want your recordings coupled on a record with recordings of an unknown or unsuccessful or controversial artist? If the answer is no, and if your agreement has a clause permitting the record company to couple your recordings with those of other artists, you may wish to modify the agreement to provide that there shall be no coupling of your recordings with those of other artists without your prior written consent, except for so-called "Best Of" or "Sampler" albums, where it is reasonable to permit the record company to release an LP album containing a maximum of two or so of your recordings with hit recordings of other artists.

Sometimes a company will rerelease old recordings of an artist and call the album "Old Hits from the 1950s," for example. The artist might feel that such a release would jeopardize his new image.

Therefore, some artists want to have the right to approve the album cover of any repackaged album.

Cross-collateralization

For purposes of our discussion, the term "cross-collateralization" means the right of the record company to recoup from you all amounts unrecouped from all sums payable to you under all contracts between you and the company. Therefore, if you have signed a recording agreement, a songwriter's agreement and a management agreement with the same person or company, that person or company would be able to recoup any unrecouped amounts under the recording agreement (for example) from any sums payable to you under the other agreements—so that you might never receive any royalties at all.

The way to prevent this situation from occurring is to provide in each agreement you sign that no amounts under that particular agreement will be cross-collateralized with any other agreements, and that each agreement will be accounted for separately by the company.

Audio-Visual Rights

Someday in the near future, people will be able to purchase a special tape record or disc record for a reasonable price, and when it is played back, they will be able to see and hear the artist performing simultaneously, or while the song is playing, images such as the ocean, trees, etc., will be seen simultaneously. There are already a few of these so called "sight and sound" devices available and in use, and as these devices are perfected and become more commercially acceptable, the rights to the artist's audiovisual recordings will likewise become more valuable.

The standard recording agreement provides that the record company has all rights including audiovisual rights to the artist's recordings. If such a provision is contained in your agreement, you may wish to have the agreement modified so that you will retain the audiovisual rights for yourself, at least, attempt to have the contract modified so that you would retain the audiovisual rights but the record company would have the "right of first refusal"— which means that you would have the right to entertain offers for your audiovisual rights from other sources, but that the record company would have the right to meet any such offer and thus acquire your audiovisual rights if it so desired.

Merchandising Rights

All of us have seen pictures of recording artists plastered on the fronts of T-shirts, on lamps, lunchboxes, and other items. The merchandising of nonrecord uses of the names, likenesses and pictures of recording artists is a multimillion-dollar-per-year business in itself. The standard recording agreement will almost always provide that the record company will have the exclusive right to exploit the merchandising rights of the artist during the term of the agreement and will pay the artist 50 percent of the net profits of the record company from the exploitation of such merchandising rights. If your contract contains a clause granting the record company the exclusive right to exploit your merchandising rights, you may wish to have such clause deleted or at least modified so that you would have the right to approve each use of your merchandising rights by the record company to prevent the indiscriminate use of your picture or name on items which may be undesirable or offensive to you. In addition, it may be advisable to have the right to exploit your merchandising rights revert to you if the record company has not exploited them or caused them to be exploited within a given period of time following the execution of your recording contract.

Soundtrack Albums

Suppose you sign a recording agreement and nothing happens with respect to your records. One day you are offered a part in a motion picture or television show, but a condition to the part being offered to you is that the company producing such show must have the right to record and release a song performed by you in the show on an LP album. If your recording agreement does not provide for this type of contingency, you could very well lose the part if the record company to whom you are signed will not permit your recorded performances to be released on such a soundtrack album. Therefore, you may want to have your recording contract modified to permit you to record for such a soundtrack album if it is a condition to obtaining a part in a movie or television show. If the record company agrees to this modification, it will most likely reserve the right to release single records of your performances from the show, which is a reasonable request and should be accepted by the producer of the show.

Promotion

After you have recorded a record for a record company, what is going to be done with the record? If there is a contractual obligation on the company's part to actively promote your record by spending at least a certain sum on the promotion over and above all other amounts such as overhead, salaries, and administrative expenses of the company, your record could obviously have a better chance to make it. Some record companies will refuse to include a provision requiring it to spend money to promote an artist's record, reasoning that if the record appears to have a chance to become a hit, the company will spend a sufficient amount of money promoting it without a provision in the agreement requiring such promotion. However, if the company releases a record that is mediocre, the fact that the company is contractually obligated to spend a certain amount of money on that particular record to promote it may make the difference between the record being a hit or a stiff.

Royalties

What percentage should you be paid as a royalty on sales of your records? How should the royalty be computed and paid? Should the royalty rate for tape records be the same as the royalty rate on disc records? What about royalties on your records sold outside of the United States or on records sold through record clubs or by means of so called "TV Broadcast Packages"?

All of the above questions plus numerous others are involved in the confusing area of royalty provisions in recording agreements.

Royalty Rate

Generally, the royalty rate payable to an unknown recording artist by a record company will be in the range of 6–8 percent of the retail list price (or the wholesale equivalent) of all such artist's records sold. Therefore, if we are discussing the sale of an LP album containing your performances which sells for $6.98, you would receive a royalty of about 42 cents for each such LP album sold on a royalty rate of 6%. Right? Wrong!

Royalty Payment on 100 Percent vs. 90 Percent of Records Sold

It is almost always the case that a record company will pay royalties on 90 percent of records sold and not on 100 percent. In the days of 78 rpm records, an average of 10 percent of records shipped would break or chip and had to be thrown away. Now, records are unbreakable, but record companies nevertheless continue the practice of paying royalties on 90 percent of records sold. Sometimes a record company will make an exception and pay an artist or producer on 100 percent of records sold, but this is usually when the artist or producer is well known. However, there is no harm in your attempting to negotiate with the company for payment to you of royalties based on 100 percent of sales especially on records sold during the option years of your contract.

Increased Royalty Rate Each Year

Since for now you are at least relatively unknown as a recording artist, your bargaining power on certain terms of your contract (such as the royalty rate during the first year of the agreement) will not be great. In the later years of your contract, definitely try for an increased royalty rate. An increase of 1–2 percent per year over that of the previous year is not an unreasonable request for you to make.

Foreign Royalties

Most record companies do not directly distribute records themselves outside of the United States but instead license the rights to manufacture and sell records in foreign countries to third-party licensees. As a result of such licensing, most record companies will not earn as much money on the sale of records by such licensees as they do on domestic sales of the same record. Naturally, the loss is passed on to the recording artist in the form of a reduced royalty. Therefore, you may expect to be paid only 50 percent of your full royalty rate on foreign sales of your records.

Foreign royalties should be based either upon the suggested retail list price of the country of sale or on the same basis as the record company is being paid by its licensee. The foreign royalty rate should not be based upon the list price of the country of manufacture because your records could be manufactured in a country where the list price is kept artificially low, thus the royalties payable to you on such sales would be effectively reduced.

Free Records

It is customary for record companies to give a certain number of free commercial copies of a particular record to record distributors when the distributors purchase a certain number of such record. For example, for each 10 LP albums sold, the record company might give the distributor 3 free copies of the album or alternatively, the record company might ship 10 commercial copies of the album to the distributor and charge him for only 7 copies. Commercial copies are those copies sold to the public as opposed to noncommercial or so-called "DJ copies" which are copies of the record labeled "not for sale."

Since, in theory, the record company does not benefit from the free records it gives to distributors, most likely there will be a provision in your agreement providing that you will not be paid on such "freebies." The problem is that you would not want too many of your records given as freebies, or you might never receive any royalties. Therefore, the number of commercial copies of each of your records that a record company has the right to give away should be limited. This can be accomplished effectively by providing in your agreement that the company's free-record policy with respect to your records will not be different from its free-record policy with respect to the majority of company's other recording artists, and further, that your records will not be utilized as so called "loss leaders." (Loss leaders are records which are given away or sold at a discount to induce the sale of records by another artist.) Finally, since many record companies allow the distributors to return all unsold records for full credit and the amount of money for such returns is deducted from the artist's royalties, your contract should provide that any records returned will be credited to records sold and records given away free in the same proportion as they were shipped to the distributor. It would not be fair for the distributor to return records that were shipped to him as free records (and on which you were not paid royalties) for credit and permit the record company to deduct the amount so credited from your royalties for the second time.

Tape Royalties

The sale of records in the form of multi-track tapes, in tape cassettes and in the form of reel-to-reel tapes is a multimillion-dollar-per-year business. With the perfection of tape playback systems, many consumers are purchasing tape records instead of the disc record counterpart because tapes are not as fragile as discs. Tapes do not scratch or warp or wear out as fast as disc records. Some record companies manufacture and sell tape records themselves, while other companies license tape rights to third parties and are paid a royalty and/or advance payment by the licensee.

Most standard recording agreements will provide that the artist will receive 50 percent of the full royalty rate on tape sales. If you are dealing with a record company which manufactures and sells tapes itself, there is no reason why you should not receive a full royalty on sales of tapes because there is no third-party licensee involved in such sales. The record company is making a full profit on the sales, and the benefit should be passed on to you. Sometimes a record company will pay the artist up to 75 percent of the full record royalty, but most companies will stand firm on the 50 percent royalty.

Record-Club Sales

In recent years, a certain segment of the record-purchasing public has been purchasing an increasing number of records through the mail by means of record clubs. Ordinarily, a record company will pay the artist 50 percent of the full record royalty on sales through record clubs because most record companies will license their record-club rights to third-party licensees. The net profit to such record companies per record will be less than if such companies would have sold such records themselves.

Some record companies manufacture and sell records through their own record clubs. In this case, you may wish to add a clause to your agreement providing for a royalty rate greater than 50 percent of the full rate on sales of your records through such company-owned record clubs since the record company is probably making more money on these sales than a record company who licenses its record-club rights to third parties.

One important point regarding sales of records through record clubs is that a record club will often give thousands of records of a hot artist away as a bonus or free record to its members to induce sales of less popular records. Unless your agreement provides otherwise, you will not be paid on the distribution of such free and bonus records. To protect yourself from this contingency, have your agreement modified to provide that you will be paid on not less than 50 percent of the aggregate number of each of your records distributed by the record club.

Packaging Deduction

Since the package containing your record or tape costs money to manufacture, it is customary for a record company to deduct such packaging costs from the price of the record or tape prior to computing royalties. Sometimes a recording contract will provide that the record company may deduct a "reasonable" amount for packaging and if this type of provision is in your contract, you may wish to have the agreement modified. Instead of a "reasonable" deduction (which could mean most anything), your agreement should provide that the deduction for packaging will not exceed the actual cost of packaging will not exceed the actual cost of packaging or 10 percent of the retail list price of each LP album and 20 percent of the retail list price per each tape record sold, whichever is less. Further, it is not customary to charge an artist with the costs of single record sleeves unless they are in color or are of a special type.

Reserves for Returns

A record company customarily allows the record distributor to whom the company has shipped records to return all unsold records for full credit. Sometimes it may take months or longer before the distributor will return its unsold records; therefore, a record company will withhold or "reserve" a portion of the royalties otherwise payable to the artist to provide for these returns. If your contract provides that the record company has the right to withhold royalties as reserves for returns, it would be a reasonable request on your part to require the company to specify in your agreement a maximum amount of your royalties it is able to withhold as a reserve for returns. For example, a request by you that the company shall not withhold more than 25 percent of your royalties as a reserve against returns is not unreasonable.

Further, the record company should not be able to withhold the reserves for an unlimited period of time and should be contractually compelled to "liquidate" the reserve within a specified time period. A clause in your agreement compelling the record company to liquidate each reserve within 12–18 months following the date such reserve was first withheld would not be an unreasonable request on your part.

The Catchall Royalty

Sometimes a record company will exploit records in certain areas (such as the licensing of records to airlines for broadcast over speakers in airplanes, etc.) not covered in your agreement. Further, there may be some new means of exploiting records devised in the future by which the record company can earn money which is not covered by your agreement. Therefore, it would be wise for you to have a clause added to your agreement providing for payment to you of 50 percent of what the record company receives from the exploitation of your recordings in connection with all uses not specified in the contract.

Also, with respect to each of the areas relating to record sales where the record company licenses record or tape rights to third parties and insists on paying you no more than 50 percent of your full royalty rate on such sales—i.e., foreign sales, tape sales and sales through record clubs, etc.—it would be wise for you to attempt to have a clause added to your contract providing for payment to you of 50 percent of what the record company receives from sales of your records through each such license or 50 percent of your full royalty rate, whichever is greater.

Accounting Provisions

Most recording contracts provide for semiannual accounting by the company to the artist. You should request that in addition to the information contained in its standard accounting statement, the company will set forth for each accounting period the amount of reserves being withheld from your royalties, the net sales of your records and tapes, both foreign and domestic, the amounts and kinds of items being recouped from your royalties or otherwise charged against your account—(packaging charges, recording costs, etc.)—, the number of "freebies" given to distributors, the number of records sold through record clubs, etc. There may be a clause in your agreement providing that you waive any objections to matters contained in an accounting statement unless you have objected to such statement within a specified period of time. You should have the right to question a faulty accounting statement *at any time* prior to the date when the statute of limitations as provided by state law with respect to such statement has elapsed. Therefore, you may want to have your agreement modified to delete any such waiver.

You should also request that your agreement contain a clause giving you the right at least once per year to audit the books and records of the record company with respect to your record sales.

TV Broadcast Packages

In the last few years, many record companies have licensed the rights to sell certain of their artists' recordings over radio and television. Since the records are usually being sold for the full price by these licensees, and since it is often the case that the record company receives a pro-rata royalty equivalent to the full retail price for such records sold, it would be wise for you to request that your contract provide that the sale of your records by means of any so-called TV Broadcast Package or any similar method will be treated as a "full-priced" sale insofar as the payment of royalties to you is concerned.

Indemnification

Your recording agreement will most likely provide that you agree to indemnify the record company from any claim made or action brought against the company relating to your services. Pursuant to such indemnification clause, you will probably be responsible for all costs of suit and attorneys' fees if such a claim is made or action is brought against the company. Further, such indemnification clause will probably permit the company to withhold all royalties payable to you in the event of such claim or action.

If your contract contains such an indemnification by you, you should request that the contract be modified to provide for a mutual indemnity so that the company will be obligated to indemnify you against any claims made or actions brought against the company or you resulting from some wrong committed by the record company. You should also have your contract modified to provide that in no event shall the company have the right to withhold royalties payable to you in an amount not reasonably related to the amount of any claim, and if the claim is brought as a result of a wrong committed by the company, the company should not have the right to withhold any of your royalties.

Performance as a Musician for Third Parties

If you are a musician as well as a singer, you will want to provide in your recording agreement that you will have the right during the term of the recording agreement to perform as a musician or sideman for third parties. The record company should have no objection to this request but it may require that except for records released by such record company that during the term of your recording agreement no credit will be given to you on any album covers or liners, etc., which restriction is reasonable.

Assignment

Many recording agreements provide that the record company has the right to assign the agreement or any rights relating to the agreement to any person, firm, or corporation. If this type of provision is in your agreement, it might be wise to have the agreement modified to provide that the record company may assign the agreement but only to a person, firm, or corporation that acquires all or a substantial portion of the stock or assets of the company to whom you are signed. Such a modification would help prevent the company to whom you are signed from assigning your agreement to just anybody while retaining all of its other artists.

Also, your contract should provide that prior to any assignment of your agreement the assignee (the one to whom your contract is being assigned) shall agree to assume all of the obligations of the company to whom you are signed in connection with your agreement, and further, that such company to whom you are signed will remain liable to you as a principal along with the assignee after the assignment.

Artist's Guarantee of Performance

Quite often, an artist will sign a recording agreement with a person or small company, and that person or company will make a deal with a large recording company for the production of masters embodying the artist's performances. This is the typical "master production deal." As a condition to the deal, the large record company will probably require the artist to sign what is called an artist's guarantee of performance. If this happens to you, remember that by signing such a guarantee of performance, the large record company will have the right to take over your recording contract so that you would be performing directly for that company if the person or company to whom you are signed should cease to be entitled to your services or fail or refuse to make your services available to the large record company pursuant to the terms of the master production agreement.

In other words, there may come a time when you could find yourself bound directly to the large record company as one of its recording artists for the duration of the term of your present agreement with the person or company to whom you are signed. Therefore it is important to analyze the artist's guarantee of performance to make certain that by signing the guarantee, you are not granting the large record company any greater rights to your services than you have already granted to the person or company to whom you are signed.

EXCLUSIVE SONGWRITER'S AGREEMENT

You may be requested to sign an exclusive songwriter's agreement. The following are some of the more basic "deal points" of which you should be aware with respect to an exclusive songwriter's agreement:

Term

If you are entering into any other agreement for your services with the same person or corporation that is requesting you to sign the songwriter's agreement, it would be a good idea to provide that the term of all the agreements will expire on the same date. In this way, when one agreement between you and the person or corporation ends, all of the agreements would end, and you would be free to sign with someone else.

Salary

Most songwriter's agreements will provide for the writer to submit a certain minimum number of musical compositions each month to the party to whom he is signed (we will call such party the "Publisher"). Therefore, it would not be unreasonable for the songwriter to request that a salary be paid to the writer each month by the Publisher.

Exploitation of the Musical Compositions.

Almost all exclusive songwriter's contracts provide that the songwriter shall assign to the Publisher 100 percent of the copyright rights in each musical composition written by the songwriter during the term of the agreement, with a royalty to be paid to the songwriter by the Publisher from the exploitation of each such musical composition.

If you find such a clause in your agreement, you may wish to provide that you shall retain a 50 percent ownership interest in the copyright in each such musical composition and/or that 100 percent of all of the rights which were assigned to the Publisher by you under the agreement will be reconveyed and assigned to you with respect to each musical composition that has not been recorded and commercially released in the United States on a record within one year following the date of submission by you to the Publisher of such musical composition. The inclusion of such a reversionary provision in your agreement would compel the Publisher either to have each song of yours recorded and released, or else you would regain all of the rights in such song.

If you are able to include a provision in your agreement providing for the retention by you of a part interest in the copyright of each song, you may wish to form your own publishing company and register it with a performing-rights organization, i.e., either Broadcast Music, Inc. (BMI) or American Society of Composers, Authors and Publishers (ASCAP), if your company qualifies for such registration. By becoming affiliated with a performing-rights society, either as a songwriter or publisher, you would be entitled to all of the benefits of such affiliation, such as the possibility of receiving advances from the society, etc.

In addition to the payment to you of royalties as a songwriter (as set forth below), you could, as co-owner of the copyrights in your songs, request that the Publisher pay you up to 50 percent of the Publisher's share of all sums relating to the exploitation of each such musical composition.

Royalty

It is customary for the songwriter to receive certain royalties and other payments in connection with the exploitation of the musical compositions that have been assigned by the writer to the Publisher.

The payment to the writer of approximately 4–5 cents per copy of sheet music sold in the United States and Canada and 50 percent of the royalties received by the Publisher from the sale of such sheet music outside the United States and Canada is standard. A royalty equal to 10 percent of the Publisher's net receipts from the sale of dance orchestrations, band arrangements, and a royalty equal to the proportionate share of 10 percent of the Publisher's net receipts from the sale of each songbook or folio printed by the Publisher are standard royalty rates.

The customary payment to the songwriter for the licensing of mechanical reproduction of the musical composition on records and tapes and from so called "synchronization rights" for the use in motion pictures is 50 percent of Publisher's net receipts received from such licensing. There should also be a clause included by you in the agreement providing that you shall receive not less than 50 percent of any advances received by the Publisher from the exploitation of any musical compositions written by you and further, that you shall receive not less than 50 percent of all amounts received by the Publisher resulting from the exploitation of any of your musical compositions for any uses not covered by the agreement.

Deductions from Royalties

Most exclusive songwriter's contracts will provide for the recoupment by the Publisher from royalties payable to the songwriter of all costs incurred by the Publisher from the exploitation of the musical compositions written by the songwriter under the contract. Costs such as demo expenses, copyright fees, legal fees, search fees, printing costs and expenses incurred by the Publisher in administering the copyrights in the musical compositions are ordinarily recouped from the songwriter's royalties.

However, since the Publisher is probably receiving an ownership interest in the copyrights in your songs under the agreement, it is not unreasonable for the Publisher to share such costs. Therefore, if your agreement provides that the Publisher has the right to recoup 100 percent of such costs from your royalties you should request that the agreement be modified so that you and the Publisher will each bear a pro-rata share of the costs in the same ratio as your and the Publisher's interest is in the copyrights in the songs.

Administration of the Copyrights

The standard exclusive songwriter's agreement will usually provide that the Publisher will have the worldwide perpetual right to administer the copyrights in the musical compositions written by the songwriter during the term of the contract, and for such administration the Publisher will usually be entitled to deduct from 10 to 20 percent of the gross receipts received by the Publisher from the exploitation of such musical compositions.

If there is such a clause in your agreement, you may wish the agreement modified to provide that no fee be charged for administration if the Publisher or a company affiliated with the Publisher administers the copyrights. This is because the Publisher is receiving either all or a portion of the copyright ownership in the songs, which includes a participation in any profits. Therefore it would not be fair to you to be charged with the administration unless the Publisher has to pay for the administration.

Accounting

Many Publishers account to their songwriters semiannually, but some Publishers will agree to account to their songwriters four times per year upon the request of the writer. Therefore, if your agreement contains a semiannual accounting provision, you may try to have your agreement modified to provide for quarterly accounting, which would be more beneficial to you.

If your agreement has a clause waiving your right to object to matters contained in a particular accounting statement unless an objection is made within a specified time after the statement has been rendered, you should have the agreement modified to provide that you may object to any accounting statement and any matters contained in such statement until such time as the statute of limitations as provided by state law has elapsed.

You may want a clause added to your agreement providing for a detailed royalty breakdown to be furnished along with each accounting statement. Finally, your agreement should provide for you to have the right to audit the books and records of the Publisher with respect to any matters relating to your musical compositions at least once per year.

Indemnification

Most songwriters' contracts provide that in the event a claim is made or an action is brought against the Publisher with respect to any of the musical compositions, the songwriter agrees to indemnify the Publisher and to pay all costs of suit and attorneys' fees. In addition, the Publisher will have the right to withhold royalties payable to the songwriter in the event such a claim or action occurs. If your contract has such an indemnification clause, you should modify the agreement to provide for a mutual indemnity whereby you would agree to indemnify the Publisher as aforesaid and the Publisher would similarly indemnify you in the event a claim or action was brought against the Publisher and/or you resulting from a wrong committed by the Publisher. Also, it would be wise to provide that in no event could the Publisher withhold royalties otherwise payable to you in an amount not reasonably related to the amount of any claim, and if the claim were brought because of the Publisher's wrong the Publisher should not be entitled to withhold any of your royalties.

Assignment

If your agreement provides that the Publisher can assign the agreement or any of Publisher's rights in the agreement to any person, firm, or corporation, you may want the agreement modified so that the Publisher can assign your agreement only to a person, firm or corporation that acquires all or a substantial portion of the stock or assets of the Publisher. This would prevent the Publisher from "selling" your agreement to a stranger without also assigning the rest of the agreements owned by the Publisher.

Also, you should provide in your agreement that the Publisher will remain liable to you as a principal along with any assignee, and further, that prior to any assignment of your agreement, the assignee must agree to perform all the Publisher's obligations to you under the agreement.

CONDITIONS TO THE EXERCISE OF OPTIONS

It is important for the recording artist to consider providing in his recording contract that the record company cannot exercise its options unless certain conditions occur. Similarly, you may wish to provide that unless certain conditions have occurred during the current period of your songwriter's contract, the Publisher cannot exercise his next option. Some suggested conditions are:

a.   A minimum number of chart records during the current year containing your songs;

b.   A minimum advance to be paid to you by the Publisher upon the exercise of each option;

c.   A minimum number of your songs recorded and released commercially on records during the current year, etc.

CROSS COLLATERALIZATION

You should provide in your agreement that nothing contained therein (including, without limitation, all sums of money) will be cross-collateralized with any other agreement, and further that the Publisher will set up a separate account for your songwriter's agreement.

DEMOS

As a general rule, a recording artist has a better chance of making a record deal with a record company if he has an agent. A good agent knows whom to see at record companies to have the artist's material listened to as well as the proper person to contact to make a record deal for the artist he represents. If you are unable to find a suitable agent to represent you, you can try dealing directly with the record company by sending your demo to the person who reviews demos at the record company.

A week or two after you have sent your demo, call the person to whom the demo was sent to see if the record company is interested. Also, if you are performing live, let the record company know where and when you are appearing when you send in the demo. This could enhance your chances of success with the record company; if your demo was well received, someone at the record company would probably want to see your live performance.

Although it is exciting to sign a record contract with a record company, a recording contract is not the end—it's just the beginning. Many artists who have signed record deals have been frustrated and disappointed when they discover that nothing has happened after the release of their record. As is the case with life in general, most of the time success is up to the individual who desires it. Therefore, the artist who is fortunate enough to sign with a record company must continue making as many personal appearances as he or she can. Also, the artist must make as many contacts as possible with important people in the record business. This can be done by making it a point to frequent places where record people congregate. A list of various record companies in the United States can be found in the Appendix.

Submission of Demos

If you are a songwriter as well as a singer, you should send a copy of your demo to music publishers as well as to record companies. If you strike out on the record-company level, you may nevertheless arouse a publisher's interest in your material. Before you send any material to a publishing company, it would be wise to contact the company and find out if material is presently being reviewed and to whom the material should be sent. A list of various music publishers can be found in the Appendix.

PERFORMING RIGHTS SOCIETIES

One of the copyright rights afforded the songwriter is the right to perform his copyrighted work for profit. Since it would be difficult for songwriters to travel around the country negotiating and collecting fees from everyone who performs their copyrighted compositions for profit, publishers and songwriters usually affiliate themselves with either the American Society of Composers, Authors and Publishers (ASCAP) or Broadcast Music, Inc. (BMI). Both ASCAP and BMI are performing-rights societies and they act as agents for publishers and songwriters to deal with and collect performance monies from radio and television stations, nightclubs, etc.

Both BMI and ASCAP require that before a songwriter is accepted as a member, he must have had at least one song published or commercially recorded, and before a publisher is accepted, the publisher must have been actively engaged in music publications which have been used or distributed on a commercial scale for at least one year. It is possible for some writers to receive advances and bonuses from BMI and ASCAP under certain conditions. You can contact ASCAP at 6430 Sunset Boulevard, Hollywood, CA 90028 or One Lincoln Plaza, New York, 10023. The address for BMI is 589 Fifth Avenue, New York, 10017 or 6255 Sunset Boulevard, Hollywood, CA 90028.

The form agreements in the Appendix (with corresponding revisions) are the standard types of agreements currently being used by many record companies, music publishing companies and personal management companies. Although the unknown artist may not be able to obtain the same kind of deal as is reflected in the revised artist's production, songwriter's or management agreements, the artist should nevertheless request that these changes be made when presented with the applicable standard "form" agreement for signature.

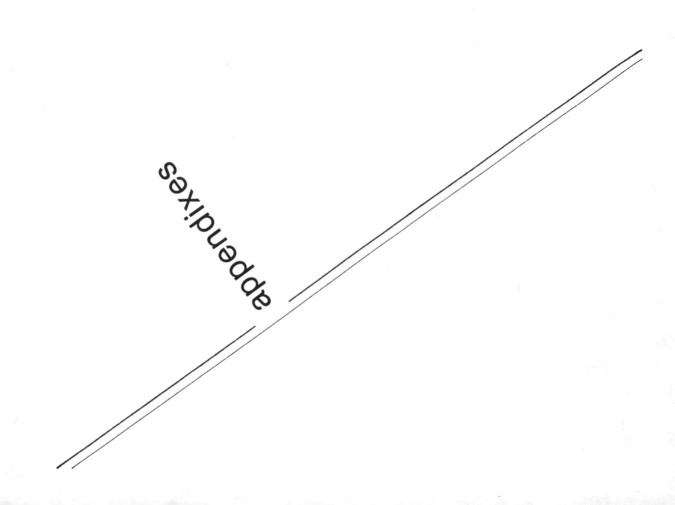

appendixes

RECORDING STUDIOS

ALABAMA

Boutwell Recording Studios, Inc.
726 South 23rd St.
Birmingham 35233
(205) 251-8889

Broadway Sound Studio
1307 Broadway St.
Sheffield 35660
(205) 381-1833

Fame Recording Studios, Inc.
603 East Avalon Ave.
Sheffield 35660
(205) 381-0801

Muscle Shoals Sound Studios
3615 Jackson Hwy.
Muscle Shoals 35660
(205) 381-2060

Music Mill Recording Studio, Inc.
1108 East Avalon Ave.
Sheffield 35660
(205) 381-5100

New London Recording Center
1817 Oxmoor Rd.
Birmingham 35209
(205) 871-4221

Prestige Productions
2717 South 19th St.
Birmingham 35209
(205) 871-7328

Rally Ranch Recording Studios
Lake Robinwood Rd.
Coker 35452
(205) 752-5067

Sound of Birmingham
3625 Fifth Ave.
Birmingham 35228
(205) 595-8497

Widget Sound Studios
3804 Jackson Hwy.
Sheffield 35660
(205) 381-1300

Wishbone Recording Studio
P.O. Box 2631 Webster Ave.
Sheffield 35660
(205) 381-1455

Woodrich Recording Studio
P.O. Box 38, George Wallace Pk. Dr.
Lexington 35648
(205) 247-3983

ALASKA

Arctic Studios
2427 East 85th
Anchorage 99507
(907) 344-7514

ARIZONA

Audio Recorders of Arizona, Inc.
3830 North Seventh St.
Phoenix 85014
(602) 277-4723

Lee Fur's Recording Studio, Inc.
25 East Glenn
Tucson 85705
(602) 792-3470

Pantheon Recording Studio
6325 North Invergordon Rd.
Paradise Valley 85253
(602) 948-5883

ARKANSAS

Pinnacle Sound Productions, Inc.
1 Warren Dr.
Little Rock 72209
(501) 565-2800

Variety Recording Studio
213 East Monroe
Jonesboro 72401
(501) 935-8820

Village Recording Studios
10 Boston Square
Fort Smith 79201
(501) 782-5051

CALIFORNIA

A & M Records
1416 North La Brea Ave.
Los Angeles 90028
(213) 469-2411

Annex Studios
1032 North Sycamore Ave.
Los Angeles 90038
(213) 464-7441

Artisan Sound Recorders
1600 North Wilcox Ave.
Los Angeles 90028
(213) 461-2751

Artists Recording Studio
1644 North Cherokee Ave.
Hollywood 90028
(213) 464-8954

Audio Arts, Inc.
5611 Melrose Ave.
Los Angeles 90038

Audio Recorders
3843 Richmond St.
San Diego 92103

Beggs/American Zoetrope Recording
916 Kearny St.
San Francisco 94133
(415) 788-8345

Bell Sound Studios
916 North Citrus Ave.
Los Angeles 90038
(213) 461-3036

Blue Bear Studios
915 Howard St.
San Francisco 94103
(415) 543-2125

Bolic Sound Studios Inc.
1310 North La Brea Ave.
Inglewood 90302
(213) 678-2632

Brandt's Recording Studio
1030 48th St.
Sacramento 95819
(916) 451-3400

Brother Studio
154 Fifth St.
Santa Monica 90401
(213) 451-5433

Burbank Studios
4000 Warner Blvd.
Burbank 91522
(213) 843-6000

Capitol Records, Inc.
1750 North Vine St.
Hollywood 90028
(213) 462-6252

Catero Sound Company
827 Folsom St.
San Francisco 94102
(415) 777-2930

Cherokee Studios
751 North Fairfax
Los Angeles 90046
(213) 653-3412

Columbia Recorders
829 Folsom St.
San Francisco 94107
(415) 397-2600

Cross-Over Recorders
2107 West Washington Blvd.
Los Angeles 90018
(213) 737-8000

Crystal-Sound Recording
1014 North Vine St.
Los Angeles 90038
(213) 466-6452

Devonshire Sound Studio
10729 Magnolia Blvd.
North Hollywood 91601
(213) 985-1945

Different Fur Music
3470 19th St.
San Francisco 94110
(415) 864-1967

Elektra Sound Recorders
962 North La Cienega Blvd.
Los Angeles 90069
(213) 655-8280

Factory Productions
P.O. Box 9246
Berkeley 94709
(415) 527-4040

Fred Fox Music Company Studio
15 South Ontario
San Mateo 94401

GBR Studios
11557 East West Ripon Rd.
Ripon 95366
(209) 599-2573

Gold Star Recording Studio
6252 Santa Monica Blvd.
Los Angeles 90038
(213) 469-1173

Golden State Recorders, Inc.
665 Harrison
San Francisco 94107
(415) 781-6306

Golden West Sound Studios
6429-½ Selma Ave.
Hollywood 90028
(213) 461-4231

Heavenly Recording & Production
    Studios
1020 35th Ave.
Sacramento 95822
(916) 428-5888

Wally Heider Recording
245 Hyde St.
San Francisco 94102
(415) 771-5780

Wally Heider Recording
1604 North Cahuenga Blvd.
Hollywood 90028
(213) 466-5474

His Master's Wheels
60 Brady St.
San Francisco 94103

Hollywood Sound Recorders
6367 Selma Ave.
Hollywood 90028
(213) 467-1411

ID Sound Studios, Inc.
1556 North La Brea Ave.
Hollywood 90028
(213) 462-6477

Kendun Recorders, Inc.
619 South Glenwood Pl.
Burbank 91506
(213) 843-8096

Larrabee Sound
8811 Santa Monica Blvd.
Los Angeles 90069
(213) 657-6750

Mantra Studio
2207 South El Camino Real
San Mateo 94403

MCA Recording Studios
100 Universal City Plaza
Universal City 91608
(213) 985-4321

Mother Music Sound Recorders
415 North Tustin Ave.
Orange 92666
(714) 639-6420

Music City Recording Studio
3250 East 14th
Oakland 94601
(415) 535-0333 or 658-5344

The Music Machine
11724 Ventura Blvd.
Studio City 91604
(213) 769-9451

Mystic Sound Studio
6277 Selma Ave.
Hollywood 90028
(213) 464-9667

Original Sound Studios
7120 Sunset Blvd.
Hollywood 90046
(213) 851-1147

Paramount Recording Studios
6245 Santa Monica Blvd.
Los Angeles 90038
(213) 461-3717

Record Plant
8456 West Third St.
Los Angeles 90048
(213) 653-0240

Sound Factory
6357 Selma Ave.
Hollywood 90028
(213) 461-3096

Star Track Recording Studio
8615 Santa Monica Blvd.
Los Angeles 90069
(213) 855-1171

Studio West
5042 Ruffner
San Diego 92111
(714) 277-4714

Sunset Sound Recorders
6650 Sunset Blvd.
Hollywood 90028
(213) 469-1186

Sunwest Recording Studios
5533 Sunset Blvd.
Hollywood 90028
(213) 463-5631

Supersound
600 East Franklin
Monterey 93940
(408) 649-4100

United Artists Recording Studio
8715 West 3rd St.
Los Angeles 90048
(213) 272-4483

United-Western Recording Studios
6000 Sunset Blvd.
Hollywood 90028
(213) 469-3983

Valentine Recording Studios
5330 Laurel Canyon Blvd.
North Hollywood 91607
(213) 769-1515

The Village Recorder
1616 Butler Ave.
Los Angeles 90025
(213) 478-8227

Whitney Recording Studio
1516 West Glenoaks Blvd.
Glendale 91201
(213) 245-6801

COLORADO

Audicom Corporation
995 South Clermont
Denver 80222
(303) 757-3377

Caribou Ranch
Nederlands 80466
(303) 258-3215

Carousel Productions Inc.
2501 Chase
Denver 80214
(303) 238-1229

Infal Recorders
2144 Champa St.
Denver 80202
(303) 892-7141

Jackson Sound Productions
1403 South Lipan
Denver 80223
(303) 722-7019

Northstar Studios
1831-½ Pearl St.
Boulder 80302
(309) 442-2001

Video Audio Artistry Corporation
1258 Bear Mountain Court
Boulder 80302
(309) 499-2001

Viking Studios Ltd.
1045 West Arizona Ave.
Denver 80223
(303) 744-6023

Western Cine Service, Inc.
312 South Pearl St.
Denver 80209
(303) 744-1017

CONNECTICUT

Connecticut Recording Studios
1122 Main St.
Bridgeport 06604
(203) 366-9168

The Gallery
442 Main St.
East Hartford 06118
(203) 569-1915

Honeywinds Productions, Ltd.
83 Goodhill Rd.
Weston 06880
(203) 226-5729

Trod Nossel Recording Studios
10 George St.
Wallingford 06492
(203) 269-4465

FLORIDA

Bee Jay Recording Studios
Box T, Winter Park
Orlando 32804
(305) 293-1781

Cajaput Sound Recorders
918 Lucas Rd.
Fort Myers 33901
(813) 481-6675

Cinemasound, Inc.
1755 N.E. 149th St.
Miami 33161
(305) 947-5611

Classic Sound & Recordings, Inc.
14130 Coral Way
Largo 33540
(813) 536-2514

Criteria Recording Studios
1755 N.E. 149th St.
Miami 33161
(305) 947-5611

Linale's Sound Studios
1995 N.E. 150th St.
North Miami 33161
(305) 944-1006

The Music Factory
567 N.W. 27th St.
Miami 33127
(305) 576-2600

National Guild Recording Studio
Carter Rd.
DeLand 32720
(904) 734-8118

Seabird Recording Studio
415 North Ridgewood Ave.
Edgewater 32032
(904) 427-2480

SRS International Recording Corporation
790 N.E. 45th St.
Fort Lauderdale 33334
(305) 772-0008

GEORGIA

Axis Sound Studios
1314 Ellsworth Industrial Dr. N.W.
Atlanta 30318
(404) 355-8680

Doppler Studios, Inc.
417 Peachtree St. N.E.
Atlanta 30308
(404) 873-6941

Master Sound Recording Studios
1227 Spring St. N.W.
Atlanta 30309
(404) 873-6425

Melody Recording Service
2093 Faulkner Rd.
Atlanta 30324
(404) 321-3886

Paragon Recording Studios
9 East Huron St.
Atlanta 60611
(404) 664-2412

PS Recording Studios
323 East 23rd St.
Atlanta 60616
(404) 225-2110

Rainbow Bridge Studios, Inc.
117 West Rockland Rd.
Libertyville 60048
(404) 362-4060

RKM Sound Studios
1200 Spring St. N.W.
Atlanta 30309
(404) 874-3668

Sound Market
664 North Michigan Ave.
Atlanta 60611
(404) 664-4335

Sound Studios
230 North Michigan Ave.
Atlanta 60601
(404) 236-4814

Streeterville Studios
161 East Grand
Atlanta 60611
(404) 644-1666

Universal Recording Corporation
46 East Walton St.
Atlanta 60611
(404) 642-6465

INDIANA

Allied Advertising Corporation
124 South Sixth St.
Richmond 47374
(317) 962-8596

Burlap Sound, Inc.
624 Walnut St.
Anderson 46012
(317) 649-3012

Commercial Features, Inc.
3650 North Washington Blvd.
Indianapolis 46205
(317) 926-5570

Corbett-Kirby Corporation
6231 Coffman Rd.
Indianapolis 46268
(317) 545-1491

The Music Mother
1330 North Illinois St.
Indianapolis 46202
(317) 638-1491

Tape Masters
5210 East 65th St.
Indianapolis 46220
(317) 849-0905

IOWA

A & R Recording Studio
2700 Ford St.
Ames 50010
(515) 232-2991

Iowa Great Lakes Recording Company
906 Ninth St.
Milford 51351
(712) 338-4482

Kajac Record Corporation
155 First St.
Carlisle 50047
(515) 989-0876

Lariam Associates, Inc.
515 28th St.
Des Moines 50314
(515) 282-8306

Triad Productions Inc.
1910 Ingersoll
Des Moines 50309
(515) 243-2125

KENTUCKY

Allen-Martin Productions
9701 Taylorsville Rd.
Louisville 40299
(502) 267-9658

Century Sound & Recording
3029 Oregon St.
Paducah 42001
(502) 554-2722

House of Truth Studio
3701 West Broadway
Louisville 40211
(502) 776-4786

Lemco Sound Studio
2518 Southview Dr.
Lexington 40503
(606) 277-1184

Sun-Ray Records
1662 Wyatt Pkwy.
Lexington 40505
(606) 254-7474

LOUISIANA

American Recording Studios
707-709 West California Ave.
Ruston 71270
(318) 255-0287

Deep South Recorders
7525 Jefferson Hwy.
Baton Rouge 70806
(504) 926-0456

Knight Recording Studio, Inc.
3116 Metairie Rd.
Metairie 70001
(504) 834-5711

La Louisianne
711 Stevenson
Lafayette 70501
(318) 234-4118

Modern Sound Studios
413 North Parkerson Ave.
Crowley 70526
(504) 783-1601

Sound City Recording
3316 Line Ave.
Shreveport 70586
(318) 861-2139

Swallow Recording Studios
434 East Main St.
Ville Platte 70586
(318) 363-2139

Ultrasonic Studios, Inc.
7210 Washington Ave.
New Orleans 70125
(504) 486-4873

MAINE

Concert Records
25 Champion Rd.
Cape Elizabeth
(207) 799-4265

EAB Recording Studio
223 Lisbon St.
Lewiston 04240
(207) 784-4944

Eight Track
South Blue Hill
South Blue Hill 04615
(207) 374-5539

MARYLAND

Blue Seas Enterprises, Inc.
P.O. Box 1633
Baltimore 21203
(301) 385-0247

DB Sound Studios, Inc.
8037 13th St.
Silver Springs 20910
(301) 589-5192

Flite Three Recording, Inc.
1130 East Cold Spring
Baltimore 21239
(301) 532-7500

Omega Recording Services
10518 Connecticut Ave.
Kensington 20795
(301) 946-4686

RMT Recording Studios
600R Holabird Ave.
Baltimore 21224
(301) 633-4224

Track Recorders, Inc.
8226 Georgia Ave.
Silver Springs 20910
(301) 589-4349

United Music Corporation
1910 Seminary Pl.
Silver Springs 20910
(301) 588-9090

MASSACHUSETTS

Dimension Sound Studios, Inc.
360 Centre St.
Jamaica Plain 02130
(617) 522-3100

Eastern Sound Recording Studios
11 Messina Ave.
Methuen 01844
(617) 685-1832

Fleetwood Recording Company, Inc.
321 Revere St.
Revere 02151
(617) 289-6800

Hermit Sound
799 Main St.
Dalton 01226
(413) 684-0898

Intermedia Sound
331 Newbury St.
Boston 02115
(617) 267-2440

Lansing Records
248 Old Windsor Rd.
Dalton 01226
(413) 684-2567

Long View Farm
Stoddard Rd.
North Brookfield 01535
(617) 867-7662

Music Designers, Inc.
1126 Boylston St.
Boston 02215
(617) 262-3546

Renaissance Church Recording Studio
71 Avenue A
Turner Falls 01376
(413) 863-9711

Shaggy Dog Studios
P.O. Box 766, Rt. 7
Stockbridge 01262
(413) 298-3737

MICHIGAN

Artie Fields Productions
9430 Woodward Ave.
Detroit 48202
(313) 873-8900

Audio Graphics
1516 Ferris Ave.
Royal Oak 48967
(313) 544-1793

Glen Roller Mills, Inc.
5402 S.W. Manitou Trail
Glen Arbor 49636
(616) 334-3223

Mutt Record Producers
27316 Michigan Ave.
Inkster 48141
(313) 565-5001

Pampa Studios
31925 Van Dyke
Warren 48093
(313) 939-3340

Pro-Gressive Productions
120 North Church St.
Kalamazoo 49006
(616) 381-1833

Sound Patterns
38180 Grand River
Farmington Hills 48024
(313) 477-6444

United Sound Systems
5840 Second Blvd.
Detroit 48202
(313) 871-2570

MINNESOTA

Artronics, Inc.
3761 North Dunlap St.
St. Paul 55112
(612) 484-1111

ASI Studios
711 West Broadway
Minneapolis 55411
(612) 521-7631

Cookhouse Recording Studios
2541 Nicollet Ave.
Minneapolis 55404
(612) 827-5441

EMC Corporation
180 East Sixth St.
St. Paul 55101
(612) 227-7366

Moon Sound Studios
2828 Dupont Ave. South
Minneapolis 55408
(612) 822-8400

Sound 80, Inc.
2709 East 25th St.
Minneapolis 55406
(612) 721-6341

MISSISSIPPI

Huff Recording
P.O. Box 2464
Laurel 39440
(601) 425-4841

Malaco Sound Recording
3023 West Northside Dr.
Jackson 39213
(601) 982-4522

MISSOURI

Archway Sound Studios
4521 Natural Bridge
St. Louis 63115
(314) 383-0067

Covern Sound Corporation
16400 East Truman Rd.
Independence 64050
(816) 836-4000

Gold Future Recording Studios
106 West Madison
St. Louis 63122
(314) 821-5537

KBK/Earth City Sound Studios
4288 Riverline Dr.
Earth City 63045
(314) 291-4840

Professional Artist Recording
2008 South 39th St.
St. Louis 63110
(314) 776-3410

Technicsonic Studios
1201 South Brentwood Blvd.
St. Louis 63117
(314) 727-1055

NEW JERSEY

Broadcast Recording Service
478 Broadway
Bayonne 07002
(201) 823-1200

Century Productions, Inc.
171 Washington Rd.
Sayreville 08872
(201) 238-5630

House of Music
1400 Pleasant Valley Way
West Orange 07052
(201) 736-3062

Quad Recording & Sound Stage
Prodigy Bldg. 6027 Rt. 130
Pennsauken 08105
(609) 662-7442

United Masterworks Recording
Company
44 Canaan Pl.
Allendale 07401
(201) 327-7737

Van Gelder Recording Studio
445 Rte. 9W
Englewood Cliffs 07632
(201) 567-4145

Vantone Recording
14 Northfield Ave.
West Orange 07052
(201) 736-3087

NEW YORK

A & R Recording, Inc.
322 West 48th St.
New York 10036
(212) 582-1070

A-1 Sound Studios, Inc.
242 West 76th St.
New York 10023
(212) 363-2603

Artcraft Recording Studios
285 East 49th St.
Brooklyn 11203
(212) 778-5150

Associated Recording Studios
723 Seventh Ave.
New York 10019
(212) 245-7640

Atlantic Recording Studio
1841 Broadway
New York 10023
(212) 484-8490

Aura Recording Studio
136 West 52nd St.
New York 10019
(212) 582-8105

Bell Sound Studios
237 West 54th St.
New York 10019
(212) 582-4812

The Big Apple
112 Greene St.
New York 10012
(212) 266-4278

Dimensional Sound, Inc.
301 West 54th St.
New York 10019
(212) 247-6010

Electric Lady Studios, Inc.
52 West 8th St.
New York 10011
(212) 777-0150

Frankford/Wayne Mastering Labs
1697 Broadway
New York 10019
(212) 582-5473

Generation Sound Studios
1650 Broadway
New York 10019
(212) 765-7400

Hit Factory, Inc.
353 West 48th St.
New York 10036
(212) 581-9590

Charles Land Studios
7 Charles St.
New York 10014
(212) 242-1479

Le Studio
143 West 51st St.
New York 10019
(212) 581-3674

Magnagraphic Studios
72 Bedford St.
New York 10014
(212) 691-2333

Magno Sound
212 West 48th St.
New York 10036
(212) 757-8857

Mastertone Recording Studios
130 West 42nd St.
New York 10036
(212) 947-2940

Mayfair Recording Studio
701 Seventh Ave.
New York 10036
(212) 581-2178

Mediasound Studios
311 West 57th St.
New York 10019
(212) 765-4700

National Recording Studios
730 Fifth Ave.
New York 10019
(212) 757-6440

Nola Sound Studios
111 West 57th St.
New York 10019
(212) 582-1417

Odo Sound Studios, Inc.
254 West 54th St.
New York 10019
(212) 757-3180

Opal Recording Studios
254 West 54th St.
New York 10019
(212) 489-6097

Plaza Sound Studios
55 West 50th St.
New York 10020
(212) 757-6111

Producers Recording Studios
45 West 54th St.
New York 10036
(212) 246-4238

The Record Plant
321 West 44th St.
New York 10036
(212) 581-6505

NORTH CAROLINA

Arthur Smith Studios
5457 Old Monroe Rd.
Charlotte 28211
(704) 536-0424

Audiofonics, Inc.
1101 Downtown Blvd.
Raleigh 27603
(919) 821-5614

Galaxie III Studios
118 Fifth St.
Taylorsville 29691
(704) 632-4735

Mega Sound Studio
P.O. Box 188
Bailey 27807
(919) 235-3362

Reflection Sound Studio
1018 Central Ave.
Charlotte 28204
(704) 377-4596

OHIO

Agency Recording
1730 East 24th St.
Cleveland 44114
(216) 621-0810

Artist's Recording Company
320 Mill St.
Cincinnati 45215
(513) 761-0011

Audio Recording Studios
601 Rockwell Ave.
Cleveland 44114
(216) 771-5112

Boddie Record Manufacturing &
Recording
12202 Union St.
Cleveland 44105
(216) 752–3340

Counterpart Creative Studios
3744 Applegate Ave.
Cincinnati 45211
(513) 661–8810

5th Floor Recording
517 West Third St.
Cincinnati 45202
(513) 651–1871

Jewel Recording Studios
1594 Kinney Ave.
Cincinnati 45231
(513) 522–9336

Mus-I-Col, Inc.
780 Oakland Park Ave.
Cleveland 43224
(216) 267–3133

NNR Recording Studio
5725 Brookpark Rd.
Cleveland 44129
(216) 749–5550

Owl Recording Studios
2551 Sunbury Rd.
Cleveland 43219
(216) 475–6309

Peppermint Productions, Inc.
803 East Indianaola Ave.
Youngstown 44502
(216) 783–2222

QCA Recording Studio
2832 Spring Grove Ave.
Cincinnati 45225
(513) 681–8400

Rite Recording Studio
9745 Lockland Rd.
Cincinnati 45215
(513) 733–5533

OKLAHOMA

Benson Sound, Inc.
3707 South Blackwelder Ave.
Oklahoma City 73119
(405) 534–4461

Producers Workshop
3604 N.W. 58th St.
Oklahoma City 73112
(405)–947–8094

OREGON

Raspberry Recording
16d Oakway Mall
Eugene 97491
(503) 687–2526

Recording Associates
5821 S.E. Powell Blvd.
Portland 97206
(503) 777–4621

Rex Recording
1931 S.E. Morrison
Portland 97206
(503) 238–4525

Rose City Sound, Inc.
1925 S.E. Morrison
Portland 97215
(503) 238–6330

Spectrum Studios Inc.
905 S.W. Alder St.
Portland 97205
(503) 248–0248

PENNSYLVANIA

Asterisk Recording
700 Wood St.
Pittsburgh 15221
(412) 731–6060

Audio Innovators, Inc.
216 Blvd. of the Allies
Pittsburgh 15222
(412) 391–6220

Brumley Artists Agency
605 Paloma Dr.
Bakersfield 93304
(805) 832-1177

California Artists Corporation
P.O. Box 11474
Fresno 93773
(209) 222-8702

Wilson Call
2200 "F" St.
Bakersfield 93301
(805) 325-1251

Celebrities, Inc.
15433 Ventura Blvd., Suite 1401
Sherman Oaks 91403
(213) 788-6362

Chartwell Artists
1901 Ave. of the Stars, Suite 670
Los Angeles 90067
(213) 553-3600

Chicory Management
6362 Hollywood Blvd.
Hollywood 90028

Concert Tour Services
9120 Sunset Blvd.
Los Angeles 90069
(213) 271-7221

Wayne Coombs Agency
8733 Sunset Blvd.
Hollywood 90069
(213) 659-5560

Creative Corporations
P.O. Box 1737
Hollywood 90028
(213) 766-2626

Creative Entertainment Associates
6911 Hayvenhurst Ave.
Van Nuys 91406
(213) 997-0338

Crescendo Agency
9165 Sunset Blvd.
Los Angeles 90069
(213) 275-1108

Crosby Music Agency
7730 Herschel Ave.
La Jolla 92037
(714) 276-7381

The Daro Agency
P.O. Box 633
Carmel Valley 93924
(408) 659-4451

Del Oro Company
3521 Grand Ave.
Oakland 94610
(415) 451-1224

A. Di Martino Production Company
6365 Selma Ave.
Hollywood 90028
(213) 463-2312

Direction Artist Managers
P.O. Box 2389
Hollywood 90028
(213) 276-2063

Manny Duran
1739 Tenth Ave.
San Francisco 94122
(415) 731-0421

Ronald L. Eisenberg Management
2700 Le Conte Ave., Suite 600
Berkeley 94709
(415) 894-1371

Franklyn Agency
999 North Doheny Dr., Suite 808
Los Angeles 90069
(213) 274-1115

Frischer Productions
16400 Ventura Blvd.
Encino 91604
(213) 784-6495

GTO Management/Recorders
8899 Beverly Blvd.
Los Angeles 90048
(213) 274-7381

Gemini Artists Management, Ltd.
9229 Sunset Blvd.
Los Angeles 90069
(213) 550-0191

Sandra Getz Agency
1727 North Crescent Heights Blvd.
Los Angeles 90069
(213) 650-1313

Heart & Soul Enterprise
P.O. Box 3808
Hollywood 90028
(714) 883-9123

The Heller-Fischel Agency
260 South Beverly Dr., Suite 308
Beverly Hills 90212
(213) 278-4787

Rob Heller Enterprise
9869 Santa Monica Blvd.
Beverly Hills 90212
(213) 553-7112

ICA Talent
9121 Sunset Blvd.
Los Angeles 90069
(213) 550-0254

Intercontinental Absurdities, Ltd.
5831 Sunset Blvd.
Los Angeles 90028
(213) 461-3277

International Artists Agency
1564 18th Ave.
San Francisco 94122
(415) 661-1962

JM Associates
8400 Sunset Blvd.
Los Angeles 90069
(213) 656-2086

Betty Kaye Productions, Inc.
2929 El Camino Ave.
Sacramento 95821
(916) 487-1923/6667

Howard King Agency
118 S. Beverly Dr., Suite 226
Beverly Hills 90212
(213) 271-7294

Kingfish
P.O. Box 1073
San Rafael 94902
(415) 457-1830

June Kingsley Artists' Management
2221 Baker St.
San Francisco 94115
(415) 931-2574

Muriel Less
142 Ninth Ave.
San Francisco 94118
(415) 386-8100

Lilienthal Programs Agency
1 Spruce St.
San Francisco 94118
(415) 221-4327

Luzane West Agency
1304 North La Brea Ave.
Inglewood 90302
(213) 295-4567

Jack McFadden
1225 North Chester Ave.
Bakersfield 93308
(805) 393-1011

Lee McRae
2130 Carleton St.
Berkeley 94704
(415) 848-5591

Reuben Mack Associates
P.O. Box 2750
Hollywood 90028
(213) 664-4341

Marianne Marshall
34 66th Pl.
Long Beach 90803
(213) 434-1374

Marshall Productions
1880 Century Park East, Suite 300
Los Angeles 90067
(213) 553-6600

Milestone Records
10th & Parker
Berkeley 94710
(415) 549-2500

Patsy Montana
1279 Studebaker Rd.
Long Beach 90815
(213) 596-0048

Monterey Peninsula Artists
P.O. Box 7308
Carmel 93921
(408) 624–4889

Musick Enterprises, Ltd.
P.O. Box 576
Burbank 91503
(213) 842–9368

NBC Booking Agency
80 Gilman Ave.
Campbell 95008
(408) 371–3434

Omac Artist Corporation
1225 North Chester Ave.
Bakersfield 93308
(805) 393–1011

Charles L. Owen
P.O. Box 842
Bakersfield 93302
(805) 871–5490

Peaceable Music
P.O. Box 77038
Los Angeles 90007
(213) 747–0938

Prestige Records
10th & Parker
Berkeley 94710
(415) 549–2500

RPM, Ltd.
400 South Beverly Dr.
Beverly Hills 90212
(213) 277–6730

Regency Artists, Ltd.
9200 Sunset Blvd., Suite 823
Los Angeles, 90069
(213) 273–7103

Howard Rose Agency
9720 Wilshire Blvd.
Beverly Hills 90212
(213) 273–6700

Dottie Ross
15300 Ventura Blvd., Suite 210
Sherman Oaks 91403
(213) 981–6988

Salle Productions
451 North Canon Dr.
Beverly Hills 90210
(213) 271–1186

San Francisco Artists
896 Folsom St.
San Francisco 94107
(415) 777–1160

George Soares Associates
12735 Ventura Blvd., Suite 15
Studio City 91604
(213) 980–0400

George Solano
2152 Mason St.
San Francisco 94133
(415) 421–3541

Special Agent Company
4924 Angeles Vista Blvd.
Los Angeles 90043
(213) 296–3870

Spectacular Productions Theatrical
  Agency
P.O. Box 15562
San Diego 92115
(714) 286–1794

Talent World Productions
8235 Santa Monica Blvd.
Hollywood 90028
(213) 656–6650

Trenda Artists
14755 Ventura Blvd.
Sherman Oaks 91403
(213) 788–4521

Vahm Entertainment Consultants
54 East Colorado Blvd.
Pasadena 91105
(213) 681–5936

Murry Weintraub
1017 North La Cienega Blvd.
Los Angeles 90069
(213) 652–3892

Lola Wilson Celebrities
139 South Beverly Dr.
Beverly Hills 90212
(213) 278–8808

Xoregos Performing Company
70 Union St.
San Francisco 94111
(415) 989-3167

COLORADO

Athena Enterprises, Inc.
1515 Monroe St.
Denver 80206
(303) 399-8681

Biscuit City Records
1106-8 East 17th Ave.
Denver 80218
(303) 832-3999

Dahlgren Artists Management
110 Cook St.
Denver 80206
(303) 320-4851

Stone County, Inc.
2107 Glenarm Pl.
Denver 80205
(303) 573-8477

Unicorn Music, Inc.
P.O. Box 11335
Denver 80212
(303) 433-1730

Reed Williams Entertainment
P.O. Box 3146
Boulder 80303
(303) 444-2560

CONNECTICUT

Act 1 Entertainments
341 Main St.
West Haven 06516
(203) 932-3405

Associated Talent Consultants
10 North Main St., Penthouse
West Hartford 06110
(203) 232-4469

Cooperative Music Consultants
53 Chamberlain St.
New Haven 06512
(203) 469-0552

Douglass Associates
17 Haynes St.
Hartford 06103
(203) 527-4980

KSM Music Productions
185 Hamilton Ave.
Watertown 06795
(203) 247-6046, (401) 232-0359

Master Talent Agency
P.O. Box 595
Hartford 06101
(203) 728-6698

Lilian Murtagh Concert Management
Box 272
Canaan 06018
(203) 824-7877

Joris Stuyck
119 June Rd.
Cos Cob 06807
(203) 322-4223

DELAWARE

Three Star Productions
201 East Village of Prestbury
Newark 19711
(302) 737-8948

DISTRICT OF COLUMBIA

Darryll Brooks
715 "G" St. N.W., Suite 306
Washington, D. C. 20001
(202) 347-3198, 783-0686

Claiborne, Inc.
2939 Van Ness St. N.W., Apt. 1217
Washington, D. C. 20008
(202) 244-3462, 347-3944

Experience Unlimited Band
1447 Howard Rd. S. E.
Washington, D. C. 20020
(202) 889-1149

Itsathang Productions
927 15th St. N.W., No. 408
Washington, D. C. 20005
(202) 638-3739

Soul City Sounds
P.O. Box 8672
Washington, D. C. 20011
(202) 882-1340

FLORIDA

Adventure Artists, Ltd.
500 Central Ave., Search Bldg.
Winter Haven 33880
(813) 299-1217

Thomas G. Barfield Management
2714 Aldine Circle
Lakeland 33801
(813) 686-6921

Bee Jay Booking Agency
Box T
Winter Park 32789
(305) 293-1781

Blade Productions
P.O. Box 12239
Gainesville 32604
(904) 372-8158

Bud Dalton
2914 Tangelo Dr.
Sarasota 33579
(813) 959-6086

George Daye, Jr.
P.O. Box 600282
North Miami Beach 33160
(305) 754-2583

Dr. Cool Productions
P.O. Box 011321
Miami 33101
(305) 672-9455

Fantasma Productions of Florida
711 South Flagler Dr.
West Palm Beach 33401
(305) 659-1216

Fusion, Inc.
4137 Malaga Ave.
Miami 33133
(305) 756-1871

Gulf Artists Productions, Inc.
1800 Amerwood Dr.
Riverview 33569
(813) 689-3944

Dick Hoekstra Agency
4747 North Ocean Blvd., Suite 225
Fort Lauderdale 33308
(305) 782-1890

Joy Productions Booking Agency
1338 Palm Beach Lakes Blvd.
West Palm Beach 33401
(305) 832-2956

Pryor-Menz Attractions
P.O. Box 9550
Panama City 32401
(904) 234-3326

Schaffer & Associates
495 S.E. Tenth Court
Hialeah 33010
(305) 888-1684

Neal Watson Attractions
2445 Ranch House Rd.
West Palm Beach 33406
(305) 686-3541

GEORGIA

Alkahest Attractions
100 Colony Sq. Bldg.
1175 Peachtree St. N.E.
Atlanta 30361
(404) 892-1843

Discovery, Inc.
3330 Peachtree Rd. N.E., Suite 239
Atlanta 30326
(404) 261-8300

Greer Agency
2343 Campbellton Rd. S.W.
Atlanta 30311
(404) 344-7504

The Hensley Agency
First Nat'l Bank Bldg.
Augusta 30902
(404) 722-8877

Susan F. Hunter
424 Princeton Way N.E.
Atlanta 30307
(404) 658-2549

Gary Monroe Promos
903 Judy Lane
Valdosta 31601
(912) 244-0651

Paragon Agency
P.O. Box 4408
Macon 31208
(912) 742-3381

HAWAII

Associated Pacific Artists
1402 Kapiolani Blvd.
Honolulu 96814
(808) 946-9028

ILLINOIS

Armageddon Bookings
P.O. Box 1232
Quincy 62301
(217) 224-1659

Robert Bauchens
41 West 987 Silver Glen Rd.
St. Charles 60174
(312) 377-0117

Beacon Artists Corporation
233 East Erie St.
Chicago 60611
(312) 787-6120

Blues Factory
7711 South Racine
Chicago 60620
(312) 488-8047

Blytham, Ltd.
P.O. Box 701
Champaign 61820
(217) 356-1857

Caroline Bowman
920 West George St.
Chicago 60657
(312) 525-5884

Jerry Butler Productions
320 East 21st St., 6th Flr.
Chicago 60616
(312) 225-0663

Scott A. Cameron Organization, Inc.
320 South Waiola Ave.
La Grange 60525
(312) 352-2026

Camil Productions
9006 South Ridgeland Ave.
Chicago 60617
(312) 374-0331

Dick/Hike Associates
4926 West Gunnison St.
Chicago 60630
(312) 545-0861

Ebony Talent Associates, Inc.
8949 South Stony Island
Chicago 60617
(312) 978-6500

Edmonds & Curley Enterprises
2800 N. Lake Shore Dr., Suite 1512
Chicago 60657
(312) 871-3334

Fountain Productions
320 East 21st St., 6th Flr.
Chicago 60616
(312) 225-0663

G & H Agent
8311 S. Crandon
Chicago 60617
(312) 221-7702

Barry Goodman
134 North La Salle St.
Chicago 60602
(312) 641-1135

Haislar Productions
311 West Main St.
Collinsville 62234
(618) 344-7910

Inner City Trade Booking
2630 East 75th St.
Chicago 60649
(312) 734-1232

Musical Enterprises
5915 North Lincoln Ave.
Chicago 60659
(312) 769–0622

National Speakers Bureau
222 Wisconsin Ave.
Lake Forest 60045
(312) 295–1122

Paramount Attractions
2 East Oak
Chicago 60611
(312) 944–2650

Peoria Musical Enterprises
1243 West Main St.
Peoria 61606
(309) 674–2195

Rapsodia Concert Management
P.O. Box 3990
Chicago 60654
(312) 472–5526

Reil-Straus Agency
4823 North Albany Ave.
Chicago 60625
(312) 539–1688

Rhythm & Blues Attractions
8959 South Oglesby Ave.
Chicago 60617
(312) 375–4276

Jimmy Richards Productions
919 North Michigan Ave.
Chicago 60611
(312) 664–1552

Red Saunders
8136 South Evans
Chicago 60619
(312) 224–4707

Soundz Productions
516 N. Milwaukee Ave.
Wheeling 60090
(312) 531–9837

Spence Stein Talent
1623 Kinsella Ave.
Belleville 62221
(618) 235–1247

Sure Thing Productions
326 East 89th Place
Chicago 60619
(312) 483–4817

TNT Productions
41 N. Vermilion St., Suites 415–17
Danville 61832
(217) 446–9120

VJD Associates
2640 West Superior St.
Chicago 60612
(312) 235–5484

INDIANA

Mark A. Briggs
12619 Thiele Rd.
Fort Wayne 46819
(219) 639–6459

Robert Hamilton
c/o Indiana Univ./Music
1825 Northside Blvd.
South Bend 46615
(219) 237–4101

Wayne Harris Enterprises
P.O. Box 18018
Indianapolis 46218

IOWA

Lyle Merriman Associates
893 Park Pl.
Iowa City 52240
(319) 338–6940, 353–3622

Operation Music Enterprises
233 West Woodland Ave.
Ottumwa 52501
(515) 682–8283

KANSAS

Great Plains Associates
P.O. Box 634
Lawrence 66044
(913) 841–4444

Mid-Continent Entertainment
P.O. Box 492
Lawrence 66044
(913) 842-0100

KENTUCKY

Joni Agency, Inc.
3805 Poplar Level Rd.
Louisville 40213
(502) 456-6655

Triangle Talent, Inc.
P.O. Box 99035
Louisville 40299
(502) 267-5466

LOUISIANA

Band Aid Entertainment
P.O. Box 3673
Baton Rouge 70821
(504) 387-5709

Reginald Brown & Associates
P.O. Box 881
Baton Rouge 70821
(504) 383-4701

Colsoul, Inc.
6227 Providence Pl.
New Orleans 70126

Entertainment Services
P.O. Drawer 6054
Monroe 71201
(318) 387-3632

Jewel Records
728 Texas St.
Shreveport 71163
(318) 222-0673

Mr. Christian Productions
P.O. Box 51828 OCS
Lafayette 70501
(318) 233-3156

Radie Productions
P.O. Box 3814
Baton Rouge 70821
(504) 766-0987

Marshall Sehorn
3809 Clemantis Ave.
New Orleans 70122
(504) 949-8386

MARYLAND

A & D Booking Agency
28 East 25th St.
Baltimore 21218
(301) 235-3235

Big B Enterprises
4176 Suitland Rd., Apt. 102
Suitland 20023
(30) 568-8608

IBB Artists Management, Inc.
8717 Hidden Hill Lane
Potomac 20854
(301) 299-8143

PHL Associates
8422 Georgia Ave., Suite 201
Silver Spring 20910
(301) 588-1330

Emily Satell Artists Management
3408 Tulsa Rd.
Baltimore 21207
(301) 944-3978

Soul Searchers
7802 Beechnut Rd.
District Heights 20028
(301) 336-6616

Sound Innovations
11213 Columbia Pike
Silver Spring 20901
(301) 593-7433

Sound Management Agency
P.O. Box 10068
Baltimore 21204
(301) 426-8639

Stable Attractions
9942 York Rd.
Cockeysville 21030
(301) 666-8722

Washington Talent Agency
11141 Georgia Ave., No. A–20
Silver Spring 20902
(301) 949-7200

MASSACHUSETTS

All-American Talent
74 Chester St.
Allston 02134
(617) 783–4100

APB
850 Boylston St.
Chestnut Hill 02167
(617) 731–0500

Avalon Productions
8 Locke St.
Cambridge 02140
(617) 492–3332

Bella Music & Theatre Associations
37 Spring St.
Somerville 02143
(617) 666–3593

Camelot Music, Inc.
74 Grove Ave.
Leeds 01053
(413) 586–4316

Ken Capurso Productions
6 Imperial Rd.
Worcester 01604
(617) 757–0269

Philip Citron Inc.
1 Wells Ave.
Newton 02159
(617) 965–4666

Clark Productions, Inc.
969 Commonwealth Ave.
Boston 02215
(617) 254–4040

Folklore Productions
739 Boylston St.
Boston 02116
(617) 267–4353

The Frothingham Management
P.O. Box 163
Weston 02193
(617) 894–7571

Don Law Agency
31 Fresh Pond Pkwy.
Cambridge 02138
(617) 547–0620

Lordly & Dame, Inc.
51 Church St.
Boston 02116
(617) 482–3593

Management in the Arts
551 Tremont St.
Boston 02116
(617) 426–2387

MR Management, Inc.
15 Lily
Nantucket Island 02554
(212) 685–9285

Pretty Polly Productions
25 Huntington Ave.
Boston 02116
(617) 266–0790

Robert Quinn Productions
P.O. Box 592, Kenmore Sta.
Boston 02215
(617) 699–4271

Eric Ross Agency
69 Newbury St.
Boston 02116
(617) 536–4827

Sweet 'N' Sour Management
259 Beacon St., No. 70
Boston 02116
(617) 267–4353

Irv Weiner Programs
1236 Great Plain Ave.
Needham 02192
(617) 449–1220

H. W. Wilson
P.O. Box 269, BBX
Boston 02117
(617) 266–1770

MICHIGAN

Ron Baltros
1800 Grindley Park
Dearborn 48126
(313) 561-4403

Cat Billue Enterprises
6434 South Dort
Grand Blanc 48439
(313) 694-1400

Black Kettle Productions
P.O. Box 2241
Saginaw 48605
(517) 792-0940, 752-2313

Circle M Talent
P.O. Box 496
Harbor Springs 49740
(616) 526-2393

DMA
22811 Mack Ave., Suite 101
St. Clair Shores 48080
(313) 773-6800

ITA
24548 Pierce
Southfield 48075
(313) 559-7630

Ollie McLaughlin
4690 Outer Dr.
Detroit 48235
(313) 864-2579

Jerry Patlow & Associates
17429 Indian Ave.
Detroit 48240
(313) 531-9330

Progressive Booking Agency
2688 West Grand Blvd.
Detroit 48208
(313) 873-1817

Punch Enterprises
567 Purdy
Birmingham 48009
(313) 642-0910

Show Biz Talent
P.O. Box 643
Escanaba 49829
(906) 786-7654

Gordon E. Strong
18035 Mark Twain
Detroit 48235
(313) 345-5089

Aaron Willis
18648 Fleming
Detroit 48221
(313) 891-6081

MINNESOTA

Ralph Beske
P.O. Box 23
Lake Park 56554
(218) 238-6611

Projects IV, Inc.
7515 Wayzata Blvd., Suite 232
Minneapolis 55426
(612) 546-0226

Marvin Rainwater
P.O. Box 256, Rte. 1
Aitkin 56431
(218) 927-2731

Schon Productions
1645 Hennepin Ave., Suite 312
Minneapolis 55403
(612) 332-6575

SRO Productions
2910 Bloomington Ave. South
Minneapolis 55407
(612) 724-3864

Variety Artists International
7200 France Ave. South, Suite 128
Minneapolis 55435
(612) 925-3440

MISSISSIPPI

Frasco Entertainment Agency
P.O. Box 4912
Jackson 39216
(601) 366-9331

Skylab Management
Box 1101
Starkville 39759
(601) 323-4586

MISSOURI

ABA
1800 Burlington St., Suite 201
North Kansas City 64116
(816) 421-1124

Classmen Enterprises
3427 Norton
Independence 64052
(816) 254-9378/0591

Continental Entertainment
734 West Port Plaza, Suite 217
St. Louis 63141
(314) 434-9400

Gypsy Moon Productions
P.O. Box 85
Columbia 65201
(314) 367-5665

Sea Cruise Productions
P.O. Box 11387
St. Louis 63105
(314) 771-7467

Top Talent, Inc.
P.O. Box 4568, Glenstone Sta.
Springfield 65804
(417) 869-6379

NEBRASKA

CID Productions
1410 Benton St.
Lincoln 68521
(402) 477-5265/6763

NEVADA

Artist Talent Corporation
3106 East Sunset Rd.
Las Vegas 89120
(702) 451-8333

Barbara Barber Artist Agency
P.O. Box L
Stateline 89449
(702) 588-6122

International Entertainment Enterprises
P.O. Box 415
Crystal Bay 89450
(702) 831-2923

John Kelly & Associates
P.O. Box 14927
Las Vegas 89114
(702) 451-1041/8081

Redbeard Presents Productions
3196 Maryland Pkwy., Suite 212
Las Vegas 89109
(702) 734-1992

NEW HAMPSHIRE

Friends Agency
Henniker 03242

NEW JERSEY

Alron Promos
26 Tweedstone Lane
Willingboro 08046
(609) 877-5662

Arts Image, Ltd.
P.O. Box 10079
Newark 07101
(201) 484-2632

Cumberland Associates
497 Cumberland Ave.
Teaneck 07666
(201) 836-0362

Dirty Martha Music
424 Lincoln Ave.
Bellmawr 08030

Kay-May Enterprises
921 Newark Ave.
Manville 08835
(201) 526-4959

Mark Kirmayer Artists' Management
100 Manhattan Ave.
Union City 07087
(201) 865-1005

Lester Productions
13 Wall St.
Rockaway 07866
(201) 627-0690

Lorna L. Litkowski
740 Watchung Ave.
Plainfield 07060
(201) 756-1196

Max Mandel
27 Serviss Ave.
E. Brunswick 08816
(201) 846-4553

Maranta Music Enterprises
P.O. Box 9
Wyckoff 07481
(201) 891-0037

John Mazzacano
P.O. Box 1049
Merchantsville 08109
(609) 795-5497

Person-to-Person Attractions
160 Goldsmith Ave.
Newark 07112
(201) 926-0615

Rev. Lawrence Roberts
13-15 Harrison St.
Nutley 07110
(201) 661-0887

Pete Salerno Enterprises
470 Sixth Ave. West
Roselle 07203
(201) 241-3681

Art Silverlight Management
502 Mountain Ave.
North Plainfield 07062
(201) 756-9220

Wooden Music Co-op
P.O. Box 1385
Merchantville 08109
(609) 662-9057

Blanche Zeller Agency
28 Chestnut Rd.
Verona 07044
(201) 239-1545

NEW MEXICO

Apollo Entertainment
Box 1119
Las Cruces 88001
(505) 526-3116

Ronald Gregory
616 Indian School Rd. N.W.
Albuquerque 87102
(505) 842-1080

Zia Talent Agency
P.O. Box 8207
Albuquerque 87108
(505) 268-6110

NEW YORK

ABC
445 Park Ave.
New York 10022
(212) 421-5200
  Branch:
9595 Wilshire Blvd., Suite 309
Beverly Hills, CA 90212
(213) 273-5600
  Branch:
6660 Biscayne Blvd.
Miami, Fla. 33138
(305) 758-2511
  Branch:
919 North Michigan Ave., Suite 2906
Chicago, IL. 60611
(312) 751-2000
  Branch:
4055 South Spencer, Suite 204
Las Vegas, NV 89109
(702) 734-8155
  Branch:
3511 Hall St., Lee Park Bldg.
Dallas, TX 75219
(214) 528-8296

Adair Productions
116 East 14th St.
New York 10003
(212) 777-3061

Admiral Talent Associates
888 Eighth Ave.
New York 10019
(212) 581-0665

Willard Alexander, Inc.
660 Madison Ave.
New York 10021
(212) 751-7070
Branch:
333 North Michigan Ave.
Chicago, IL 60601
(312) 236-2460

Alkebu Lan Productions
250 Madison St.
Brooklyn 11216
(212) 857-6557

APA
120 West 57th St.
New York 10019
(212) 581-8860
Branch:
9000 Sunset Blvd., Suite 315
Los Angeles, CA 90069
(213) 273-0744
Branch:
203 North Wabash
Chicago, IL 60601
(312) 664-7703

Associated Concert Artists
2109 Broadway, Suite 17-18
New York 10023
(212) 595-5891

ATI
888 Seventh Ave.
New York 10019
(212) 977-2300
Branch:
118 South Beverly Dr.
Beverly Hills CA 90212
(213) 278-9311

ATV, Inc.
205 Mariners Way
Copiague 11726
(516) 842-0416

Ayteen Entertainment Enterprises
3298 Cherrywood Dr.
Wantagh 11793
(516) 221-0007

Dina Bader Associates
444 East 82nd St.
New York 10028
(212) 861-4042

Banner Talent Associates
1650 Broadway, Suite 611
New York 10019
(212) 581-6900

Bari & Bennett Productions
17 West 67th St.
New York 10023

Herbert Barrett Management
1860 Broadway
New York 10023

Richard Barri
344 West 89th Street
New York 10024
(212) 877-7507

Harry Beall Management
119 West 57th St.
New York 10019
(212) 586-8135

Doug Belscher Agency
P.O. Box 385
Branchport 14418
(315) 536-3571

M. Bichurin Concerts
Carnegie Hall, Suite 609
New York 10019
(212) 586-2349

Eastman Boomer Management
157 West 57th St., Suite 504
New York 10019
(212) 582-9364

Herbert Breslin
119 West 57th St.
New York 10019
(212) 581-1750

CAMI
165 West 57th St.
New York 10019
(212) 397-6900

Royce Carlton, Inc.
866 United Nations Plaza
New York 10017
(212) 355-7931

Castalia Enterprises, Inc.
32 Jones St.
New York 10014
(212) 989-1644, 243-0360

Castrataro, Herman & Beinin
110 East 59th St.
New York 10022
(212) 758-3102

Max Cavalli
232 Martense St.
Brooklyn 11226
(212) 856-3308

Cecada Productions
P.O. Box 669
Woodstock 12498
(914) 679-6069/7788

Charter Producers
666 Fifth Ave.
New York 10019
(212) 489-0680

Chimera Foundation
33 East 18th St.
New York 10003

Circustime, Inc.
157 West 57th St.
New York 10019
(212) 265-5864

Joyce Ellyott Clarke
14 Winthrop St.
Brooklyn 11225
(212) 462-6439

George Cochran
150 West 87th St.
New York 10024
(212) 799-7890

Coffee-House Circuit
159 West 53rd St.
New York 10019
(212) 247-3257

Colbert Artists Management
111 West 57th St.
New York 10019
(212) 757-0782

Cone/Susman Artists Representatives
14 East 60th St.
New York 10022
(212) 688-0895

Counterpoint/Concerts, Inc.
10 Munson Court
Huntington Station 11746
(516) 549-1443

Country Talent Agency
1458 Buffalo Rd.
Rochester 14624
(716) 328-5565

Creative Funk Music, Inc.
122-21 Merrick Blvd.
St. Albans 11434
(212) 978-6400

Critic's Choice Artists Management
1697 Broadway
New York 10019
(212) 245-9250

CTA
59 Locust Ave.
New Rochelle 10801
(914) 576-1100

DNP
1271 Ave. of the Americas
New York 10020
(212) 397-1881

Faye Dean
400 East 52nd St., Rm. 9F
New York 10022
(212) 753-2492

Nicholas Degloma Talent Agency
33 Cherry St.
Geneva 14456
(315) 789-7310

A. Demos
666 Fifth Ave., 10th Flr.
New York 10019
(212) 489-0687

Thea Dispeker Artists' Representative
59 East 54th St.
New York 10022
(212) 421-7676

David Dodds
33-05 90th St.
Jackson Heights 11372
(212) 639-6718, 564-3250

Enchanted Door Management
Box 544
New Rochelle 10801
(914) 576-1211

The Entertainment Bureau
3785 Broadway, Suite 1
New York 10032
(212) 234-6431

Entertainment Projects, Inc.
29 East 61st St.
New York 10022
(212) 371-7395

John Fisher
155 West 68th St.
New York 10023
(212) 362-4372

Frycek Productions
22 Pierces Rd.
Newburgh 12550
(914) 561-6700

Robert M. Gewald Management, Inc.
2 West 59th St.
New York 10019
(212) 753-0450

Larney Goodkind
30 East 60th St.
New York 10022
(212) 355-6560

Great Lakes Booking & Management
1455 Hertel Ave.
Buffalo 14216
(716) 837-5581

Leonard Green Productions
157 West 57th St.
New York 10019
(212) 265-5864

Guardian Productions
201 West 54th St.
New York 10019
(212) 581-5398

Gunhill Road Enterprises
P.O. Box 41
Yonkers 10710
(212) 671-2716

Gus Enterprises
4109 Barnes Ave.
Bronx 10466
(212) 547-5539

Hairy Lip Productions
133 Fifth Ave.
New York 10003
(212) 675-4078

Margaret Hanks
c/o Herbert H. Lehman College
Dance Off., Gymnasium, Rm. 117
Bronx 10468
(212) 960-8404

Robert Harris
Carnegie Hall, Suite 1101
154 West 57th St.
New York 10019
(212) 924-5079

HI Enterprises, Inc.
200 West 57th St., Rm. 1307
New York 10019
(212) 247-4230

Kazuko Hillyer International, Inc.
250 West 57th St.
New York 10019
(212) 581-3644

Hit Factory
353 West 48th St.
New York 10036
(212) 581-9590

Hans J. Hofmann Management
200 West 58th St.
New York 10019
(212) 246-1557

Mel Howard Presents
143 East 27th St.
New York 10016
(212) 889–8460

Steve Huhta
c/o Phil Jordan
P.O. Box 178
Spencer 14883
(607) 589–4933

Hurok Concerts
1370 Ave. of the Americas
New York 10019
(212) 245–0500

Branch:
9200 Sunset Blvd.
Los Angeles, CA 90046
(213) 278–4141

Saeko Ichinohe & Company
116 West 69th St.
New York 10023
(212) 362–0532

ICM
40 West 57th St.
New York 10019
(212) 586–0440

Jacquet, Inc.
112–44 179th St.
St. Albans 11433
(212) 658–3455

Dick James Music, Inc.
119 West 57th St.
New York 10019
(212) 581–3420

Jay Artist Representatives
387 East Main St.
Rochester 14604
(716) 454–3170

Joyce Agency
435 East 79th St.
New York 10021
(212) 988–3371

JR Productions
1620 Niagara Falls Blvd., Suite 285
Tonawanda 14150
(716) 838–6330

Ed Joyner Enterprises
200 West 135th St., Rm. 203-A
New York 10030
(212) 926–9996

Melvin Kaplan, Inc.
85 Riverside Dr.
New York 10024
(212) 877–6310

Karass Media Productions
24 Horatio St., 3rd Flr.
New York 10014
(212) 675–0992

Albert Kay Associates
58 West 58th St., No. 31E
New York 10019
(212) 593–1640

Kee Talent
34 Spring St.
Cambridge 12816
(518) 677-3872

Keishval Enterprises, Inc.
1650 Broadway, Suite 1105
New York 10019
(212) 757–7890

Bruce King Foundation
160 West 73rd St.
New York 10023
(212) 877–6700

Kolmar-Luth Entertainment
1776 Broadway
New York 10019
(212) 581–5833

Mark La Roche Management
203 Columbus Ave., Apt. 3C
New York 10023
(212) 362–1288

Laurel Theatre Productions
P.O. Box 53, Radio City Sta.
New York 10019
(201) 833–0403

Dodie Lefebre
498 West End Ave.
New York 10024
(212) 724–8143

106

Jacques Leiser
155 West 68th St.
New York 10023
(212) 595-6414

Richard Lescsak
60 West 68th St.
New York 10023
(212) 874-5152

Milton Levy Company
119 West 57th St., Suite 818
New York 10019
(212) 757-7755

Judith Liegner Artists Management
1860 Broadway, Suite 1610
New York 10023
(212) 582-5795

Long Island Institute of Music
78-39 Parsons Blvd.
Flushing 11366

Ludwig Lustig & Florian, Ltd.
111 West 57th St.
New York 10019
(212) 586-3976

Lyra Management, Inc.
160 West 87th St.
New York 10023
(212) 582-5300

Joe McHugh
24 Horatio St., 3rd Flr.
New York 10014
(212) 675-0992

Martin Machat
1501 Broadway
New York 10019
(212) 563-6440

Magna Artists Corporation
1370 Ave. of the Americas
New York 10019
(212) 489-8027

Robert Marinaccio
134 Duane St.
New York 10013
(212) 732-1219

Matthews/Napal, Ltd.
270 West End Ave., Apt. 3E
New York 10023
(212) 873-2121

Maurel Enterprises, Inc.
225 West 34th St., Suite 1012
New York 10001
(212) 564-6656

Maximus Agency Corporation
39 West 55th St.
New York 10019
(212) 581-4144

Ralph Mercado Management
1674 Broadway, Suite 1674
New York 10019
(212) 541-7950

Rae Metzger Management
110 West 96th St., Suite 9D
New York 10025
(212) 749-5464

Lee Moore
P.O. Box 134
Wynantskill 12198
(518) 283-2213

William Morris Agency, Inc.
1350 Ave. of the Americas
New York 10019
(212) 586-5100
   Branch:
151 El Camino Dr.
Beverly Hills, CA. 90212
(213) 274-7451
   Branch:
435 North Michigan Ave.
Chicago, IL 60611
(312) 467-1744

Musical Artists
119 West 57th St.
New York 10019
(212) 586-2747

Muskrat Productions, Inc.
59 Locust Ave.
New Rochelle 10801
(914) 636-0809

New Arts Management
713 Washington St.
New York 10014
(212) 691-5434

New York Coffee Circuit
159 West 53rd St.
New York 10019
(212) 247-3187

Nod-Out Talent, Ltd.
2527 James St.
Syracuse 13206
(315) 437-1151

Anne J. O'Donnell Management
353 West 57th St.
New York 10019
(212) 581-1184

Peter Paul
1 Rockefeller Plaza
New York 10020
(212) 489-6120

PCA
234 North Central Ave.
Hartsdale 10530
(914) 428-5840

Performing Artservices
463 West St.
New York 10014
(212) 989-4953

Kay Perper Management
152 West 58th St.
New York 10019
(212) 765-2515

Podium Management Associates
75 East 55th St.
New York 10022
(212) 752-4653

Michael Podoli Concert
171 West 71st St.
New York 10023
(212) 877-1001

James Powers Professional Artists
55 West 42nd St.
New York 10036
(212) 594-2807

Premier Talent Associations
888 Seventh Ave.
New York 10019
(212) 757-4300

Presentations
91 Central Park West
New York 10023
(212) 874-3085

Python Productions
120 Central Park South
New York 10019
(212) 541-5795

QBC
1650 Broadway, Suite 1410
New York 10019
(212) 489-1400
   Branch:
6430 Sunset Blvd., Suite 916
Los Angeles, CA 90028
(213) 462-2383

RD III Ventures
20 Welwyn Pl.
Great Neck 11021
(516) 482-4683

Riva, Inc.
260 West End Ave., Suite 7-A
New York 10023
(212) 874-4378

Rochester Talent Unlimited
346 Ridge Rd. East
Rochester 14621
(716) 342-1670

Rock International, Ltd.
41 West 36th St.
New York 10018
(212) 564-0089

Charles R. Rothschild Productions
330 East 48th St.
New York 10017
(212) 421-0592

Jim Rouse
1674 Broadway, Suite 309
New York 10019
(212) 541-7950

Safier-Barry Agency
667 Madison Ave.
New York 10021
(212) 838–4868

Frank Salomon Associates
201 West 54th St., Suite 4C
New York 10019
(212) 581–5197

Sardos Artist Management
180 West End Ave.
New York 10023
(212) 874–2559

David Schiffmann
57 West 68th St.
New York 10023
(212) 877–8111

Eric Semon Associations
111 West 57th St., Suite 1619
New York 10019
(212) 765–1310

Arthur Shafman International
521 Fifth Ave.
New York 10017
(212) 873–1559

Pete Shanaberg
37 West 87th St.
New York 10019
(813) 367–4135

Shaw Concerts, Inc.
1995 Broadway
New York 10023
(212) 595–1909

Sir Productions
130 West 57th St.
New York 10019
(212) 765–7620

Sheldon Soffer Management
130 West 56th St.
New York 10019
(212) 757–8060

Ruth K. Solomon & Associates
4544 Fieldston Rd.
Riverdale 10471
(212) 546–9323

Spectrum Concertbureau
205 East 63rd St.
New York 10021
(212) 753–9527

Strata-East Associates
156 Fifth Ave., Suite 612
New York 10010
(212) 691–9294

Supreme Artists
888 Eighth Ave.
New York 10019
(212) 582–4600

Sutton Artists Corporation
505 Park Ave.
New York 10022
(212) 832–8302

Paul Szilard Productions
161 West 73rd St.
New York 10023
(212) 799–4756

Thames Talent, Ltd.
1345 Ave. of the Americas
New York 10019
(212) 541–6740

Three Brothers Music
1 Rockefeller Plaza
New York 10020

Tin Bar Amusement Corporation
15 Central Park West
New York 10023
(212) 586–1015

Tornay Management
250 West 57th St.
New York 10019
(212) 246–2270

Branch:
P.O. Box 2750
Hollywood, CA 90028
(213) 664–4341

Torrence/Perrotta Management
1860 Broadway
New York 10023
(212) 541–4620

Universal Attractions, Inc.
888 Seventh Ave., Suite 401
New York 10019
(212) 582-7575

Valex Agency
P.O. Box 241
Ithaca 14850
(607) 273-3931

Vincent Attractions
119 West 57th St.
New York 10019
(212) 765-3047

Norby Walters Associates
410 Jericho Tnpk.
Jericho 11753
(516) 822-9100

Samuel B. Waterboy & Associates
P.O. Box 546
Potsdam 13676
(315) 265-8938

Raymond Weiss Artist Management
300 West 55th St.
New York 10019
(212) 581-8478

Wendel Artists Management
95 Commercial St.
Plainview 11803
(516) 938-3498

Jack Whittemore
80 Park Ave.
New York 10016
(212) 986-6854

World-Wide Theatre Corporation
142 West End Ave., Suite 28-U
New York 10023
(212) 787-4681

Young Concert Artists
75 East 55th St.
New York 10022
(212) 759-2541

NORTH CAROLINA

Entertainers Unlimited
421 Briarbend Dr.
Charlotte 28209
(704) 327-1639

Hit Attractions, Inc.
P.O. Box 682
Charlotte 82230
(704) 372-3955

North-South Arts
Box 10273, Salem Sta.
Winston-Salem 27108
(919) 768-2821

Talent Attractions
156 Tunnel Rd.
Asheville 28805
(704) 253-4161

OHIO

Ajaye Entertainment Corporation
2181 Victory Pkwy.
Cincinnati 45206
(513) 221-2626

Ariba Down Talents
P.O. Box 7079
Columbus 43205
(614) 252-5075

Bracy & Bracy
24700 Center Ridge Rd.
Cleveland 44145

Hylo Brown
Box 80, Rte. 2
Jackson 45640
(614) 286-4095

Capsoul Booking Agency
1640 Franklin Ave.
Columbus 43205
(614) 252-2626

Consolidated Entertainment
276 Fairwood
Columbus 43205
(614) 253-4830

Dynamic Entertainment Inc.
494 South Yearling
Columbus 43213
(614) 237-6321

Elwood Emerick Management
596 Crystal Lake Rd.
Akron 44313
(216) 666-2036

Four Seasons Enterprises
506 E. Prospect St.
Girard 44420
(216) 545-6501

Nat Greenberg
200 East Town St.
Columbus 43215
(614) 244-3291

Dave Howell
Box 217
Oak Hill 45656
(614) 682-6592

Marcia Hulen
c/o Terry Waldo
504 South Lazelle St.
Columbus 43206
(614) 224-5828

Lake Front Talent Agency
P.O. Box 2395
Sandusky 44870
(419) 626-4987

Lee-Fam Enterprises
16303 Stockbridge Ave.
Cleveland 44128
(216) 991-2693

MEE
236-½ Valley St.
Youngstown 44505
(216) 747-7205

Roy Moore
1225 Avondale, Suite 4
Sandusky 44870
(419) 625-1527

Andi Noble
171 Parkway St.
Struthers 44471
(216) 755-7253

ONL Enterprises
1 First National Plaza, Suite 630
Dayton 45402
(513) 223-0657

Savage Productions
1002 West Centerville Rd.
Dayton 45459
(513) 433-6446

Cliff Smith
2131 West 105th
Cleveland 44102
(216) 631-7340

Herbe Smith Music
1512 West Dorothy Lane
Dayton 45409
(513) 298-8640

Tunesmith Music
203 East Sycamore St.
Columbus 43206
(614) 444-1808

OKLAHOMA

Al Good Artists Bureau
2500 N.W. 39th St.
Oklahoma City 73112
(405) 947-1503

Jim Halsey Co., Inc.
3225 South Norwood Ave.
Tulsa 74135
(918) 663-3883
   Branch:
9046 Sunset Blvd.
Los Angeles, CA 90069
(213) 278-3397
   Branch:
901 18th Ave. South
Nashville, TN 37212
(615) 320-1240

OREGON

Bob Oquist Talent Agency
3617 S. W. Hume St.
Portland 97219
(503) 245-5219

PENNSYLVANIA

American Artist, Inc.
13th & Walnut Sts., Suite 303
Philadelphia 19107

Aquarian Associates, Inc.
100 Forbes Ave., Suite 880
Pittsburgh 15222
(412) 391-9640

Robert Arrow Music Enterprises
130 South 18th St.
Philadelphia 19103
(215) 561-3838

Billy Bryant
2449 Glenarm Ave.
Pittsburgh 15226
(412) 561-9189

Command Performance
4025 Rte. 8
Allison Park 15101
(412) 487-3800

DMI Enterprises
2628 Welsh Rd., Suite 110
Philadelphia 19152
(215) 698-9578

Entertainment Corporation of America
401 N. Broad St., Suite 830
Philadelphia 19108
(215) 922-5599

Father Maple, Inc.
P.O. Box 15642
Pittsburgh 15244
(412) 766-5088

Golden Music, Media & Management
P.O. Box 275
East Stroudsburg 18301
(717) 424-5081

Lila Lou Hallman
1226 Kay Circle
West Chester 19380
(215) 696-3727

Harlequin Enterprises
4030 Windsor St.
Pittsburgh 15217
(412) 421-6197

Jolly Joyce Agency
2028 Chestnut St.
Philadelphia 19103
(215) 564-0982

Andrew King & Associates
2519 Brown St.
Philadelphia 19130
(215) 763-2300

Jim McClelland
2316 Lombard St.
Philadelphia 19146
(215) 546-0700

Media V Entertainment
Fourth & Northampton Sts., Suite 600
Easton 18042
(215) 258-2308

Ernie Pep Theatricals
3162 Denfield Pl.
Philadelphia 19145
(215) 755-6708

Philadelphia International Records
309 S. Broad St.
Philadelphia 19107
(215) 985-0900

Process Talent Management
439 Wiley Ave.
Franklin 16323
(814) 432-4633

Joanne Rile Management
119 North 18th St.
Philadelphia 19103
(215) 569-4500

Bruce Rohrback & Company
907 North Front St.
Harrisburg 17102
(717) 232-8651

Sixuvus Productions
P.O. Box J
Aliquippa 15001
(412) 846-0170

Telecon Talent Group
P.O. Box 55
Philadelphia 19107
(215) 928-0520

Vokes Booking Agency
P.O. Box 12
New Kensington 15068
(412) 274-4620

Wright Management Agency
122 Host Inn, 4751 Lindle Rd.
Harrisburg 17111
(717) 939-0471

RHODE ISLAND

Mrs. George H. Utter
Box 520
Westerly 02891

SOUTH CAROLINA

Boss Attractions
P.O. Box 11457
Columbia 29211
(803) 794-0574

Bennie Brown Productions
P.O. Box 5702
Columbia 29205
(803) 788-5734

Fred E. Daniel
P.O. Box 441
Spartanburg 29301
(803) 582-8715

The Joe Phillips Organization
P.O. Box 5981
Greenville 29607
(803) 288-6587

TENNESSEE

Acuff-Rose Artists Corporation
2510 Franklin Rd.
Nashville 37204
(615) 297-5366

AQ Talent, Inc.
903 18th Ave. South
Nashville 37212
(615) 329-9194

Ask Talent Agency
P.O. Box 12744
Nashville 37212
(615) 385-2059

Atlas Artist Bureau, Inc.
217 East Cedar St.
Goodlettsville 37072
(615) 859-1343

Cliff Ayers Productions
1009 16th Ave. South
Nashville 37212
(615) 256-1693

Beaverwood Talent Agency
133 Walton Ferry Rd.
Hendersonville 37075
(615) 824-2820

Century II
P.O. Box 1701
Nashville 37212
(615) 244-9222

Gentry Crowell
Lebanon 37087
(615) 444-2967

Ted Cunningham
3114 Radford Rd.
Memphis 38111
(901) 327-8187

Tex Davis, Ltd.
530 West Main St.
Hendersonville 37075
(615) 824-6565

Billy Deaton Talent Agency
1314 Pine St.
Nashville 37203
(615) 244-4259

Dharma Productions, Inc.
807 Redwood Dr.
Nashville 37220
(615) 834-0474

Ford Agency
P.O. Box 635
Nashville 37202
(615) 383-8318

Bill Goodwin Agency
P.O. Box 144
Madison 37115
(615) 868-5380

Hitsburgh Talent Agency
P.O. Box 195
Gallatin 37066
(615) 452-1479

Wes Holland Agency
1511 Sigler St.
Nashville 37203
(615) 255-8375

Interstate Talent Agency
1513 Hawkins St., Suite 108
Nashville 37203
(615) 259-3213

Jack D. Johnson Talent
P.O. Box 40484
Nashville 37204
(615) 383-6564

Grandpa Jones Enterprises
Box 167B, Rte. 3
Goodlettsville 37072
(615) 859-1920

Key Talent, Inc.
805 16th Ave. South
Nashville 37203
(615) 242-2461

Shorty Lavender Talent Agency
1217 16th Ave. South
Nashville 37212
(615) 244-5265

Alan Lawler
2500 Mount Morial, Suite 402
Memphis 38118
(901) 363-0312

Buddy Lee Attractions, Inc.
806 16th Ave. South, Suite 300
Nashville 37203
(615) 244-4336
    Branch:
666 Farnam Bldg., 1613 Farnam St.
Omaha, NB 68102
(402) 346-7369
    Branch:
888 Seventh Ave.
New York, NY 10019
(212) 247-5216

Jerry Lee Lewis & Co.
1717 West End Blvd., Suite 322
Nashville 37203
(615) 320-1187

Don Light Talent, Inc.
1100 17th Ave. South
Nashville 37212
(615) 244-3900

Hubert Long International
1513 Hawkins St.
Nashville 37203
(615) 244-9550

Mimosa Productions
358 E. Parkway North, Suite 2
Memphis 38112
(901) 324-4120

Moeller Talent, Inc.
P.O. Box 15364
Nashville 37215
(615) 244-4292

Monya Music
1712 Beechwood
Nashville 37212
(615) 297-8556

Music City Attractions
1513 Hawkins St., Suite 108
Nashville 37203
(615) 259-3213

Nashboro Records
1011 Woodland St.
Nashville 37206
(615) 227-5081

Nashville International Talent
1006 17th Ave. South
Nashville 37212
(615) 254-1049

National Artist Attractions
5577 Glenwild
Memphis 38117
(901) 685-8331

Newtone Music Agency
P.O. Box 15325
Nashville 37215
(615) 297-4950

Nova Agency
910 17th Ave. South
Nashville 37212
(615) 254-1384

One Niters, Inc.
111 Lyle Ave.
Nashville 37203
(615) 244-1145

Deanie Parker
2693 Union Ext.
Memphis 38112
(901) 458-4421

Roger Talent Enterprises
1024 16th Ave. South
Nashville 37212
(615) 327-3644

Skylite Talent
P.O. Box 350
Nashville 37202
(615) 244-7404

Bobby Smith Productions
P.O. Box 8156
Nashville 37207
(615) 865-4759

Sundown Pete
P.O. Box 1483
Kingsport 37660

The Taliesyn Agency
1870 Union Ave.
Memphis 38104
(901) 274-0056

Joe Taylor Artist Agency
2401 Granny White Pike
Nashville 37204
(615) 385-0035

Top Billing, Inc.
P.O. Box 12514
Nashville 37212
(615) 383-8883

United Talent
1907 Division St.
Nashville 37203
(615) 244-9412

Shannon Williams
1011 Woodland St.
Nashville 37206
(615) 227-5081

TEXAS

The Adams Company
P.O. Box 822
Forth Worth 76101
(817) 926-8637

Alamo Promotions
1534 Bandera Rd.
San Antonio 78228
(512) 432-0983

Americartists, Inc.
22 World Trade Center
Houston 77002
(713) 224-8000

Arsak Music Agency
P.O. Box 1293
Amarillo 79105
(806) 353-1791, 352-1617

Bob Bailey
210 North Adams Ave.
Odessa 79761
(915) 332-0605

Ray Brondo Productions
P.O. Box 28542
Dallas 75228
(214) 279-8674

Johnny Bush Attractions
102 West Rampart, Q-104
San Antonio 78216
(512) 341-0443

Ken-Ran Enterprises
3039 West Northwest Hwy., Suite 105
Dallas 75220
(214) 350-6647

Steven Long & Associates
5102 Meadow Lane
Dickinson 77539
(713) 762-8434, 337-2966

LSI Management
3410 Ave. R
Lubbock 79412
(806) 774-5590

Montgomery Booking Agency
8914 Georgian Dr.
Austin 78753
(512) 836-3201

Moon-Hill
P.O. Box 4945
Austin 78765
(512) 452-9411

On Stage Productions
258 Westoak
San Antonio 78227
(512) 674-8795

Ray Price Booking Agency
P.O. Box 34886
Dallas 75234
(214) 387-1101

STA Productions
6222 North Central Expwy, Suite 200
Dallas 75206
(214) 691-5521

Showco Management
9011 Governor's Row
Dallas 75247
(214) 630-1188

Spirit Sound, Inc.
208 Pennsylvania St.
Big Lake 76932
(915) 884-2298

UTAH

Vandermeide Associates
3904 Hallmark Dr.
Salt Lake City 84119
(801) 298-6382

VERMONT

Linda Cooper
P.O. Box 2012
South Burlington 05401
(802) 864-4466/0350

VIRGINIA

Briarwood Talent
2030 N. Oakland St.
Arlington 22207
(703) 527-2692

Check Productions, Inc.
936 Moyer Rd.
Newport News 23602
(804) 877-0762

Dynamic Booking
P.O. Box 25654
Richmond 23260
(814) 355-3186

Jim Gemmill Productions
1205 West Main St., Suite 208
Richmond 23220
(804) 358-1373

Lenis Guess
633 West 35th St.
Norfolk 23508
(804) 625-3120

International Artists Alliance
P.O. Box 131
Springfield 22150
(703) 451-1404

Kings Entertainment Enterprises
P.O. Box 168
Roanoke 24002
(703) 342-7088, 344-2192

Lendel Agency
Rte. 2
Warrenton 22186
(703) 347-2496

Sound by Guy Productions
5136 Duke St.
Alexandria 22304
(703) 751-4767

Southern Booking & Management
P.O. Box 4251
Virginia Beach 23454
(804) 428-6407

United Entertainment
P.O. Box 3161
Norfolk 23514
(804) 623-7880

Willis Talent Service
P.O. Box 5471
Roanoke 24012
(703) 563-9238

World Wide Promos
613 West 35th St.
Norfolk 23508
(804) 623-5657

WASHINGTON

George Carlson & Associates
4106 Arcade Bldg.
Seattle 98101
(206) 623-8045

Helen Jensen Artists Management
716 Joseph Vance Bldg.
Third & Union
Seattle 98101
(206) 622-7896, 523-0382

Olympic Artists Management
P.O. Box 15302, Wedgewood Sta.
Seattle 98115
(206) 523-1554

Jack Roberts Agency
17522 Bothell Way N.E.
Bothell 98011
(206) 485-6511

WEST VIRGINIA

Socrates Enterprises
3600 West St.
Weirton 26062
(304) 748-3743

WISCONSIN

Adamany & Toler
520 University Ave., Rm. 125
Madison 53703
(608) 251-2644

Contemporary Talent
P.O. Box 5510
Milwaukee 53211
(414) 765-0440

MCT
P.O. Box 1812
Madison 53701
(608) 251-3606

McMillan & Clary Talent
P.O. Box 1812
Madison 53701
(608) 251-3606

Performers/Entertainment, Inc.
P.O. Box 11715
Milwaukee 53211
(414) 964-5740

Phyllis Stringham Concert Management
425 Mountain Ave.
Waukesha 53186
(414) 542-7197

Gary Van Zeeland Talent
1750 Freedom Rd.
Little Chute 54140
(414) 788-5222

Larry G. Youngsteadt
P.O. Box 11715
Milwaukee 53211
(414) 964-5740

CANADA

Studio City Musical
10534 109th St., Rm. 201
Edmonton, Alta. T5H 3B2
(403) 426-5801

Sudra Talent & Bookings
9844 106th St.
Edmonton, Alta.
(403) 423-2140

Axis Entertainment
P.O. Box 3404
Vancouver, B.C. V6B 3Y4
(604) 922-2770

Jake Doell
2190 West 12th Ave.
Vancouver, B.C. V6K 2N2
(604) 736-7626

Robert Meyer Artist Management
4493 Emily Carr Dr.
Victoria, B.C.
(604) 658-8373

Mushroom Records
1234 West Sixth Ave.
Vancouver, B.C.
(604) 736-7207

Overture Concerts
960 Richard St.
Vancouver, B.C.
(604) 685-6188

Studio 3 Productions
2190 West 12th Ave.
Vancouver, B.C.
(604) 736-7626

Hungry I Agency
403-265 Portage Ave.
Winnipeg, Man. R3B 2C5
(204) 947-0092

Jim Millican
380 Assiniboine Ave., No. 3
Winnipeg, Man.
(204) 667-2338

Dick Nolan
Box 9072, Sta. B
St. Johns, Newfoundland
(709) 437-5931

Yorke's Entertainment Contacts
5639 Spring Garden Rd., Suite 300
Halifax, N.S.
(902) 429-0174

Ahed Music Corporation
142 Sparks Ave.
Willowdale, Ont. M2H 2V9
(416) 499-5000

Peter Beauchamp
33 Madison Ave.
Toronto, Ont. M5R 2S2
(416) 967-3696

Lawrence Bennett
957 Broadview
Toronto, Ont. M4K 2R5
(416) 423-7016

Gary Buck
c/o Broadland Music
1 Valleybrook Dr.
Don Mills, Ont.
(426) 449-6432

CIT
Box 443
Waterloo, Ont. N2J 4V3
(519) 579-2250

Canadian General Artists
10 Northfield Rd.
Scarborough, Ont. M1G 2H4
(416) 439-4800

Columbia Records of Canada
1121 Leslie St.
Don Mills, Ont. M3C 2J9

Concept 376, Ltd.
57 Spadina Ave., Suite 201
Toronto, Ont. M5V 2J2
(416) 366-8535

Concerts Canada
151 Sparks St.
Ottawa, Ont. K1P 5V8
(613) 237-3400

Daffodil Records
2400 Eglinton Ave. West
Toronto, Ont. M6M 1S6
(416) 654-1906

Donat Mittoo Music
35 Esterbrooke, Suite 602
Toronto, Ont. M2J 2C6
(416) 494-1966

Dram Agency, Ltd.
P.O. Box 413
Waterloo, Ont. N2J 1P5
(519) 576-9760

Barry Haugan
225 Mutual St.
Toronto, Ont. M5B 2B4
(416) 363-3443

Hokee Productions Ltd.
RR 1
Churchill, Ont. L0L 1K0
(705) 456-3707

Marathong Music, Inc.
1145 Bellamy Rd.
Scarborough, Ont.
(416) 438-5147

Mid Week Music
501 King St. East
Oshawa, Ont.
(416) 576-1561

Bert Mitford
100 Richmond St. West, Suite 422
Toronto, Ont.
(416) 366-3377

Music Shoppe International
44 Upjohn Rd.
Don Mills, Ont.
(416) 445-9240

Gary Mutch
c/o WEA Music, A&R Dept.
40 Scollard St.
Toronto, Ont.
(416) 920-2246

Naja, Inc.
1560 Bayview Ave., Suite 102
Toronto, Ont.
(416) 482-4827

John Sinclair
110 Indian Road Crescent
Toronto, Ont. M6P 2G3
(416) 766-5450

Smile Records
542 Mount Pleasant Rd.
Toronto, Ont. M45 2M7
(416) 485-1157

Star Agency
1957 Silverberry Crescent
Mississauga, Ont. L5J 1C8
(416) 625-1037

Syncona
369 Berkeley St.
Toronto, Ont.
(416) 962-4960

3 Hats Productions
576 Huron St.
Toronto, Ont.
(416) 922-7541

Charlie Underhill
77 Overbank Crescent
Don Mills, Ont.
(416) 449-9371

Ross White
969 Fraser Dr.
Burlington, Ont.
(416) 868-0080

Albert-Pare Assocs.
P.O. Box 246, Westmount Sta.
Montreal, P.Q. H3Z 2T2
(514) 849-6374

Barclay Records
1265 Ducharme Ave.
Montreal, P.Q. H2V 1E6
(514) 273-2883

Gary Cape
123 Silver Birch Rd.
Dollard Des Ormeaux, P.Q.
(514) 684-9000

Francoise Chartrand, Inc.
9323 De Chateaubriand
Montreal, P.Q. H2M 1Y2
(514) 382-2210

Jacques Chenier
214 Brunswick Blvd.
Pointe Clare, P.Q.
(514) 697-7440

Corporation Image
440 Pl. Jacques Cartier, Suite 4
Montreal, P.Q.
(514) 871-1707

Eldon Associates International Ltd.
3465 Cote des Neiges, Suite 1
Montreal, P.Q. H3H 1T7
(514) 932-4123

Gallant-Robertson
7 Burton Ave.
Montreal, P.Q., H32 1J6
(514) 482-4933

Good Noise Records
163 St. Paul St. East
Montreal, P.Q. H2Y 1G8
(514) 871-9323

Ben Kaye Associates
4824 Cote des Neiges, Suite 38
Montreal, P.Q. H3V 1G4
(514) 739-4774

Kebec Spec.
273 Carre St. Louis
Montreal, P.Q. H2X 1A3
(514) 288-7224

Jean-Claude Lord
8199 Louis XIV
St. Leonard, P.Q.
(514) 321-7980

Guy Roy (Productions)
1700 Rue Berri, Suite 3106
Montreal, P.Q.
(514) 845-0263

Sonoshow
166 St. Amable St.
Old Montreal, P.Q.
(514) 866-1510

PERSONAL MANAGERS

ARKANSAS

Black Oak Arkansas, Inc.
General Delivery
Oakland 72661
(501) 431-8551

Sweet Tater Enterprises
General Delivery
Oakland 72661
(501) 431-8551

CALIFORNIA

Aarons Enterprises, Inc.
9655 Wilshire Blvd., Suite 320
Beverly Hills 90212
(213) 278-7620

Adam's Dad Management Company
827 Folsom St.
San Francisco 94107
(415) 777-2930

Alive Entertainments
8530 Wilshire Blvd., Suite 306
Beverly Hills 90211
(213) 657-4380

AMP
7033 Sunset Blvd.
Hollywood 90028
(213) 462-5655

Artists Group, Inc.
825 Las Palmas Road
Pasadena 91105
(213) 684-1313

Peter Asher Management, Inc.
644 North Doheny
Los Angeles 90069
(213) 273-9433

Backstage Management, Inc.
8919 Sunset Blvd.
Los Angeles 90069
(213) 659-8340

Bag-O-Bucks
113 Steuart
San Francisco 94105
(415) 495-3141

John Baruck
1046 Carol Dr.
Los Angeles 90069
(213) 278-2981

Daniel Ben Av
9200 Sunset Blvd., Suite 1220
Los Angeles 90069
(213) 271-5171

BK Management
1131 Alta Loma, Suite 337
Los Angeles 90069
(213) 659-6585

BKM, Inc.
9200 Sunset Blvd., Suite 1207
Los Angeles 90069
(213) 271-6265

Black Bull Presentations
6255 Sunset Blvd.
Los Angeles 90028
(213) 468-3455

Branch:
1780 Broadway, Suite 1000
New York, NY 10019
(212) 586-7120

BNB Associates, Ltd.
9454 Wilshire Blvd.
Beverly Hills 90212
(213) 273-7020

Patrick Boyle & Associates
7033 Sunset Blvd.
Hollywood 90028
(213) 462-0883

Al Bunetta Management
4121 Wilshire Blvd., Suite 312
Los Angeles 90010
(213) 385-0882

Paul Cantor Enterprises, Ltd.
144 South Beverly Dr.
Beverly Hills 90212
(213) 274-9222

Caribou Management Corporation
8600 Melrose Ave.
Los Angeles 90069
(213) 659-1301

Allan Carr Enterprises, Inc.
P.O. Box 69670
Los Angeles 90069
(213) 274-8518

Cavallo-Ruffalo Management
9615 Brighton Way, Suite 212
Beverly Hills 90210
(213) 274-8071

Ray Charles Enterprises
2107 West Washington Blvd., Suite 203
Los Angeles 90018
(213) 737-8000

Chrysalis Management
9255 Sunset Blvd., Suite 201
Los Angeles 90069
(213) 550-0171

Branch:
360 East 6th St.
New York, NY 10021
(212) 535-1292

Clayton Enterprises
8730 Sunset Blvd.
Los Angeles 90069
(213) 659-5186

Herb Cohen Management
5831 Sunset Blvd.
Hollywood 90028
(213) 461-3277

Jerry Cohen
9465 Wilshire Blvd.
Beverly Hills 90212
(213) 274-9387

Bruce Cohn Management
P.O. Box 878
Sonoma 95476
(707) 938-4060

Cornelius-Griffey Entertainment
  Company
9200 Sunset Blvd., Penthouse 15
Los Angeles 90069
(213) 550-8623

Mike Curb Productions.
280 South Beverly Dr., Suite 311
Beverly Hills 90212
(213) 278-3208

Joan L. Danto
7260 Hillside Ave.
Los Angeles 90046
(213) 874-4166

Day 5 Productions
216 Chatsworth Dr.
San Fernando 91340
(213) 365-9371

Bea Donaldson
P.O. Box 7088
Burbank 91510
(213) 851-0609

Dubow/Mirell Personal Management
6551 Commodore Sloat Dr.
Los Angeles 90048
(213) 933-3780

George Bullets Durgom
9229 Sunset Blvd., Suite 615
Los Angeles 90069
(213) 278-8820

EL Management
9229 Sunset Blvd., Suite 625
Los Angeles 90069
(213) 656-8802

Robert Ellis and Associates
8272 Sunset Blvd., Suite 22
Los Angeles 90046
(213) 656-1082

Norman Epstein Management
644 North Doheny
Los Angeles 90069
(213) 271-5181

Martin Erlichman
10202 West Washington Blvd.
Culver City 90230
(213) 836-3000

Far-Out Management, Ltd.
7417 Sunset Blvd.
Hollywood 90046
(213) 874-1300

David Forest Co., Inc.
7060 Hollywood Blvd., Suite 505
Los Angeles 90028
(213) 464-9241

Freeman and Doff, Inc.
8732 Sunset Blvd., Suite 250
Los Angeles 90069
(213) 659-4700

Ken Fritz Management
8450 Melrose Place
Los Angeles 90069
(213) 651-5350

Front Line Management
8380 Sunset Blvd., Suite 307
Los Angeles 90069
(213) 685-6600

Gelb and Associates
2233 Nichols Canyon Rd.
Hollywood 90046
(213) 874-1555

David Gershenson
9538 Brighton Way
Beverly Hills 90210
(213) 278-2343

Global Entertainment Industries, Inc.
1440 Veteran Ave., Suite 503
West Los Angeles 90024
(213) 477-3369

GNP Crescendo
8560 Sunset Blvd.
Los Angeles 90069
(213) 659-7433

Joe Gottfried Management
15456 Cabrito Road
Van Nuys 91406
(213) 873-2842

Bill Graham Management
201 11th St.
San Francisco 94103
(415) 864-0815

Norman Granz
451 North Canon Dr.
Beverly Hills 90210
(213) 271-1186

Grateful Dead Productions
P.O. Box 1073
San Rafael 94902
(415) 457-6300

Grelf-Garris Management
8467 Beverly Blvd.
Los Angeles 90048
(213) 653-4780

Bernie Gross
9000 Sunset Blvd., Suite 710
Los Angeles 90069

Forest Hamilton Personal Management
9229 Sunset Blvd., Suite 700
Los Angeles 90069
(213) 273-3710

Hartmann and Goodman
1500 Crossroads of the World
Hollywood 90028
(213) 461-3461

Seymour Heller & Associates
9200 Sunset Blvd.
Los Angeles 90069
(213) 273-3060

Stephen Hill
6255 Sunset Blvd.
Los Angeles 90028
(213) 468-3708

ICA Talent
9100 Sunset Blvd., #210
Los Angeles 90069
(213) 550-0254

Jackson-Arons Enterprises
6255 Sunset Blvd., Suite 1023
Hollywood 90028
(213) 466-7325

Quincy Jones Productions
1416 North La Brea Ave.
Los Angeles 90028
(213) 469-2411

Katz-Gallin-Cleary Enterprises
9255 Sunset Blvd., #1115
Los Angeles 90069
(213) 273-4210

Kaufman and Levine
P.O. Box 589
Berkeley 94701
(415) 527-6527

Monte Kay Management
9229 Sunset Blvd.
Beverly Hills 90069
(213) 278-7981

Don Kelly Organization
1474 North Kings Road
Los Angeles 90069
(213) 656-4787

Kessler-Grass Management
449 South Beverly Dr., #108
Beverly Hills 90212
(213) 227-3484

Bob Kirkland
6255 Sunset Blvd., #1005
Hollywood 90028
(213) 469-2951

Kudo III Management
8250 Wilshire Blvd., #300
Beverly Hills 90212
(213) 278-2916

Larry Larson Association, Inc.
8732 Sunset Blvd., #600
Los Angeles 90069
(213) 652-8700

Larter Enterprises
9440 Santa Monica Blvd., #740
Beverly Hills 90210
(213) 278-3156

Buddy Lee Attractions
14755 Ventura Blvd.
Sherman Oaks 91403
(213) 788-4521

LeMond-Zetter
3853 Stone Canyon Ave.
Sherman Oaks 91403
(213) 872-0481

   Branch:
850 7th Ave.
New York, NY 10019
(212) 765-0810

John Levy Enterprises
8570 Hollywood Blvd.
Los Angeles 90069
(213) 656-6184

Richard O. Linke Associates,
   Incorporated
4055 Kraft Ave.
Studio City 91604
(213) 760-2500

Lookout Management
9120 Sunset Blvd.
Los Angeles 90069
(213) 278-0881

Sam J. Lutz Artists Management
1626 North Vine St.
Hollywood 90028
(213) 469-1993

The Management Company
9000 Sunset Blvd., Suite 705
Los Angeles 90069
(213) 273-4005

Management Council, Ltd.
14827 Ventura Blvd., #216
Sherman Oaks 91403
(213) 986-8862

Management I Inc.
1900 Ave. of the Stars, #1600
Los Angeles 90069
(213) 277-5253

Management Three
9644 Wilshire Blvd.
Beverly Hills 90212
(213) 550-7100

Branch:
1345 Ave. of the Americas
New York, NY 10019
(212) 752-1563

Sy Marsh, Ltd.
2029 Century Park E., #3590
Beverly Hills 90067
(213) 553-6895

Rod McKuen Enterprises
8440 Santa Monica Blvd.
Los Angeles 90069
(213) 656-7311

Con Merten and Associates
7235 Hollywood Blvd., #221
Hollywood 90046
(213) 874-1002

Arnold Mills & Associates
8271 Sunset Blvd.
Los Angeles 90069
(213) 657-2024

Multi Media Management
6252 Sunset Blvd.
Hollywood 90028
(213) 657-3390

New Direction
9255 Sunset Blvd., #526
Los Angeles 90069
(213) 550-7205

October Management
6255 Sunset Blvd.
Los Angeles 90028
(213) 468-3459

Omac Artists Corporation
1225 North Chester Ave.
Bakersfield 93308
(805) 393-1000

Brian Panella Management
838 West Knoll Dr., #122
West Hollywood 90069
(213) 657-2600

Radin Associates
9255 Sunset Blvd.
Los Angeles 90069
(213) 550-8170

Branch:
P.O. Box MMMM
Southampton, NY 11968
(516) 283-9100

Jess Rand, Inc.
9460 Wilshire Blvd.
Beverly Hills 90212
(213) 275-6000

John Reid Enterprises, Inc.
211 South Beverly Dr., #200
Beverly Hills 90212
(213) 275-5221

Renaissance Management Corporation
433 North Camden Dr.
Beverly Hills 90210
(213) 273-4162

Bud Robinson Productions, Inc.
1100 North Alta Loma Rd., #707
Los Angeles 90069
(213) 652-3242

Wally Roker Management
8560 Sunset Blvd., #800
Los Angeles 90069
(213) 659-7022

Glen Ross Management
6290 Sunset Blvd., #304
Hollywood 90068
(213) 463-1344

Kal Ross Management, Inc.
2029 Century Park East, #3585
Los Angeles 90067
(213) 553-9757

Howard Rothberg, Ltd.
1706 North Doheny Dr.
Los Angeles 90069
(213) 273-9100

Alfred Schlesinger
6230 Sunset Blvd.
Hollywood 90028
(213) 462-6011

Scotti Brothers Entertainment
9229 Sunset Blvd., #616
Los Angeles 90069
(213) 274-7853

Selective Artists
15250 Ventura Blvd., #1100
Sherman Oaks 91403
(213) 995-0105

Mel Shayne Enterprises, Inc.
8271 Sunset Blvd., #209
Los Angeles 90069
(213) 659-9977

Solo Enterprises
1900 Ave. of the Stars, #1600
Los Angeles 90067
(213) 277-5253

Stardust Enterprises
2650 Glendower Ave.
Los Angeles 90064
(213) 660-2553

Stream Associates
P.O. Box 856
San Luis Obispo 93406
(805) 544-3500

Norton Styne Co., Inc.
148 South Beverly Dr.
Beverly Hills 90212
(213) 274-9475

Tentmakers Corporation
1411 North St. Andrews Place
Los Angeles 90004
(213) 464-9222

Total Experience Management
6226 Yucca St.
Hollywood 90028
(213) 462-6585

Twin Trumpets Productions
6430 Sunset Blvd., #1531
Los Angeles 90069
(213) 462-6803

Wald-De Blasio
9120 Sunset Blvd.
Los Angeles 90069
(213) 273-2192

Mimi Weber Management
9738 Arby Dr.
Beverly Hills 90210
(213) 278-8440

Ron Weisner Management, Inc.
9200 Sunset Blvd., #808
Los Angeles 90069
(213) 550-0570

Wolfhead Productions, Inc.
12776 Hollyridge Dr.
Hollywood 90068
(213) 469-2739

Stanford Zucker & Associates
9350 Wilshire Blvd.
Beverly Hills 90212
(213) 274-6703

COLORADO

Feyline Management
8933 East Union, #250
Englewood 80110
(303) 773-6000

CONNECTICUT

Media Consulting Corporation
54 Main St.
Danbury 06810
(203) 792-8880

DISTRICT OF COLUMBIA

Cellar Door Management
1201 34th St. N.W.
Washington, DC 20007
(202) 337-3389

Roberta Flack Enterprises
244 "G" St. S.W.
Washington, DC 20024
(202) 628-5350

GEORGIA

Phil Walden & Associates
535 Cotton Ave.
Macon 31201
(912) 745-8511

HAWAII

Associated Pacific Artists
1402 Kapiolani Blvd., #40
Honolulu 96816
(808) 946-9028

ILLINOIS

Al Curtis Entertainment
5200 Main St.
Skokie 60076
(312) 679-7397

KENTUCKY

Triangle Talent, Inc.
P.O. Box 99035
Louisville 40299
(502) 267-5466

LOUISIANA

Tillman Franks Enterprises
521 Louisiana Bank Bldg.
Shreveport 71101
(318) 221-5886

Al Hirt Enterprises
809 St. Louis St.
New Orleans 70112
(504) 525-6167

MARYLAND

Jack Berry Enterprises
7316 Wisconsin Ave.
Bethesda 20014
(301) 657-8048

MASSACHUSETTS

Backstage Ltd.
36 Elliott Drive
Lowell 01852
(617) 458-0027

MICHIGAN

Al Nalli Productions
312 North Ashley
Ann Arbor 48104
(313) 769-5454

Punch Enterprises, Inc.
567 Purdy
Birmingham 48009
(313) 642-0910

MINNESOTA

Projects IV, Inc.
7515 Wayzata Blvd., #110
Minneapolis 55426
(612) 546-0226

MISSOURI

Good Karma Product
4218 Main St.
Kansas City 64111
(816) 531-3857

NEVADA

Vic Beri Productions
2739 Polar Court
Las Vegas 89121
(702) 457-2425

NEW JERSEY

Rick Martin Productions
5130 Blvd. East
West New York 07093
(201) 348-1647

NEW YORK

Buddy Allen Management, Inc.
65 West 55th St.
New York 10019
(212) 581-8988

Benjamin Ashburn
39 West 55th St., Penthouse South
New York 10019
(212) 246-0385

Aucoin Management, Inc.
645 Madison Ave.
New York 10022
(212) 826-8800

AWB, Inc.
240 Central Park South
New York 10019
(212) 586-1324

Branch:
9155 Sunset Blvd., Suite 3
Los Angeles, CA 90069
(213) 550-8644

Bandana Enterprises, Ltd.
654 Madison Ave., Suite 609
New York 10021
(212) 758-2122

Sid Bernstein Productions, Ltd.
44 West 51st St.
New York 10020
(212) 765-1415

Marion F. Billings
605 Park Ave.
New York 10021
(212) 249-1368

Jackie Bright, Ltd.
850 7th Ave.
New York 10019
(212) 247-2930

James Brown Enterprises
810 7th St.
New York 10019
(212) 977-7273

Century Artists Bureau, Inc.
866 Third Ave.
New York 10019
(212) 752-3920

Champion Entertainment Corporation
105 West 55th St., Suite 7A
New York 10019

Cy Coleman Enterprises
161 West 54th St., Suite 503
New York 10019
(212) 757-9547

Peter Dean
161 West 54th St.
New York 10019
(212) 265-0789

Desert Moon Enterprises
850 7th Ave.
New York 10019
(212) 765-8840

Peter Duchin Orchestras, Inc.
400 Madison Ave.
New York 10017
(212) 753-4393

Mallory Factor Associates, Inc.
1500 Broadway
New York 10036
(212) 869-1600

Phil Farrell Associates
35 West 53rd St.
New York 10019
(212) 757-4140

Danny Fields
745 5th Ave.
New York 10022
(212) 755-9490

Peter Glick
c/o Tellurian Music, Inc.
1350 Avenue of the Americas
New York 10019
(212) 582-8021

Danny Goldberg
140 West 79th St.
New York 10024
(212) 598-0888

Greenfield Associates, Inc.
1 Rockefeller Plaza
New York 10020
(212) 245-8130

Greengrass Enterprises, Inc.
505 Park Ave.
New York 10022
(212) 421-8415

Albert B. Grossman
P.O. Box 135
Bearville 12409
(914) 697-7303

Hampton Artists Corporation
6925 Exeter St.
Forest Hills 11375
(212) 261-8133

Mickey Harman Productions
1500 Broadway, 21st Flr.
New York 10036
(212) 354-8900

Fred Heller
40 Cedar Ave.
Dobbs Ferry 10522
(914) 693-1091

Ted Hook
1065 Lexington Ave.
New York 10021
(212) 628-6099

Marc Howard Productions
1200 East 53rd St.
Brooklyn 11234
(212) 763-1189

Val Irving
114 East 61st St.
New York 10021
(212) 755-8932

David Jonas
101 West 57th St.
New York 10019
(212) 247-5140

Jerry Katz
527 Madison Ave.
New York 10022
(212) 752-0850

Kirshner Enterprises
1370 Sixth Ave.
New York 10019
(212) 489-0440

LaMonica Management, Inc.
10 Park Ave., Suite 7H
New York 10016
(212) 889-7000

Leber-Krebs, Inc.
65 West 53rd St.
New York 10019
(212) 756-2600

Joseph Lodato
111 West 57th St.
New York 10019
(212) 541-5030

Steve Metz
1650 Broadway
New York 10019
(212) 757-7780

Arthur Miller
1501 Broadway, #1803
New York 10036
(212) 730-1444 or 1445

Gordon Mills
1 Rockefeller Plaza
New York 10020
(212) 245-8130

Music Media Management Corporation
P.O. Box 366
West Nyack 10994
(914) 359-7550

Rick Newman
67-66 108th St.
Forest Hills 11375
(212) 520-1259

Gerald W. Purcell Associates, Ltd.
133 Fifth Ave.
New York 10003
(212) 475-7100

Joseph Rapp Enterprises
1650 Broadway
New York 10019
(212) 581-6162

Rollins, Joffe and Morra, Inc.
130 West 57th St.
New York 10019
(212) 382-1940

Phil Schapiro, Inc.
157 West 57th St.
New York 10019
(212) 581-6830

George Scheck Enterprises
161 West 54th St.
New York 10019
(212) 586-6767

Jack Segal Enterprises, Inc.
850 7th Ave.
New York 10019
(212) 265-7489

Sidney A. Seidenberg, Inc.
1414 Ave. of the Americas
New York 10019
(212) 421-2021

Sir Productions, Inc.
130 West 57th St.
New York 10019
(212) 765-7620

Kuno Sponholz
350 West 55th St.
New York 10019
(212) 265-3777

Harry Steinman
15 Central Park West, #1208
New York 10023
(212) 751-2156

Robert Stigwood Organization (RSO)
1775 Broadway
New York 10019
(212) 975-0700

Swan Song, Inc.
444 Madison Ave., 35th Flr.
New York 10022
(212) 752-1330

Tedlem Associates, Ltd.
200 West 57th St.
New York 10018

Thruppence, Ltd.
119 West 57th St.
New York 10019
(212) 541-5580

Tin-Bar Amusement Corporation
15 Central Park West
New York 10023
(212) 586-1015

Charles Tishman Enterprises
2211 Broadway
New York 10024
(212) 873-8213

T-Neck
1650 Broadway, #1401
New York 10019
(212) 882-5430

Tunny Enterprises, Inc.
315 West 57th St.
New York 10019
(212) 581-5455 or 5456

Wartoke Concern
250 West 57th St.
New York 10019
(212) 245-5587

OHIO

Belkin Productions, Inc.
28001 Chagrin Blvd., Suite 205
Cleveland 44115
(216) 456-5990

OKLAHOMA

Jim Halsey Co., Inc.
3225 South Norwood Ave.
Tulsa 74135
(918) 663-3883

PENNSYLVANIA

Denny Somach Productions
525 North Broad St.
Allentown 18104
(215) 820-9090

WMOT Productions
1307 Vine St.
Philadelphia 19107
(215) 922-6640

TENNESSEE

Acuff-Rose Publications, Inc.
2510 Franklin Road
Nashville 37204
(615) 385-3031

Al Gallico Music Corporation
50 Music Square West
Nashville 37203
(615) 327-2773

Waylon Jennings, Ltd.
1117 17th Ave. South
Nashville 37212
(615) 327-3840

Jack D. Johnson Talent, Inc.
P.O. Box 40484
Nashville 37204
(615) 383-6564

Lavender-Blake
1217 16th Ave. South
Nashville 37212

Jerry Lee Lewis Talent
1717 West End, Suite 322
Nashville 37203
(615) 320-1187

Lisa Music Productions
P.O. Box 1062
Nashville 37202
(615) 327-4667

Loretta Lynn Enterprises
7 Music Circle North
Nashville 37203
(615) 259-2021

Prima-Donna Enterprises
P.O. Box 15385
Nashville 37215
(615) 373-2390

Jerry Reed Enterprises
805 18th Ave. South
Nashville 37203
(615) 327-3818

Shelby Singleton Corporation
3106 Belmont Blvd.
Nashville 37212
(615) 385-1960

Sound 70 Management, Inc.
1719 West End Ave. #111
Nashville 37203

Top Billing, Inc.
P.O. Box 12514
Nashville 37212
(615) 383-8883

TEXAS

Music Enterprises
5626 Brock
Houston 77023
(713) 926-4431

Ray Price Enterprises
P.O. Box 34886
Dallas 75234
(214) 387-1101

WASHINGTON

Albatross Productions
P.O. Box 86558
Seattle 98166
(206) 246-9400

CANADA

Bruce Allen Talent Promotions, Ltd.
12 Water St., #108
Vancouver, B.C. V6B 1A5
(604) 688-7274

David Coutts Personal Management
1659 Bayview Ave.
Toronto, Ont. M4G 3C1
(416) 485-1157

Bob Ezrin
125 Scollard St.
Toronto, Ont.
(416) 916-0164

Allan Katz
128 Shutr St.
Toronto, Ont. M4G 3C1
(416) 868-6269

U.S. RECORD
COMPANIES

ALABAMA

Ansap Records
P.O. Box 10612
Birmingham 35204

Cartee Music Corporation
1108 East Avalon Ave.
Muscle Shoals 35660

Branch:
Sunset Vine Tower
6290 Sunset Blvd.
Hollywood, CA 90028

Branch:
21 Music Circle East
Nashville, TN 37203

Everlovin Corporation, Inc.
P.O. Box 4007
Huntsville 35802

Hemphill Recording
544 Bessemer Super Hwy.
Midfield 35228

JB Records International, Inc.
Box 7221
Mobile 36607

McDowell Records
828 South Lawrence St.
Montgomery 36104

Orbit Records
100 Harvard Ave.
Gadsden 35901

Raven Records
P.O. Box 1766
Dothan 36301

ARIZONA

Canyon Records, Inc.
4143 North 16th St.
Phoenix 85016

Dads Tunes
P.O. Box 26637
Tempe 85282

NuTop Record, Inc.
4750 North Central, P-1
Phoenix 85012

Pantheon Desert Records
6325 North Invergordon Rd.
Scottsdale 85253

Recital Records
4640 East Lewis
Phoenix 85008

Suncountry Productions, Inc.
14 East Second St.
Tucson 85705

Up With People
3103 North Campbell Ave.
Tucson 85719

World Jazz Records
4350 East Camelback
Phoenix 85018

ARKANSAS

Combined Marketing Associates
10 Boston Square
Fort Smith 72901

Jamdan Publishing Company
1119 East Broadway
West Memphis 72301

Razorback of Arkansas
9207 Malabri Dr.
Little Rock 72209

Robbins Records
Box 157, Rte. 1
Magazine 72943

Thrust/Byblos Record Productions
4208 West 19th
Little Rock 72204

CALIFORNIA

A Record Company
1608 Argyle
Hollywood 90028

ABC Records, Inc.
8255 Beverly Blvd.
Los Angeles 90048

AD & A Records
P.O. Box 1412
Hollywood 90028

A & M Records, Inc.
1416 North La Brea Ave.
Hollywood 90028

Abattoir Records
(Kahuku Productions)
1680 North Vine St., Suite 900
Hollywood 90028

Accent Records
6533 Hollywood Blvd.
Hollywood 90028

Acoustic Records of America
2700 Benedict Canyon Dr.
Beverly Hills 90210

Advent Productions
P.O. Box 635
La Habra 90631

Alshire International
1015 Isabel St.
Burbank 91502

Alva Records
3929 Kentucky Dr.
Los Angeles 90068

American Variety International, Inc.
9220 Sunset Blvd., Suite 224
Los Angeles 90069

Anahuac (Discos)
6331 Santa Monica Blvd.
Hollywood 90019

Lee Anderson Enterprises
P.O. Box 4141
North Hollywood 91607

Anpre Records
802 East Ocean Ave.
Lompoc 93436

Danny Antell Productions
521 West Bradley
El Cajon 92020

April Twenty-Two Productions
9000 Sunset Blvd., Suite 1119
Los Angeles 90069

Arhoolie Records, Inc.
10341 San Pablo Ave.
El Cerrito 94530

Ariola America, Inc.
8671 Wilshire Blvd.
Beverly Hills 90211

Arriba Records
2525 West Pico Blvd.
Los Angeles 90006

Artists of America Records, Inc.
21636 Ventura Blvd.
Woodland Hills 91365

Ashton Records
358 31st St.
Hermosa Beach 90254

Audio Arts, Inc.
5611 Melrose Ave.
Los Angeles 90038

Azteca Records, Inc.
1015 Isabel St.
Burbank 91502

Bal Records
Box 369
La Canada 91011

Balboa Record Company
16027 Sunburst St.
Sepulveda 91343

Bald Ego
Box 31451
San Francisco 94131

Barnaby Records
816 North La Cienega Blvd.
Los Angeles 90069

Base Recordings
2048 Charle St.
Costa Mesa 92627

Bay Records
1516 Oak St., Suite 320
Alameda 94501

Bel-Ad Records
4307 South Broadway
Los Angeles 90037

Beserkley Records
1199 Spruce St.
Berkeley 94707

Birthright Records
3101 South Western Ave.
Los Angeles 90018

Blackjack Records
P.O. Box 3367
Hollywood 90028

Blue Canyon Records
100 Granville Ave.
Los Angeles 90049

Blue River Records
6223 Selma Ave., Suite 125
Hollywood 90028

Bomp Records
Box 7112
Burbank 91510

Briar Records
7460 Melrose Ave.
Los Angeles 90046

Brother Records, Inc.
3621 Sepulveda Blvd., Suite 3
Manhattan Beach 90266

CMH Records, Inc.
P.O. Box 39439
Los Angeles 90039

Cabot Entertainment Companies
P.O. Box 3901
Hollywood 90028

Cadet Records, Inc.
5810 South Normandie Ave.
Los Angeles 90044

California Artists Corporation
P.O. Box 11474
Fresno 93773

Calliope Records, Inc./Festival
Records, Inc.
15910 Ventura Blvd., Suite 603
Sherman Oaks 91403

Calvary Records, Inc.
174 North Maple Ave.
Fresno 93702

Capitol Records, Inc.
1750 North Vine St.
Hollywood 90028

Branch:
1370 Ave. of the Americas
New York, NY 10019

Branch:
38 Music Square East
Nashville, TN 37203

Carapan Productions, Inc.
17029 Chatsworth St.
Granada Hills 91344

Caribou Records
8600 Melrose Ave.
Los Angeles 90069

Carousel Records, Inc.
1273-½ North Crescent Heights
Los Angeles 90046

Casablanca Records & Film Works
8255 Sunset Blvd.
Los Angeles 90046

Cassandra Records
2027 Parker St.
Berkeley 94704

Celestial Records
1560 North La Brea, Suite M
Hollywood 90028

Charade Records, Inc.
1310 East Kern St.
Tulare 93274

Chattahoochee Record Company
16038 Ventura Blvd.
Encino 91436

Chrysalis Records
9255 Sunset Blvd., Suite 212
Los Angeles 90069

Cinema Prize, Inc.
8192 Universal Plaza Station
Universal City 91608

Cin-Kay Record Company
15130 Ventura Blvd., No. 202
Sherman Oaks 91403

Claridge Records
6381 Hollywood Blvd.
Hollywood 90028

Cobra Records
P.O. Box 2144
Winnetka 91306

Concert Company
P.O. Box 531
Lynwood 90262

Concord Jazz, Inc.
P.O. Box 845
Concord 94522

Contemporary Records, Inc.
8481 Melrose Pl.
Los Angeles 90069

Coronado Record Company
897 Walker Ave.
Oakland 94610

Corral Records
8560 Sunset Blvd., Suite 800
Los Angeles 90069

Country Porn Records
P.O. Box 7142
Berkeley 94707

Cream Records
8025 Melrose Ave.
Los Angeles 90046

Creative World, Inc.
1012 South Robertson Blvd.
Los Angeles 90035

Criterion Music Corporation
6124 Selma
Hollywood 90028

Crossover Records Company
2107 West Washington Blvd.
Los Angeles 90018

Branch:
120 East 56th St.
New York, NY 10022

Crystal Record Company
P.O. Box 65661
Los Angeles 90065

Crystal Clear Records, Inc.
225 Kearny St., Suite 200
San Francisco 94108

Damount Corporation
315 South Beverly Dr., Suite 400
Beverly Hills 90212

Daybreak Distribution Corporation
6725 Sunset Blvd., Suite 402
Hollywood 90028

Dejay "Gold" Records & Productions
859 North Hollywood Way
Burbank 91505

Delos Records, Inc.
855 Via de la Paz
Pacific Palisades 90272

Richard Delvy Enterprises, Inc.
8127 Elrita Dr.
Los Angeles 90046

Discocorp
P.O. Box 771
Berkeley 94701

Discos Latin International, Inc.
1646 South Vermont
Los Angeles 90006

DiscReet Records, Inc.
5831 Sunset Blvd.
Hollywood 90028

Disneyland-Vista Records
350 South Buena Vista St.
Burbank 91521

Documentary Recordings
P.O. Box 24605
Los Angeles 90024

Dore Records
1608 Argyle
Hollywood 90028

Doric Recording Group, Inc.
P.O. Box 282
Monterey 93940

Dorn Records
20531 Plummer St.
Chatsworth 91311

E & G Productions
2858 West Pico Blvd.
Los Angeles 90006

Eagle Record Company
P.O. Box 1102
Burbank 91507

Educational Film Systems
11566 San Vicente Blvd.
Los Angeles 90049

Educational Media Associate of
America, Inc.
P.O. Box 921
Berkeley 94701

Elektra/Asylum/Nonesuch Records
962 North La Cienega
Los Angeles 90069

Elm Records
P.O. Box 1100
Westminster 92683

El Rauncho Records
P.O. Box 28402
San Jose 95159

Encore Records
P.O. Box 343
Santa Monica 90406

Era Records Ltd.
9460 Wilshire Blvd.
Beverly Hills 90212

Essar Records
P.O. Box 38444
Hollywood 90028

Everest Recording Group
10920 Wilshire Blvd.
Los Angeles 90024

Express Records
P.O. Box 3763
Hollywood 90028

FADA Record Production
844 West 107th
Los Angeles 90044

Fairmont Records
P.O. Box 3392
Santa Monica 90504

Falconer Records
P.O. Box 2217
Inglewood 90205

Fama Records
377 South First St.
San Jose 95113

Fanatasy/Prestige/Milestone
10th & Parker Sts.
Berkeley 94710

Wes Farrel Organization
9200 Sunset Blvd., Suite 620
Los Angeles 90069

FEL Publications, Ltd.
1925 South Pontius Ave.
Los Angeles 90025

Maynard Ferguson Music, Inc.
305 North Foothill Rd.
Ojai 93023

Fermata International Melodies, Inc.
Sunset-Vine Tower, Suite 616
Hollywood 90028

Festival Records & Distribution
15910 Ventura Blvd., Suite 603
Sherman Oaks 91403

Fidelity Sound Recordings
23 Don Court
Redwood City 94062

Forest Bay Record Company
703 Canham Rd.
Santa Cruz 95060

49th State Hawaii Record Company
P.O. Box 371
Redlands 92373

Freckle Records
P.O. Box 31319
San Francisco 94131

Full Moon Records
9126 Sunset Blvd.
Los Angeles 90069

GNP Crescendo Records
8560 Sunset Blvd., Suite 603
Los Angeles 90069

Garden Record Company
9000 Sunset Blvd.
Los Angeles 90069

Gas Records
2716 West Pico Blvd.
Los Angeles 90006

Gem Records
Box 9726, West Gate Sta.
San Jose 95117

Genesis Records, Inc.
1641 18th St.
Santa Monica 90404

Glendale Records
731 West Wilson
Glendale 91203

Golden Gate Records
2494 Mission
San Francisco 94410

Marc Gordon Productions
1022 North Palm Ave.
Los Angeles 90069

Gramophone Records Company
Box 921
Beverly Hills 90213

Granite Records
6255 Sunset Blvd., Suite 723
Los Angeles 90028

Grassroots Project Unlimited
P.O. Box 4689
San Francisco 94101

Guitar Player Records
Box 615
Saratoga 95008

HDM Records
1777 North Vine St.
Hollywood 90028

Happy Fox Records
1530 Gower, Suite 7
Hollywood 90028

Harlequin Records
P.O. Box 20201
San Diego 92120

Harmony Club Records
P.O. Box 925
Hollywood 90068

Haven Records, Inc.
6255 Sunset Blvd., Suite 709
Hollywood 90028

Haze Record Company
1617 North El Centro
Hollywood 90028

L. Herbst Investment Trust Fund
c/o Antejo Corporation
P.O. Box 1659
Beverly Hills 90213

Heritage Singers USA, Inc.
P.O. Box 1358
Placerville 95667

Eric Hilding Enterprises
715 Timor Court
San Jose 95127

Hindsight Records
P.O. Box 480306
Los Angeles 90048

Hit Machine Records
P.O. Box 20692
San Diego 92120

Horizon Publishing Company
13615 Victory Blvd., Suite 216
Van Nuys 91401

Horoscope Records
P.O. Box 811
Santa Monica 90406

Bobbie Horwitz Productions
16700 Chatsworth St., Suite H-2
Granada Hills 91344

International Artists Group
6420 Wilshire Blvd.
Los Angeles 90048

Jansco Records
P.O. Box 807
Northridge 91328

Janus Records
8776 Sunset Blvd.
Los Angeles 90069

Jet Records, Inc.
2 Century Plaza, Suite 4414
2049 Century Park East
Los Angeles 90067

Paul Johnson Productions
P.O. Box 552
Woodland Hills 91365

Joyce Records
5500 West Jefferson Blvd.
Los Angeles 90016

Jucu Recordings
Box 2161
North Hollywood 91602

Kaleidoscope Records
P.O. Box O
El Cerrito 94530

Kangaroo Records
302 East Dewey
San Gabriel 91776

Katie the Great
P.O. Box 19215A
Los Angeles 90019

Kicking Mule Recording Company
P.O. Box 3233
Berkeley 94703

Koala Records, Inc.
9255 Sunset Blvd.
Los Angeles 90069

Laff Records
4218 West Jefferson Blvd.
Los Angeles 90016

Landers-Roberts, Inc.
9255 Sunset Blvd.
Los Angeles 90048

Ray Lawrence, Ltd.
P.O. Box 1987
Studio City 91604

Lighthouse Records
65 Loval Ave.
San Rafael 94901

Little Angel Records
1844 Westhime Ave.
Westwood 96137

Little David Records Company, Inc.
9229 Sunset Blvd., Suite 901
Los Angeles 90069

Little Star Records
723 North Seward
Los Angeles 90038

Loadstone & Open Record Company
163 Orizaba Ave.
San Francisco 94132

Lu Tall Records
P.O. Box 6162
Long Beach 90806

MCA Records, Inc.
100 Universal City Plaza
Universal City 91608

C.P. MacGregor Recording Studios
729 South Western Ave.
Los Angeles 90006

Lee Magid, Inc.
19657 Ventura Blvd.
Tarzana 91360

Majega Records
240 East Radcliffe Dr.
Claremont 91711

Manna Records
2111 Kenmere
Burbank 91504

Marantha! Music Company
3001 Sunflower
Santa Ana 92704

Marsel Records, Inc.
6464 Sunset Blvd., Suite 910
Los Angeles 90028

Marzique Music Company
5752 Bowcroft St.
Los Angeles 90016

Masterscores
1335 North Detroit, Suite 103
Hollywood 90046

Mastertrack Records
8899 Beverly Blvd.
Los Angeles 90048

Mercantile Productions
P.O. Box 2271
Palm Springs 92262

Mirror Ball Discs
958 West Edgemont Dr.
San Bernardino 92405

Montclair Records
13755 Bayliss Road
West Los Angeles 90049

Monterey Records
P.O. Box 8497
Universal City 91608

Moonstone International Records
P.O. Box 946
Hollywood 90028

Motown Record Corporation
6255 Sunset Blvd.
Hollywood 90028

Mushroom Records, Inc.
8833 Sunset Blvd.
Los Angeles 90069

Music First Productions
243 South Ave. 50
Los Angeles 90042

Musimex, Inc.
2596 West Pico Blvd.
Los Angeles 90006

Mystic Records
6277 Selma Ave.
Hollywood 90028

Nashville West Productions
124 Country Side Dr.
Bakersfield 93308

Nautilus Recordings
761 Shell Beach Rd.
Shell Beach 93449

New Wine Productions
P.O. Box 544
Lomita 90717

October Records
1474 North Kings Rd.
Los Angeles 90069

Ode Records, Inc.
1416 North La Brea
Hollywood 90028

Olinger Music Productions
11110 Los Alamitos, Suite 215
Los Alamitos 90720

Olivia Records, Inc.
P.O. Box 70237
Los Angeles 90070

Orfeon Records, Inc.
2837 West Pico Blvd.
Los Angeles 90006

Original Sound Records
7120 Sunset Blvd.
Hollywood 90046

Orion Master Recordings, Inc.
5840 Busch Dr.
Malibu 90265

Outstanding Records
P.O. Box 2111
Huntington Beach 92647

PBR International
7033 Sunset Blvd.
Los Angeles 90028

Pablo Records
451 North Canon Dr.
Beverly Hills 90210

The Pacific Arts Corporation
P.O. Box 5547
Carmel 93921

Pacific Records
9200 Sunset Blvd.
Hollywood 90069

Paramount-West Enterprises
8010 Second St.
Paramount 90723

Parasound, Inc.
680 Beach St.
San Francisco 94109

Pausa, Inc.
9255 Sunset Blvd., Rm. 509
Los Angeles 90069

Peaceable Music
3525 Encinal Canyon Rd.
Malibu 90205

Pelican Records
214 Marine St.
Santa Monica 90405

Pirate Records
P.O. Box 49204, Barrington Sta.
Los Angeles 90049

Playboy Records, Inc.
8560 Sunset Blvd.
Los Angeles 90069

Pleason Records
1727 Roanoke Ave.
Sacramento 95838

Point Blank Productions
2017 Walnut Creek Pkwy.
West Covina 91791

Puerto Vallarta (Discos)
13615 Victory Blvd.
Van Nuys 91401

QCA
P.O. Box 1127
Burbank 91507

Quinto Records
4423 Ledge Ave.
Touluca Lake 91602

RSO Records & Tapes, Inc.
8335 Sunset Blvd.
Los Angeles 90069

Rage Records Company
19826 Wadley Ave.
Carson 90746

Rainbo Record Manufacturing
  Corporation
1738 Berkeley St.
Santa Monica 90404

Ranwood Records, Inc.
9034 Sunset Blvd.
Los Angeles 90069

Bill Rase Productions, Inc.
955 Venture Court
Sacramento 95825

Raven Record Company
P.O. Box 20037
Sacramento 95820

R'Cade Record Corporation
3090 North Lincoln Ave.
Altadena 91001

Recorded Treasures, Inc.
P.O. Box 1278
North Hollywood 91604

Redwood Records
565 Doolan Canyon Dr.
Ukiah 95482

Regency Records
9454 Wilshire Blvd., Suite 500
Beverly Hills 90212

Renaissance Records
13422 Oxnard St.
Van Nuys 91401

Renfro Records
1148 Tremaine Ave.
Los Angeles 90019

Reuben Records
8537 Sunset Blvd., No. 2
Los Angeles 90069

Rhythms Productions
Box 34485
Los Angeles 90034

Rivera Enterprises
1908-1910 Mission St.
San Francisco 94103

Rocket Record Company
211 South Beverly Dr.
Beverly Hills 90212

Rogo Records
8721 West Sunset Blvd.
Los Angeles 90069

Rollin' Rock Records, Inc.
6777 Hollywood Blvd., 9th Flr.
Hollywood 90029

Round Robin Records
19142 Keswick St.
Reseda 91335

Roxy Records, Inc./Platinum Plus
  Record Corporation
9465 Wilshire Blvd.
Beverly Hills 90212

Russell Records, Inc.
1403 Callens Rd.
Ventura 93003

SIPRA
1617 El Centro Ave., Suite 5
Los Angeles 90028

S & M Records
6777 Hollywood Blvd., 9th Flr.
Hollywood 90028

SRI Records
231 Emerson
Palo Alto 94301

Safari Record Company
139 Maryland St.
El Segundo 90245

San Diego Jazz Club
322 Forward St.
La Jolla 92037

San Diego Recording Company
Box 23113
San Diego 92115

Scolaron Records
P.O. Box 441
Northridge 91324

Scrimshaw Records
6943 Valjean Ave.
Van Nuys 91406

1750 Arch, Inc.
1750 Arch St.
Berkeley 94709

Sheffield Lab, Inc.
P.O. Box 5332
Santa Barbara 93108

Shelter Recording Company
5112 Hollywood Blvd.
Hollywood 90027

Sierra Records
7460 Melrose Ave.
Los Angeles 90046

Sonata Records
4304 Del Monte Ave.
San Diego 92107

Sonic Arts Corporation
665 Harrison St.
San Francisco 94107

Sonrise Mercantile Corporation
22802 Pacific Coast Hwy.
Malibu 90265

Sonyatone Records
P.O. Box 567
Santa Barbara 93102

Soul Set Productions
1218 Hollister Ave.
San Francisco 94124

Soul Train Records
9200 Sunset Blvd.
Los Angeles 90069

Sound-Off Records
200 North Long Beach Blvd.
Compton 90221

Hal Southern Productions
Box 4234
Panorama City 91412

Sparrow Records, Inc.
8587 Canoga Ave.
Canoga Park 91304

Specialty Records, Inc.
8300 Santa Monica Blvd.
Los Angeles 90069

Spectrum Records
P.O. Box 757
San Carlos 94070

Spina Music
2232 Vista Del Mar Place
Hollywood 90068

SpinIt Records
3008 Belden Dr.
Los Angeles 90068

Stanyan Record Company
8440 Santa Monica Blvd.
Hollywood 90069

Stinson Records
P.O. Box 3415
Granda Hills 91344

Styletone Records
254 East 29th St., Suite 7
Los Angeles 90011

Sunbeam Records, Inc.
13821 Calvert St.
Van Nuys 91401

Suncat Records
P.O. Box 1212
Redondo Beach 90278

Sunrise Records
1845 West Empire Ave.
Burbank 91504

Surf City Records
5460 White Oak Ave., Suite G-338
Encino 91316

Sutton-Miller, Ltd.
8913 Sunset Blvd.
Los Angeles 90069

Sweet Earth Sound
P.O. Box 1339
Downey 90240

Takoma Records, Inc.
P.O. Box 5369
Santa Monica 90405

Tally Records, Inc.
3811 River Blvd.
Bakersfield 93305

Tao Records
P.O. Box 504
Bonita 92002

R. Dean Taylor Productions
6515 Sunset Blvd., Suite 309
Hollywood 90028

20th Century Records
8544 Sunset Blvd.
Los Angeles 90069

UPCO Music
1050 Plymouth Dr.
Sunnyvale 94087

Uncle Jim O'Neal
P.O. Box A
Arcadia 91006

United Artist Records
6920 Sunset Blvd.
Los Angeles 90028

VRA Records
1224 North Vine St.
Hollywood 90038

The Van Winkle Enterprise
1549 North Vine St., Suite 20
Hollywood 90028

Varese International
P.O. Box 148
Glendale 91209

Vee Jay International Music
131 East Magnolia Blvd.
Burbank 91502

Vincent Enterprises, Inc.
16692 Bolsa Chica, Suite A
Huntington Beach 92649

WILD
P.O. Box 38391
Hollywood 90038

Waltner Enterprises
14702 Canterbury
Tustin 92680

Warner Brothers Records, Inc.
3300 Warner Blvd.
Burbank 91510

Warner-Spector Records, Inc.
P.O. Box 69529
Los Angeles 90069

Wenra Record Company
2801 Santa Clara Ave.
Alameda 94501

West Records
P.O. Box 2851
Hollywood 90028

Western American Record Company
830 South Live Oak Park Rd.
Fallbrook 92028

Western News Records
619-A Buck
Vacaville 95688

Whitfield Records
8719 Santa Monica Blvd.
Los Angeles 90069

Fran Williamson Productions, Inc.
256 South Robertson Blvd.
Beverly Hills 90211

Wilwin Records
P.O. Box 1669
Carlsbad 92008

Wooden Nickel Records, Inc.
6521 Homewood Ave.
Los Angeles 90028

Youngheart Music Education Service
P.O. Box 22784
Los Angeles 90027

Ziv International, Inc.
600 North Sepulveda Blvd.
Bel Air 90049

COLORADO

Bel-J Productions, Inc.
1085 West Arizona Ave.
Denver 80223

Biscuit City Enterprises, Inc.
1106 East 17th Ave.
Denver 80218

Curtain Call Records, Inc.
778 South Pearl St.
Denver 80209

The Fisherman, Inc.
P.O. Box AA
Woodland Park 80863

Great American Music Machine
1130 West Evans
Denver 80223

Northstar Studios, Inc.
P.O. Box D
Boulder 80302

Wesley Records
P.O. Box 10044
Denver 80210

Wormwood Projects
1540 Lehigh St.
Boulder 80303

CONNECTICUT

Broadway Baby Demos-Broadway/
  Hollywood Recordings–Take Home
  Tunes
Box 496
Georgetown 06829

Cook Labs, Inc.
375 Ely Ave.
South Norwalk 06854

Esoteric, Inc.
26 Clark St.
East Hartford 16108

Folk-Legacy Records, Inc.
Sharon Mountain Rd.
Sharon 06069

Innisfree Records, Inc.
70 Turner Hill Rd.
New Canaan 06840

Listening Library, Inc.
1 Park Ave.
Old Greenwich 06870

Lone Star Record Corporation
c/o Neil Reshen
54 Main St.
Danbury 06810

Pharoah Record Corporation
1260 East Main St.
Meriden 06450

Randall Records
29 Elaine Rd.
Milford 06460

Shower Records
P.O. Box 371
Rocky Hill 06067

Fred Weinberg Productions, Inc.
16 Dundee Rd.
Stamford 06903

Wildwood Entertainment
114 West Maiden Ln.
Monroe 06468

DELAWARE

Fleurette Records
P.O. Box 34
Claymont 19703

DISTRICT OF COLUMBIA

Arrest Records
1420 "K" St., N.W.
Washington, DC 20005

Black Fire Records
P.O. Box 38054
Washington, DC 20020

Heavy Sound Productions
P.O. Box 2875
Washington, DC 20013

Histown-Disko Record Corporation
327 Upshur St. N.W.
Washington, DC 20011

Independence Corporation of America
226 Massachusetts Ave.
Washington, DC 20001

Mir-A-Don Records, Inc.
5333 Astor Pl. S.E.
Washington, DC 20019

Showtime
P.O. Box 40074
Washington, DC 20016

FLORIDA

Adam Productions, Inc.
2501 South Ocean Dr.
Hollywood 33022

Aladdin Record Company
835 North Federal Hwy.
Fort Lauderdale 33304

Aquila Record Corporation
6730 Taft St.
Hollywood 33024

Art Records Manufacturing Company
991 S.W. 40 Ave.
Fort Lauderdale 33318

Banditt Records, Inc.
410 Woodfern Ave.
Mary Esther 32569

Beantown Records
206 East Jordan St.
Pensacola 32503

Bee Jay Booking Agency & Recording
   Studios, Inc.
P.O. Box T
Winter Park 32790

Calmex SrL
P.O. Box 014092
Flagler Station
Miami 33101

DGJ Records, Inc.
P.O. Box 010772
Miami 33101

Dana Publishing Company
1130 Stillwater Dr.
Miami Beach 33141

Dit Dot Records
155 N.W. 28th Ave.
Pompano Beach 33060

Empire Records & Tapes
1945 N.E. Fifth St.
Deerfield Beach 33441

Florida Independent Record Corporation
31 N.E. 161st St.
North Miami Beach 33162

GRS Records Company
1236 East India, Dept. 7
Tampa 33602

Godell Music Company, Inc.
1545 S.W. Eighth St.
Miami 33135

GoodSounds Records, Inc.
1755 N.E. 149th St.
Miami 33181

Happy House Productions
P.O. Box 8265
Naples 33940

International Broadcasting Systems
1703 Acme St.
Orlando 32805

Jay Jay Record & Tape Company
35 N.E. 62nd St.
Miami 33138

Jemkl Record Corporation
P.O. Box 460
Miami 33168

Kubaney Publishing Corporation
1305 West 46th St., No. 222
Hialeah 33012

Miami Recordings & Distributing
  Corporation
2819 N.W. Seventh Ave.
Miami 33127

Microfon America
8155 N.W. 103rd
Hialeah Gardens 33016

Music Factory, Inc.
567 N.W. 27th St.
Miami 33127

Palmetto Records
741 N.W. 137th St.
North Miami 33168

Panart International, Inc.
477 West 27th St.
Hialeah 33010

Parnaso Records Company, Inc.
8170-74 N.W. 103rd St.
Hialeah Gardens 33016

Quadraphonic Talent, Inc.
P.O. Box 630175
Miami 33163

Record Distributor of America
780 West 27th St.
Hialeah 33010

Request Records
3800 South Ocean Dr.
Hollywood 33019

Summit Sound System Company
4962 104th Way North
St. Petersburg 33708

TK Productions, Inc.
495 S.E. 10th Court
Hialeah 33010

Universal Evangelistic Miracle & Music
  Fellowship
P.O. Box 795
Bonifoy 32425

Velvet Records, Inc.
10128 N.W. 80th Ave.
Hialeah Gardens 33016

GEORGIA

Atlantis Records
230 Peachtree St., N.W.
Atlanta 30303

Atteiram Productions, Inc.
P.O. Box 606
Marietta 30061

Bang-Bullet Records, Inc.
2107 Faulkner Rd.
Atlanta 30324

Boblo Records & Sound Studio, Inc.
3807 Norwich St.
Brunswick 31520

Capricorn Records, Inc.
535 Cotton Ave.
Macon 31208

Dance-A-Thon Records
1957 Kilburn Dr.
Atlanta 30324

Dewdrop Records
1324 Old Yatesville Rd.
Thomaston 30286

Golden River Records
Steadman Road
Tallapoosa 30176

Gusman Company
P.O. Box 9202
Savannah 31402

Gwen Record Service
P.O. Box 3388
Albany 31701

Jazzology-GHB Records
3008 Wadsworth Mill Pl.
Decatur 30032

Money Records Company
6232 Lynridge Dr.
Columbus 31904

New Spirit Productions, Inc.
174 11th St. N.E.
Atlanta 30309

Note Records, Inc.
799-½ Martin Luther King Dr.
Atlanta 30314

Owl Record Company
P.O. Box 557
Lithia Springs 30057

Progressive Records
Box 986, Rte. 4
Tifton 31794

RJL Enterprises
2020 Riverside Dr.
Macon 31208

Ralph's Radio Music
Demorest 30535

Rose Records Company, Inc.
651-F Morosgo Dr. N.E.
Atlanta 30324

Scaramouche Records
P.O. Drawer 1967
Warner Robins 31093

Scorpio Records
1314 Ellsworth Industrial Dr.
Atlanta 30318

2-Mac Records
P.O. Box 7729
Atlanta 30337

Utopian Enterprises, Inc.
P.O. Box 5314
Macon 31208

HAWAII

ETS Record Company
P.O Box 932
Honolulu 96808

Hula Records, Inc.
Warehouse No. 3
1020 Auahi St.
Honolulu 96826

Music of Polynesia, Inc.
Moana Bldg., Suite 919
Honolulu 96814

Panini Records/Panini Productions
P.O. Box 15808
Honolulu 96815

Singergia, Inc.
46-003 Alaloa St.
Kaneohe 96744

Surfside Hawaii, Inc.
1412 Colburn St.
Honolulu 96817

Tropical Music, Inc.
P.O. Box 1494
Honolulu 96806

IDAHO

American Heritage Music Corporation
1208 Everett St.
Caldwell 83605

Jenero Record Company
P.O. Box 121
Soda Springs 83276

ILLINOIS

Balkan Music Company
6917 West Cermak Rd.
Berwyn 60402

Beacon Artists Corporation
233 East Erie St.
Chicago 60611

Big Rock Recording
1311 North Lake
Aurora 60507

Birch Records
Box 92
Wilmette 60091

Bold Records
5824 West Madison
Chicago 60644

Boogie Man Records, Inc.
P.O. Box 727
Oak Park 60303

Brown Productions
180 West Washington, Suite 1202A
Chicago 60602

CJ Record Company
4827 South Prairie Ave.
Chicago 60615

Cha-Cha Records
15041 Wabash Ave.
South Holland 60473

Chi-Town Records
2123 North Seminary Ave.
Chicago 60614

Clay Pigeon Records
P.O. Box 20346
Chicago 60620

Communication Records
7212 South Wabash Ave.
Chicago 60619

Curtom Records, Inc.
5915 North Lincoln Ave.
Chicago 60659

Daniels Eight Record Company
P.O. Box 266
River Forest 60305

Delmark Records
4243 North Lincoln
Chicago 60618

Dharma Records
117 Rockland Rd.
Libertyville 60048

Entr'act Recording Society
1220 North State, No. 402
Chicago 60610

Fleur-De-Lis Records
2513 North Major
Chicago 60639

Flying Fish Records
3320 North Halsted
Chicago 60657

Franne Records
P.O. Box 8135
Chicago 60680

HNH Records, Inc.
820 David St., Suite 222
Evanston 60201

Happy Day Records
2630 North Mannheim
Franklin Park 60131

International Recording Company
1649 West Evergreen Ave.
Chicago 60622

JermA Records Company
1410 East 72nd St.
Chicago 60619

Jezreel, Inc.
2058 First St.
Highland Park 60035

Kiderian Records Productions
4926 West Gunnison
Chicago 60930

LK Records
1936 North Clark St.
Chicago 60614

Lakco Record Company
3902 North Ashland Ave.
Chicago 60613

Lindberg Records
1445 Sunset Ridge Rd.
Glenview 60025

Masterton Records
4770 North Lincoln Ave.
Chicago 60625

Mod-Art Records
10358 South Forest Ave.
Chicago 60628

Nessa Records
5404 North Kimball Ave.
Chicago 60625

North Street Productions
1757 North Mohawk
Chicago 60614

Ovation Records
1249 Waukegan Rd.
Glenview 60025

PA Enterprises, Inc.
875 North Michigan, Suite 5404
Chicago 60611

Pan American Records, Inc.
3751 West 26th
Chicago 60623

Phonogram, Inc./Mercury Records
1 IBM Plaza
Chicago 60611

Polish Record Center
3055 Milwaukee Ave.
Chicago 60618

Stage Production Records
189 West Madison
Chicago 60602

Ultra-Nova Productions, Ltd.
501 East Providence Rd.
Palatine 60067

VEL Records & Music Group
P.O. Box 1218
Chicago 60690

Vocab, Inc.
3071 South Broad St.
Chicago 60608

Xavier Records, Ltd.
P.O. Box 59
Medinah 60157

INDIANA

Bar-B-Q Records, Inc.
114 South Grant
Bloomington 47401

Basic Records
1309 Celesta Way
Sellersburg 47172

Easy Prize Records
615 Preston Dr.
South Bend 46615

Seven Hills Recording Company
905 North Main St.
Evansville 47711

TRC Records
1330 North Illinois St.
Indianapolis 46202

Village Records, Inc.
6325 Guilford Ave.
Indianapolis 46220

IOWA

Fanfare Records
900 County Line Rd.
West Des Moines 50265

Iowa Great Lakes Recording Company
906 Ninth St.
Milford 51351

Kajac Record Corporation
155 First St.
Carlisle 50047

2–J Records, Inc.
1115 South Lillian
Ottumwa 52501

KANSAS

Antique-Catfish Records
Box 192
Pittsburg 66762

Jay Bird Records
P.O. Box 140
Parsons 67357

Mouth Music Company
P.O. Box 3142
Lawrence 66044

Rabbitt Record Company
P.O. Box 1997
Wichita 67201

Stone Post Record Company
Box 1213
Emporia 66801

Tempo Records
1900 West 47th Pl.
Mission 66205

KENTUCKY

Allen-Martin Productions, Inc.
9701 Taylorsville Rd.
Louisville 40299

June Appal Recordings
Box 743
Whitesburg 41858

McLain Family Band
CPO 1322
Berea 40404

LOUISIANA

Beach Records, Inc.
Box 154, Rte. 2
Gonzales 70737

Big Deal Records Company
711 Greenwood Ave.
Cheneyville 71325

Boquet-Orchid Enterprises
P.O. Box 4220
Shreveport 71104

Centaur Records, Inc.
P.O. Box 23764
Baton Rouge 70893

Cord Records
Box 7422
Shreveport 71107

Flat Town Music Company
434 East Main
Ville Platte 70586

Goldband Recording Studio
313 Church St.
Lake Charles 70601

Great Southern Record Company
P.O. Box 30029
New Orleans 70190

Jewel Recording Corporation
P.O. Box 1125
Shreveport 71163

King Walk
Box 15094
New Orleans 70115

La Louisanne/BooRay Record
   Distributors
707 Stevenson St.
Lafayette 70501

Land O' Jazz Records
P.O. Box 26393
New Orleans 70126

Lanor Records
329 North Main
Church Point 70525

Modern Sound Studio Productions
413 North Parkerson Ave.
Crowley 70526

New Orleans Records
1918 Burgundy St.
New Orleans 70116

Sound City Recording
3316 Line Ave.
Shreveport 71104

Stone Records
316 Riverside Mall
Baton Rouge 70801

Worldstar Records
P.O. Box 2609
Lafayette 70502

MAINE

Audem Records
146 Parkway South
Brewer 04412

Event Records
Rte. 302
Westbrook 04092

MARYLAND

Adelphi Records, Inc.
Box 288
Silver Spring 20907

Audio-Video Concepts, Inc.
6909 Old Alexander Ferry Rd.
Clinton 20735

Country Showcase America
11350 Baltimore Ave.
Beltsville 20705

Dawn Productions
Box 535
Belair 21014

Dimitri Music Company
7859 Bastille Pl.
Severn 21144

Discount Record & Book Shop
9093 Comprint Court
Gaithersburg 20760

Kaymar Records
P.O. Box 624
Ellicott City 21043

Songs by Sommers
P.O. Box 322
Silver Spring 20907

MASSACHUSETTS

AcoustoGraphic Records
1 Simpson's Ln.
Edgartown 02539

Back Door Records
909 Beacon St.
Boston 02215

Cambridge Records, Inc.
125 Irving St.
Framingham 01701

Casa Grande Records/Don-Mar
 Records/Shawmut Records
P.O. Box 113
Woburn 01801

Clear Light Productions, Inc.
P.O. Box 391
Newton 02158

Continental Recordings, Inc.
210 South St.
Boston 02111

Cookin' Records
19 Ledge Hill Rd.
West Roxbury 02132

Elf Records, Ltd.
P.O. Box 404, Astor St. Sta.
Boston 02123

Evening Star Productions
1955 Massachusetts Ave.
Cambridge 02140

Full Sail Productions
1126 Boylston St.
Boston 02215

Marjo Records, Inc.
739 Boylston St., Rm. 407
Boston 02116

Pathways of Sound, Inc.
102 Mt. Auburn St.
Cambridge 02138

Penco Record Company
428 Wood St.
New Bedford 02745

Periscope Record Company
129 Bishop St.
Brockton 02402

Rat Records
528 Commonwealth Ave.
Boston 02215

Rocky Coast Records
125 Main St.
Reading 01867

Romantic Records
P.O. Box 83
Medford 02153

Rounder Records Corporation
186 Willow Ave.
Somerville 02144

Sine Qua Non Productions
1 West St.
Fall River 02720

Standard–Colonial Records
Bldg. 8, 6 Gill St.
Woburn 01801

Rik Tinory Productions
622 Rte. 3A
Cohasset 02025

Varulven Record Company
39 Beverly Rd.
Arlington 02174

MICHIGAN

Big Mack Records
1300 Robin Rd.
Muskegon 49445

Blind Pig Records
208 South First
Ann Arbor 48103

Davida Recording & Publishing
 Company
9700 Burnette
Detroit 48204

Endeavor Records
30064 Annapolis Circle
Inkster 48141

Fish-Head Records
P.O. Box 399
Bay City 48706

Fortune & Hi-Q Records
3942 Third Ave.
Detroit 48201

Funhouse Associates
17651 Annchester
Detroit 48219

Ghost Records
1905 Pesos Pl.
Kalamazoo 49008

Heavy Hank Productions
1644 Glynn Court
Detroit 48206

Holy Spirit Records
27335 Penn St.
Inkster 48141

Jessup Records, Inc.
3150 Francis St.
Jackson 49203

La Val Record Company
226 North Burdick
Kalamazoo 49006

Lucky's Kum-Ba-Ya Records
Box 6
Brohman 49312

MSK Productions, Inc.
8880 Hubbell Ave.
Detroit 48228

Magnetic Video Corporation
23434 Industrial Park Court
Farmington Hills 48024

Neostat Music Company
425 Bryn Mawr
Birmingham 48009

Old Homestead Record Company
Box 100
Brighton 48116

Olenik Records
G–10282 North Saginaw Rd.
Clio 48420

Pyramid Records
20855 Pickford
Detroit 48219

Record & Music People, Inc.
635 Elm St.
Birmingham 48011

Singcord Recordings
1415 Lake Dr. S.E.
Grand Rapids 49506

Sound, Inc.
56880 North Ave.
New Haven 48048

Stag Records, Inc.
P.O. Box 04069
Detroit 48204

Vandalia Records
Box 32 Rte. 2, Quaker St.
Vandalia 49095

We Productions, Inc.
14744 Puritan
Detroit 48227

Westbound Records, Inc.
19631 West Eight Mile Rd.
Detroit 48219

Wheelsville Records
17544 Sorrento
Detroit 48235

MINNESOTA

ASI Records
711 Broadway
Minneapolis 55411

Banjar Records, Inc.
7440 University Ave., N.E.
Minneapolis 55432

Black Gold Records
226 South Cedar Lake Rd.
Minneapolis 55405

Cognito Productions
7515 Wayzata Blvd., No. 110
Minneapolis 55426

Cookhouse Recording Studio
2541 Nicollet Ave. South
Minneapolis 55404

The Good Sound Factory
1415 North Lilac Dr.
Minneapolis 55422

K-tel International, Inc.
11311 K-Tel Dr.
Minnetonka 55343

Sherwin Linton Entertainment
226 Cedar Lake Rd. South
Minneapolis 55405

Metrobeat Productions, Inc.
P.O. Box 755
Minneapolis 55440

Mill City Records
P.O. Box 3759
Minneapolis 55403

Sanskrit Records
7515 Wayzata Blvd., No. 110
Minneapolis 55426

Shadow Records
3346 Hennepin
Minneapolis 55408

Shi Shi Wu Ai Records, Inc.
8120 Oakland Ave. South
Bloomington 55420

Slade Record Company
Box 536
Crookston 56716

Sweet Jane, Ltd.
Snake Trail
Cushing 56443

Symposium Records
204 Fifth Ave. S.E.
Minneapolis 55414

MISSISSIPPI

Axent Ltd.
700 West Jackson St.
Biloxi 39533

Malaco, Inc.
3023 West Northside Dr.
Jackson 39213

Mitchell Recording Company
Box 67, Rte. 7, Ridge Rd.
Columbus 39701

National Foundation of Music
Box 414, Rte. 3, Hwy. 82 West
Columbus 39701

Sundown Records
Box 258, Rte. 1
Carriere 39426

Talk of the Town Recording
408 West Pascagoula
Jackson 39203

MISSOURI

American Audioport
1407 North Providence Rd.
Columbia 65201

Country Stream Music & Record
  Company
P.O. Box 2644
St. Louis 63116

Dirty Shame Records
4552 Shenandoah
St. Louis 63110

ELJ Record Company
1344 Waldron Ave.
St. Louis 63130

Gospel Chimes Records
5612 West Florissant Ave.
St. Louis 63120

Ken Keene International
2028 South 39th St.
St. Louis 63110

NMI Productions Corporation
516 West 75th St.
Kansas City 64114

Nada Music
P.O. Box 248
Lutesville 63762

Release Records
P.O. Box 234
St. Louis 63166

St. Lou-E Blu Records
4412 Natural Bridge
St. Louis 63115

NEBRASKA

Flin-Flon Music
Box 103
Mullen 69152

MJ Recording, Inc.
Dodge 68633

NEVADA

Lotus Music Corporation
P.O. Box 5606
Las Vegas 89102

Luba Records
P.O. Box 42696
Las Vegas 89104

NEW HAMPSHIRE

Marvel Records Company
852 Elm St.
Manchester 03101

NEW JERSEY

All Platinum Record Company, Inc.
96 West St.
Englewood 07631

American Tape Corporation
1116 Edgewater Ave.
Ridgefield 07657

Andira Record Corporation
41 Central Ave.
Newark 07102

Argus Record Productions
P.O. Box 58
Glendora 08029

Century Productions, Inc.
171 Washington Rd.
Sayreville 08872

Country Pie Records
132 Spring St.
Newton 07860

Country/Politan Records
735 Lincoln Blvd.
Middlesex 08846

Deliverance Records
621 Clinton Ave.
Newark 07108

Delwood Music Company, Inc.
160 South Leswing Ave.
Saddle Brook 07662

Disco Record Company, Inc.
467 Mundet Pl.
Hillside 07205

Eric Records
1120 Crown Point Rd.
Westville 08093

Farr Records
Box 1098
Somerville 08876

Folkraft Publishing Company, Inc.
10 Fenwick St.
Newark 07114

Glori Records, Inc.
110 Academy St.
Jersey City 07302

H & L Records Corporation
532 Sylvan Ave.
Englewood Cliffs 07632

HMR Productions, Inc.
574 West Court
Scotch Plains 07076

Jim Hall Productions
5 Aldom Circle
West Caldwell 06007

Historical Records, Inc.
P.O. Box 4204
Jersey City 07304

Jersey Coast Agents, Ltd.
72 Thorne Pl.
West Keansburg 07734

Joka Records, Inc.
403 Summit St.
Vineland 08360

Latin Percussion Ventures, Inc.
454 Commercial Ave.
Palisades Park 07650

LeMans Record Company
331 Triangle Rd.
Somerville 08876

Lucifer Records, Inc.
P.O. Box 263
Hasbrouck Heights 07604

MSI Recording Studio, Inc.
6015 Pleasant Ave.
Pennsauken 08110

Maranta Music Enterprises
P.O. Box 9
Wyckoff 07481

Mickey Records
26 Mountain Ave.
Dover 07801

Nirvana Records
1145 Green St.
Manville 08835

PM Records, Inc.
20 Martha St.
Woodcliff Lake 07675

Passport Records, Inc.
3619 Kennedy Rd.
South Plainfield 07080

Peter Pan Industries
145 Komorn St.
Newark 07105

Phoenix Jazz Records, Inc.
P.O. Box 3
Kingston 08528

Rob-Lee Music
P.O. Box 1385
Merchantville 08109

Savoy Records, Inc.
625 Pennsylvania Ave.
Elizabeth 07201

Sir Lion Records Company
455 West Hanover St.
Trenton 08618

Springboard International
   Records, Inc.
947 U.S. Hwy. 1
Rahway 07065

Springwater Productions, Ltd.
P.O. Box 203
Princeton 08540

The Stacy-Lee Label
425 Park St.
Hackensack 07601

Trutone Records
163 Terrace St.
Haworth 07641

Virginia Recording Company
209 Main St.
Fort Lee 07024

Volare Records, Inc.
P.O. Box 325
Englewood 07631

NEW MEXICO

Tom Bee Productions
P.O. Box 8207
Albuquerque 87108

Goldust Records Company
115 East Idaho Ave.
Las Cruces 88001

Hurricane Enterprises
1927 San Mateo N.E.
Albuquerque 87110

Indian House
Box 472
Taos 87571

Little Richie Johnson Agency
Box 3
Belen 87002

Space Records
2037 Alvarado Dr. N.E.
Albuquerque 87110

NEW YORK

AA Records
250 West 57th St.
New York 10019

Abkco Records, Inc.
1700 Broadway
New York 10019

J. Albert & Son Pty, Ltd.
4 East 52nd St.
New York 10022

Amerama, Inc.
250 West 57th St.
New York 10019

American Album & Tape, Inc.
850 Seventh Ave.
New York 10019

American Themes & Tapes, Inc.
240 West 55th St.
New York 10019

Amherst Records
355 Harlem Rd.
Buffalo 14224

Ansonia Records, Inc.
802 Columbus Ave.
New York 10025

Chuck Antony Music, Inc.
425 Broad Hollow, Suite 411
Melville 11746

Apon Records Co., Inc.
P.O. Box 3082, Steinway Sta.
44-16 Broadway
Long Island City 11103

Arista Records, Inc.
6 West 57th St.
New York 10019

   Branch:
9220 Sunset Blvd.
Los Angeles, CA 90069

Arlo Records Company
7653 Telephone Rd.
LeRoy 14482

Artemis Records, Ltd.
157-52 96th St.
Howard Beach 11414

Atlantic Recording Corporation
75 Rockefeller Plaza
New York 10019

Audiofidelity Enterprises, Inc.
221 West 57th St.
New York 10019

Audiorama Records Corporation
658 10th Ave.
New York 10036

Avant Garde Records
250 West 57th St.
New York 10019

Avoca Musical Industries
P.O. Box 494
Wheatley Heights 11798

Bareback Records, Inc.
1650 Broadway
New York 10019

Barrier Records
P.O. Box 1109
White Plains 10017

Nelson Barry Recordings, Inc.
319 East 44th St.
New York 10017

Beam Junction Records
360 East 72nd St.
New York 10021

Bearsville Records, Inc.
75 East 55th St.
New York 10022

Bente Records
382 Central Park West, Suite 2D
New York 10025

Berlitz Publications, Inc.
866 Third Ave.
New York 10022

Big Boro Records Corporation
1700 Broadway
New York 10019

Big Sound Records
175 Thompson St.
New York 10012

Big Tree Enterprises, Ltd.
75 Rockefeller Plaza
New York 10019

Biograph Records, Inc.
16 River St.
Chatham 12037

Eubie Blake Music Recording
284-A Stuyvesant Ave.
Brooklyn 11221

Blue Labor Records
Box 1262
New York 10009

Blue Sky Records, Inc.
745 Fifth Ave., Suite 1802
New York 10022

Bornand Music Box Company
139 Fourth Ave.
Pelham 10803

Bourne Company
1212 Ave. of the Americas
New York 10036

Brasilia Records & Tape Corporation
29 West 56th St.
New York 10036

Brookville Marketing Corporation
420 Lexington Ave.
New York 10017

Brownstone Records
c/o ATI
888 Seventh Ave.
New York 10019

Brunswick Recording Corporation
888 Seventh Ave.
New York 10019

Bryan Records
1 East 42nd St.
New York 10017

Buddah Records, Inc.
810 Seventh Ave.
New York 10019

CBS Records
51 West 52nd St.
New York 10019

Branch:
1801 West Century Park West
Los Angeles, CA 90067

Branch:
49 Music Square West
Nashville, TN 37203

CMS Records, Inc.
12 Warren St.
New York 10017

Caedmon
505 Eighth Ave.
New York 10018

Capitol Star Artist, Inc.
1458 Buffalo Rd.
Rochester 14624

Carillon Records, Inc.
521 Fifth Ave.
New York 10017

Cartoon Records
c/o Enchanted Door
301 North Ave.
New Rochelle 10801

Centaur Records
82 Aldin St.
Rochester 14619

Choice Records, Inc.
245 Tilley Pl.
Sea Cliff 11579

Coco Records, Inc.
1700 Broadway
New York 10019

Collegium Sound Systems
35–41 72nd St.
Jackson Heights 11372

Colony Records
470 Smith St.
Farmingdale 11735

Columbia Special Productions
51 West 52nd St.
New York 10019

Commodore Record Company, Inc.
3 Kensington Oval
New Rochelle 10805

Composers Recordings, Inc.
170 West 74th St.
New York 10023

Connoisseur Society, Inc.
390 West End Ave.
New York 10024

Conversa-phone Institute, Inc.
225 West 34th St.
New York 10001

Copperfield's Enterprises, Ltd.
2339 Jericho Turnpike
Garden City Park 11040

R.D. Cortina Company
136 West 52nd St.
New York 10019

Country International Records
315 West 57th St.
New York 10019

Countrywide Tape & Record
Distributors
200 Robbins Ln.
Jericho 11753

Creative Funk Music, Inc.
122-21 Merrick Blvd.
St. Albans 11434

Crescendo Record Company
37-25 Crescent St.
Long Island City 11101

Crosseyed Bear Records
286 Brompton Rd.
Buffalo 14221

DJM Records
119 West 57th St., Suite 400
New York 10019

D & M Sound Corporation
185 West End Ave.
New York 10023

Davis Records
518 West 50th St.
New York 10019

De-Lite Records
200 West 57th St.
New York 10019

Dellwood Records
200 West 57th St.
New York 10019

Desert Moon Records
1697 Broadway
New York 10019

Desmar Music, Inc.
155 Ave. of the Americas
New York 10013

Discolando Records & Tapes
Corporation
718-20 10th Ave.
New York 10019

Domino Records
37 Odell Ave.
Yonkers 10701

Dragon Records
2805 Creston Ave.
Bronx 10468

Dyer-Bennet Records
792 Columbus Ave.
New York 10025

ESP-Disck, Ltd.
5 Riverside Dr., Suite 2-C
New York 10023

Earth Sound Music/TAJ Enterprises
469 Rockaway Parkway
Brooklyn 11212

El-Ay Records, Inc.
312 Lagoon Dr. West
Lido Beach 11561

Ember Enterprises, Inc.
747 Third Ave., 27th Floor
New York 10017

Erva Records
200 West 57th St., Suite 1404
New York 10019

FFO Communications, Inc.
Box 313, Kingsbridge Sta.
Bronx 10463

Famous Door Records
40-08 155th St.
Flushing 11354

Fania Records, Inc.
888 Seventh Ave.
New York 10019

Fiesta Record Company, Inc.
1619 Broadway
New York 10019

Fiorucci, Inc.
125 East 59th St.
New York 10022

Fist-O-Funk, Ltd.
293 Richard Court
Pomona 10970

Folkways Records
43 West 61st St.
New York 10023

Friends & Company
108 Sherman Ave.
New York 10034

Gale Electronics of America
348 East 84th St.
New York 10028

Garfort Inc. Corporation
1650 Broadway
New York 10019

Gillette-Madison Company
17 East 48th St.
New York 10017

Glad Hamp Records, Inc.
1955 Broadway
New York 10023

Glenn Productions & Promos
157 West 57th St.
New York 10010

Golden Crest Records, Inc.
220 Broadway
Huntington Station 11746

Gomelsky Eggers Music Company
595 Madison Ave.
New York 10022

Gospel Records, Inc.
P.O. Box 90, Rugby Sta.
Brooklyn 11213

Great Gramaphone Records
240 West 55th St.
New York 10019

Groove Merchant International, Inc.
515 Madison Ave.
New York 10022

Haven Records
233 West 42nd St.
New York 10036

Henry Street Records, Inc.
124 Montague St.
Brooklyn Heights 11201

Herwin Records, Inc.
P.O. Box 306
Glen Cove 11542

Hot Damn Records Corporation
130 West 42nd St.
New York 10036

Improvising Artists, Inc.
26 Jane St.
New York 10014

India Navigation Company
35 River Rd.
Grandview 10960

Institute for Language Study
136 West 52nd St.
New York 10019

International Book & Record
   Distributors
31–83 34th St.
Astoria 11102

International Music Consultants
888 Seventh Ave.
New York 10019

Jazz Composers' Orchestra Association
6 West 95th St.
New York 10025

Jody Records
2226 McDonald Ave.
Brooklyn 11223

Johnson Record Company
1619 Broadway
New York 10019

Just Sunshine, Inc.
36 East 61st St.
New York 10021

Kid Cus'n Record Company
P.O. Box 182, Midwood Sta.
Brooklyn 11230

Kirshner Entertainment Corporation
1370 Ave. of the Americas
New York 10019

Koko Enterprises, Inc.
888 Seventh Ave.
New York 10019

Kool Kat Productions
39 South Main St.
Spring Valley 10977

LIRS Classics
72 Orange St.
Brooklyn 11201

Laurie Records, Inc.
20–F Robert Pitt Dr.
Monsey 10977

Legrand-Norfolk International
177 Rte. 304
New City 10956

Lifesong Records, Inc.
488 Madison Ave.
New York 10022

Branch:
9229 Sunset Blvd.
Los Angeles, CA 90069

Lifetime Recordings
133 North St.
Rochester 14604

Little Guy Records
1513 Eighth St.
Niagara Falls 14305

London Records, Inc.
539 West 25th St.
New York 10001

Lovinn Label Records
35 West 92nd St.
New York 10025

Loypriquan Ltd.
39 West 55th St.
New York 10019

Lyrichord Discs, Inc.
141 Perry St.
New York 10014

Magna-Glide Record Corporation
323 East Shore Rd.
Great Neck 11023

Mainstream Records, Inc.
1700 Broadway
New York 10019

Manhattan Records
65 West 55th St.
New York 10019

Maria Records
P.O. Box 3770, Grand Central Station
New York 10017

Marlo Record Company
Box 39, RD 1
Utica 13502

Mayjams Collegiate Records
P.O. Box 46, Morningside Sta.
New York 10026

Met Richmond Latin Record Sales
1637 Utica Ave.
Brooklyn 11234

Michele Audio Corporation
Andrew Street Rd.
Massena 13662

Midsong International Records, Inc.
1650 Broadway
New York 10019

Millenium Records
3 West 57th St.
New York 10019

Mirror Records, Inc.
645 Titus Ave.
Rochester 14617

Monitor Recordings, Inc.
156 Fifth Ave.
New York 10010

Monmouth Evergreen Records
1697 Broadway, Suite 1201
New York 10019

Montuno Records, Inc.
1470 Broadway, Times Square
New York 10036

Muse Records
160 West 71st St.
New York 10023

Music Inn
169 West Fourth St.
New York 10014

Music Minus One Music Group
43 West 61st St.
New York 10023

Musicanza Corporation
2878 Bayview Ave.
Wantagh 11793

Music Resources International
    Corporation
161 West 54th St., Suite 601
New York 10019

Musicor Records, Inc.
870 Seventh Ave., Suite 348
New York 10019

Mustevic Sound Records
193-18 120 Ave.
Jamaica 11412

Newbery Award Records/Miller-Brody
    Productions
342 Madison Ave.
New York 10017

Noodle Records Corporation
39 West 55th St.
New York 10019

Nova Recordings
150 Fifth Ave., Suite 717
New York 10011

OHB Records Company
224 Haddon Rd., Suite 100
Woodmere 11598

Old Town Record Corporation
41-43 39th St.
Long Island City 11104

Otoao Records Company
    International, Ltd.
214 West 96th St.
New York 10025

Overseas Wax
1650 Broadway
New York 10019

PTO Record Company
111 East Ave., Suite 228
Rochester 14604

Painted Smiles Records
116 Nassau St.
New York 10038

Paredon Records
P.O. Box 889
Brooklyn 11202

Pecan Pie Music, Inc.
300 East 74th St., Apt. 32C
New York 10021

Peer-Southern Organization
1740 Broadway
New York 10019
    Branch:
6922 Hollywood Blvd.
Los Angeles, CA 90028
    Branch:
150 S.E. Second St., Rm. 1409
Miami, FL 33131
    Branch:
7 Music Circle North
Nashville, TN 37203

Peters International, Inc.
619 West 54th St.
New York 10019

Pickwick Records
135 Crossways Park Dr.
Woodbury 11797

Playette Corporation
301 East Shore Rd.
Great Neck 11023

Polka Towne Music
211 Post Ave.
Westbury 11590

Polydor, Inc.
810 Seventh Ave.
New York 10019

Polygram Corporation
450 Park Ave.
New York 10022

Prelude Records
200 West 57th St.
New York 10019

Private Stock Records
40 West 57th St.
New York 10023

QMO Sales, Inc.
331 Willis Ave.
Mineola 11501

RCA Records
1133 Ave. of the Americas
New York 10036

RCI Records
P.O. Box 126
Elmsford 10523

R & R Records, Inc./Ren Rome
663 Fifth Ave.
New York 10022

Radio Music Productions
600 Ridgewood Ave.
Brooklyn 11203

Radiola Company, Inc.
P.O. Box H
Croton-on-Hudson 10520

Rae-Cox Records, Inc.
1674 Broadway
New York 10019

Rainbow Room
30 Rockefeller Plaza
New York 10020

Ram Records
213 Park Ave. South
New York 10003

Rashid Sales Company
191 Atlantic Ave.
Brooklyn 11201

Record Guild of America
144 Milbar Blvd.
Farmingdale 11735

Recorded Anthology of American
   Music (New World Records)
3 East 54th St.
New York 10022

Red Diamond Record Company
42 Chapman Ave.
Auburn 13021

Red Greg Enterprises
1650 Broadway, Suite 714
New York 10019

Red Rooster Records
Box 300
Mount Marion 12456

Regal Records
Heaton Rd. and Oak Dr.
Monroe 10950

Rego Irish Records & Tapes
84–48 63nd Dr.
Middle Village 11379

Revonah Records
Box 217
Ferndale 12734

Rico Records Productions Corporation
748 10th Ave.
New York 10019

Right On! Records USA
408 West 115th St., Suite 2-W
New York 10025

Roadshow Records Corporation
850 Seventh Ave.
New York 10019

Rockmasters, Inc.
177 Rte. 304
New City 10956

Roper Records, Inc.
45–15 21st St.
Long Island City 11101

Roulette Records, Inc.
17 West 60th St.
New York 10023

Rubber Records, Ltd.
130 West 57th St., Suite 6–D
New York 10019

Salsoul Records
240 Madison Ave.
New York 10016

Sam Records, Inc.
41–45 39th St.
Long Island City 11104

Sandcastle Records
157 West 57th St.
New York 10019

San-Lyn Records
414 Cortland Ave.
Syracuse 13205

Sceneville Industries
78–08 88th Ave.
Woodhaven 11421

A. Schroeder International, Ltd.
25 West 56th St.
New York 10019

Serenus Corporation
P.O. Box 267
Hastings-on-Hudson 10706

Sesame Street Records
1 Lincoln Plaza
New York 10023

Silver Blue Records
401 East 74th St.
New York 10021

Silver City Records
P.O. Box 8633
Rochester 14619

Sirco Records, Inc.
22 Pine St.
Freeport 11520

Sire Records, Inc.
165 West 74th St.
New York 10023

Solid Sound Records
30 Lark Dr.
Woodbury 11797

Spanish Music Center, Inc.
319 West 48th St.
New York 10036

Spiral Records, Inc.
17 West 60th St., Rm. 715
New York 10023

Spivey Records
65 Grand Ave.
Brooklyn 11205

Spoken Arts, Inc.
310 North Ave.
New Rochelle 10801

Spring Records, Inc.
161 West 54th St.
New York 10019

Standy Records, Inc.
760 Blanding St.
Utica 13501

Steady Records
846 Seventh Ave.
New York 10019

Strata-East Records, Inc.
156 Fifth Ave.
New York 10010

Surf Enterprises, Inc.
84A Rte. 66
East Nassau 12062

Swallow Tail Records
Box 843
Ithaca 14850

Syntonic Research, Inc.
175 Fifth Ave.
New York 10010

TR Records, Inc.
747 10th Ave.
New York 10018

TSG Records
502 Park Ave.
New York 10022

TWC Entertainment Corporation
GPO Box 2021
New York 10001

Tappan Zee Records
888 Seventh Ave.
New York 10019

Creed Taylor, Inc.
1 Rockefeller Plaza
New York 10020

Tobill Entertainment Corporation
107 Delaware Ave.
Buffalo 14202

Tomato Music Company, Ltd.
505 Park Ave.
New York 10022

Total Sound, Inc.
1133 Ave. of the Americas
New York 10036

Toy Records
P.O. Box 219, Radio City Sta.
New York 10019

Trix Records, Inc.
Drawer AB
Rosendale 12472

UK Records, Inc.
315 West 57th St., Suite 3H
New York 10019

United Polka Artists, Inc.
Box 1
Florida 10921

Thomas J. Valentino, Inc.
151 West 56th St.
New York 10036

Vanguard Recording Society
71 West 23rd St.
New York 10010

Veevo Record Company
54 West 74th St., Suite 402
New York 10023

Versatile Records, Ltd.
39 West 55th St., Penthouse North
New York 10019

Virgin Records, Inc.
43 Perry St.
New York 10019

Vox Productions, Inc.
211 East 43rd St.
New York 10017

WATT Works, Inc.
6 West 95th St.
New York 10025

WEA International, Inc.
75 Rockefeller Plaza
New York 10019

West End Music Industries, Inc.
254 West 54th St.
New York 10019

White-Card Record Company
101 North Hamilton Ave.
Lindenhurst 11757

Win Records, Inc.
41–43 39th St.
Long Island City 11104

Windfall Records
1790 Broadway
New York 10019

Woodbury Records
Box 402
Woodbury 11797

Worldtone Music, Inc.
230 Seventh Ave.
New York 10011

Worldwide Music Services
1966 Broadway
New York 10023

Xanadu Records, Ltd.
3242 Irwin Ave.
Kingsbridge 10463

Yazoo Records, Inc.
245 Waverly Pl.
New York 10014

Yellow Bee Productions, Inc.
245 Waverly Pl.
New York 10014

Zim Records
P.O. Box 158
Jericho 11753

NORTH CAROLINA

Carolina Records
1605 Park Dr.
Raleigh 27605

Charma Records, Inc.
103 Mimosa Dr.
Chapel Hill 27514

Galaxie III Studios
118 Fifth St.
Taylorsville 28681

Mazingo's
P.O. Box 11181
Charlotte 28209

New Dimension Recordings
218 West Broad St.
Statesville 28677

Parchment Records
P.O. Box 22106
Greensboro 27420

Playhouse Records
126 South Main St.
Monroe 28110

Reflection Sound Production, Inc
1018 Central Ave.
Charlotte 28204

Stark Records & Tape Company
628 South St.
Mount Airy 27030

Teena Joy Records
P.O. Box 302
Wilmington 28401

NORTH DAKOTA

Drum Records, Inc.
Box 347
Fargo 58102

Marycords
Box 48
Powers Lake 58773

OHIO

Aesthetic Artist Records
P.O. Box 144
Mid-City Station
Dayton 45402

Atmosphere Productions
420 Prospect Ave., Suite 300-A
Cleveland 44115

Audio Technica US, Inc.
33 Shiawassee Ave.
Fairlawn 44313

Belkin Productions, Inc.
28001 Chagrin Blvd.
Cleveland 44122

Boddie Record Manufacturing &
   Recording, Inc.
12202 Union Ave.
Cleveland 44105

Centaurian Records, Inc.
3291 East 119th St.
Cleveland 44120

Cleveland International Records
P.O. Box 783
Willoughby 44094

Courthouse Records
1391 New London Rd.
Hamilton 45013

Dani Records
P.O. Box 315
Cleveland 44127

Delta International Records
1584 East 31st
Cleveland 44114

Destiny Records
P.O. Box 2094
Sheffield Lake 44054

Diablo Record Company
3518 Champlain Ave.
Youngstown 44502

Fairweather Corporation
P.O. Box 435
Cambridge 43725

Fraternity Recording Corporation
3744 Applegate Ave.
Cincinnati 45211

Galactic Enterprises
1285 Parkamo Ave.
Hamilton 45011

Hillside Records
948 Studer Ave.
Columbus 43206

Incentive Productions
639 Bulen Ave.
Columbus 43205

Jalyn Recording Company
1806 Brown St.
Dayton 45409

Kare Records, Inc.
1391 Oakland Park Ave.
Columbus 43224

King Bluegrass Records
4766 Glendale-Milford Rd.
Cincinnati 45242

Melody Recording Studio
1912 St. Clair St.
Hamilton 45011

Neon Recording Company
6701 Hope Ave.
Cleveland 44102

Ohio Records
P.O. Box 655
Hudson 44236

Owl Recording Studios, Inc.
2551 Sunbury Rd.
Columbus 43219

Pamlyn Records
P.O. Box 6211
Cleveland 44101

QCA Records, Inc.
2832 Spring Grove Ave.
Cincinnati 45225

Red Onion Records
P.O. Box 366
Dayton 45401

Rite Record Productions
9745 Lockland Rd.
Cincinnati 45215

M.R. Sand & Company
6211 Milan Rd.
Sandusky 44870

Tammy Jo Records, Inc.
1044 Lilly Ave. N.E.
Canton 44646

Telarc Records
4150 Mayfield Rd.
Cleveland 44121

Vetco Records
5825 Vine St.
Cincinnati 45216

OKLAHOMA

Alvera Record Company
P.O. Box 9304
Tulsa 74060

Blackland Records
P.O. Box 7349
Tulsa 74105

Boyd Records
2609 N.W. 36th St.
Oklahoma City 73112

Compo Record Company
105 Burk Dr.
Oklahoma City 73115

OREGON

Kastle Productions
4647 S.W. Pendleton
Portland 97221

Sunny Day Productions
1931 S.E. Morrison
Portland 97214

PENNSYLVANIA

Aljean Records
RD 4
Myerstown 17067

Annuit Coeptis Music Records & Tapes
Ltd.
2933 River Rd.
Croydon 19020

Arcade Music Company
3010 North Front St.
Philadelphia 19133

Arzee Music Company
3010 North Front St.
Philadelphia 19133

Associated Recording Companies
2250 Bryn Mawr Ave.
Philadelphia 19131

Branch:
9229 Sunset Blvd.
Los Angeles, CA 90069

Blue Diamond Company
Box 102C, Chubbic Rd.
Canonsburg 15317

Cargo Record Company
8227 Williams Ave.
Philadelphia 19150

Colosseum Records, Ltd.
134 South 20th St.
Philadelphia 19103

Country Star, Inc.
439 Wiley Ave.
Franklin 16323

Crimson Dynasty Record Corporation
P.O. Box 271
Jenkintown 19046

Dante Records
71 Smithbridge Rd.
Glen Mills 19342

Dee Productions of Philadelphia
1445 North Hills Ave.
Willow Grove 19090

Dee-Bee Recording Service
South Camp St. Ext.
Windsor 17366

East Coast Records, Inc.
P.O. Box 5363
Philadelphia 19142

Educator Records
P.O. Box 490
Wayne 19087

Fee Bee Record Company
4517 Wainwright Ave.
Pittsburgh 15227

Future Gold Records, Inc.
1834 West Chelstenham Ave.
Philadelphia 19126

Golden Crest Records, Inc.
P.O. Box 9, Walker Rd.
New Oxford 17350

Gotham Record Corporation
925 North Third St.
Philadelphia 19123

Jamie/Guyden Distributing Corporation
919 North Broad St.
Philadelphia 91923

Jeree Records
1469 Third St.
New Brighton 15066

Danny Luciano Productions
6133 Elmwood Ave.
Philadelphia 19142

McKinnon Records
P.O. Box 691
Reading 19601

Marjon Records, Inc.
159 Easton Rd.
Sharon 16146

Maycon Records
5306 West Columbia Ave.
Philadelphia 19131

New Wave Records
10 North Third St.
Philadelphia 19106

North American Music Industries, Inc.
300 Brook St.
Scranton 18501

Omnisound, Inc.
Delaware Water Gap 18327

Page Recording Company
604 Broad St.
Johnstown 15906

Parr-X Corp.
8809–11 Rising Sun Ave.
Philadelphia 19115

Philadelphia International Records
309 South Broad St.
Philadelphia 19107

Record Rendezvous, Inc.
134 South 20th St.
Philadelphia 19103

Ripsaw Record Company
121 North Fourth St.
Easton 18042

Branch:
320 West 30th St.
New York, NY 10001

St. Clair Productions
485 Fort Couch Rd.
Pittsburgh 15241

Skyrocket Records
2065 Kennedy St.
Philadelphia 19124

Stentorian Productions
P.O. Box 1945
Philadelphia 19105

The Sunshine Group, Ltd.
800 South Fourth St.
Philadelphia 19147

Sure Music & Record Company, Inc.
P.O. Box 94
Broomall 19008

Vantage Recording Company
P.O. Box 212
Pottstown 19464

Vokes Record Company
P.O. Box 12
New Kensington 15068

Wave Records
5635 Verona Rd.
Verona 15147

Wham Bam Records
525 North Broad St.
Allentown 18104

White Rock Records, Inc.
401 Wintermantle Ave.
Scranton 18505

Wine Records
3307 Laurel Dr.
Glenshaw 15116

SOUTH CAROLINA

Freedom Records, Ltd.
P.O. Box 888
Easley 29640

The Herald Association, Inc.
Wellman Heights
Johnsonville 29555

Mark Five Recording
10 Michael Dr.
Greenville 29610

Mother Cleo Productions
P.O. Box 521
Newberry 29108

Sivatt Music Company, Inc.
P.O. Box 1079, Hwy. 153
Easley 29640

Wagon Wheel Records
Box 266, Rte. 1
Georgetown 29440

Wesjac Record Enterprises
P.O. Box 743
Lake City 29560

TENNESSEE

Aaron Records
P.O. Box 4796
Nashville 37216

Air Trans Records, Inc.
P.O. Box 28835
Memphis 38128

American Cowboy Songs, Inc.
The Homeplace
Mount Juliet 37122

Ashley Record Company
249 Bluegrass Dr.
Hendersonville 37075

The Benson Company
365 Great Circle Road
Nashville 37228

Boot Records, Inc.
P.O. Box 12647
Nashville 37212

Brite Star
728 16th South
Nashville 37203

Brougham Records
107 Music City Circle
Nashville 37214

Caprice Records, Inc.
907 Main St.
Nashville 37206

Casino Records, Inc.
3100 Walnut Grove, Suite 515
Memphis 38111

Buzz Cason Productions
2804 Azalea Pl.
Nashville 37204

Catron Records
726 East McLeeore
Memphis 38106

Chuck Chellman Company
1201 16th Ave.
Nashville 37212

Commercial Distributing Corporation
(CDC)
2535 Franklin Rd.
Nashville 37204

Con Brio Records
49 Music Square West, Suite 407
Nashville 37202

Concorde Records
P.O. Box 196
Nashville 37202

Delta Record Company, Inc.
11 Music Circle South
Nashville 37115

Dial Records, Inc.
P.O. Box 1273
Nashville 37203

Direct Disc
16 Music Circle South
Nashville 37203

Johnny Dollar Records
P.O. Box 4690
Nashville 37216

Eagle International Records
1108 16th Ave. South
Nashville 47313

Elbejay Enterprises, Inc.
P.O. Box 40544
Nashville 37204

50 States/Charta Records
44 Music Square East, Suite 107
Nashville 27102

4 Star Records, Inc.
49 Music Square West
Nashville 37212

Fretone Records, Inc.
3114 Radford
Memphis 38114

GRT Records
1226 16th Avenue South
Nashville 37212

Glolite Enterprises
625 Chelsea
Memphis 38107

Goldmont Music, Inc.
24 Music Square East
Nashville 37203

Gospel Crusade
Box 2194
Memphis 38101

Gusto Records, Inc.
220 Boscobel St.
Nashville 37213

HSE Records, Inc.
1707 Church St.
Nashville 37203

James Hendrix Enterprises
P.O. Box 90639
Nashville 37209

Hickory Records, Inc.
2510 Franklin Rd.
Nashville 37204

IRDA
55 Music Square West
Nashville 37203

International Marketing &
  Management Corporation
P.O. Box 1776
Nashville 37203

Gene Kennedy Enterprises
2125 Eighth Ave. South
Nashville 37204

King of Music
38 Music Square East
Nashville 37203

LS Records
120 Hickory St.
Madison 37115

Louisiana Hayride Records, Inc.
1708 Grand Ave.
Nashville 37212

Messenger Records
P.O. Box 931
Memphis 38101

Monument Record Corporation
21 Music Square East
Nashville 37203

Music City Workshop, Inc.
38 Music Square, East, Suite 115
Nashville 37203

NRS Records & Tapes, Inc.
P.O. Box 22653
Nashville 37202

Nashboro Record Company
1011 Woodland St.
Nashville 37206

Nashville International Corporation
20 Music Square West
Nashville 37203

National Rock Distribution
50 Music Square West, Suite 804
Nashville 37203

Nationwide Sound Distributors, Inc.
P.O. Box 2362
Nashville 37202

Nu-Sound Records
2012 Beech Ave.
Nashville 37204

Paragon Associates, Inc.
803 18th Ave. South
Nashville 37202

Park Avenue Gospel Productions
3109 Park Ave.
Memphis 38111

Ram Records
397 Saundersville Rd.
Old Hickory 37138

Recorded Memories, Inc.
1107 Whiting St.
Memphis 38117

Record Productions of America
50 Music Square West, Suite 401
Nashville 37203

Republic Records, Inc.
815 18th Ave. South
Nashville 37203

Rice Records, Inc.
29 Music Square East
Nashville 37203

Room Service Productions
Box 12457
Nashville 37212

Savage Records
P.O. Box 22993
Nashville 37202

Scorpio Enterprises
38 Music Square East
Nashville 37203

Shannon Records, Inc.
P.O. Drawer 1
Madison 37115

Shelby Singleton Corporation
3106 Belmont Blvd.
Nashville 37212

Skylite-Sing, Inc.
1008 17th Ave. South
Nashville 37212

Soul Country & Blues, Inc.
P.O. Box 110546
Nashville 37211

Soundwaves Records
1204 Elmwood
Nashville 37212

Sovereign Records
55 Music Square West
Nashville 37203

Spindrift Records
P.O. Box A
Trezevant 38258

Star Track Records
Box 89, RR 1, Riverside Dr.
Mount Juliet 37122

Starcrest Records Ltd.
50 Music Square West, Suite 901
Nashville 37203

Superior Sound Studio
Rockland Rd.
Hendersonville 37075

Supreme Record Company
110 21st Ave. South
Nashville 37203

Tee Vee Records, Inc.
2002 Richard Jones Rd.
Nashville 37215

Terock Records
P.O. Box 4740
Nashville 37216

Triune Music, Inc.
824 19th Ave. South
Nashville 37203

Up-Trend Music & Publishing
   Corporation
4225 Harding Rd., Suite 112
Nashville 37205

World International Group, Inc.
22 Music Square West
Nashville 37203

World Wide Music, Inc.
1300 Division St.
Nashville 37203

Worldwide Sound Distributors, Inc.
147 Jefferson Ave., Suite 1010
Memphis 38103

Zodiac Records, Inc.
21 Music Circle East
Nashville 37203

TEXAS

Action Records
P.O. Box 9470
Fort Worth 76107

Almanac Record Company
P.O. Box 13661
Houston 77019

Autumn International Records
3810 Cavalier St.
Garland 75042

BCL Enterprises, Inc.
1002 Hoefgen St.
San Antonio 78210

BLT Records
3507 West Vickery
Fort Worth 76107

Beau-Jim Agency, Inc.
301 Plantation Dr.
Lake Jackson 77566

Bellaire Record Sales
4900 Bissonnet
Bellaire 77401

Bollman International Records
P.O. Box 28553
Dallas 75228

Chisholm Record Company
508 East Loop 340
Waco 76705

Christi Records
P.O. Box 1152
Fort Worth 76110

Cochise Record Company
P.O. Box 1415
Athens 75751

Contract Record Corporation
2404 East Houston St.
San Antonio 78202

DC Sound Enterprises
5677-D Westcreek Dr.
Fort Worth 76133

Del-Mar Records, Inc.
Box 237
Lancaster 75146

Falcon Record Company
821 North 23rd
McAllen 78501

Freddie Records
1316 North Chaparral St.
Corpus Christi 78401

John Hall Records
P.O. Box 13344
Fort Worth 76118

Happy Jazz Records, Inc.
P.O. Box 66
San Antonio 78205

Hare Music Company
P.O. Box 1209
Andrews 79714

Inergi Records
1300 Texas Ave.
Houston 77002

Isle City Records
411 Kempner
Galveston 77550

Jive in the Hills
c/o OK Books & Records
137 East Sixth St.
Austin 78701

Joey Record Manufacturing Company
6703 West Commerce
San Antonio 78227

Lake Country Music
P.O. Box 1073
Graham 76046

Longhorn Ballroom, Inc.
P.O. Box 17667
Dallas 75217

Long Neck Records
6004 Bull Creek Rd.
Austin 78757

MBA Productions
8914 Georgian Dr.
Austin 78753

Marsal Productions, Inc.
2015 Castroville Rd.
San Antonio 78237

Marullo Productions, Inc.
1121 Market St.
Galveston 77550

Maudi Records
3113 South University
Fort Worth 76109

Mulberry Square Records
10300 North Central Expwy.
Dallas 75231

Music Enterprises, Inc.
5626 Brock
Houston 77023

NAP Records, Inc.
3941 Don Juan
Abilene 79605

National Records
3410 Ave. 4
Lubbock 79412

National Music Enterprises
P.O. Box 35855
Houston 77035

New England Records
Drawer 520
Stafford 77477

Oakridge Music Recording Service
2001 Elton Rd.
Fort Worth 76117

Old Hat Records
P.O. Box 54
Mansfield 76063

Pantego Sound Studios
2310 Raper Blvd.
Pantego 76013

Priority Records
2300 Lincoln Ave.
Fort Worth 76106

Radio & Television Commission of the
Southern Baptist Convention
6350 West Freeway
Fort Worth 76116

Rainbow Sound, Inc.
2721 Irving Blvd.
Dallas 75207

Resco Records, Inc.
614 Dennis
Houston 77006

Ridge Runner Records
3035 Townsend Dr.
Fort Worth 76110

Don Schafer Promos
P.O. Box 57291
Dallas 75207

Silicon Music
222 Tulane St.
Garland 75041

Sixpence Productions
6115 Red Bird Court
Dallas 75232

Stoneway Records, Inc.
2817 Laura Koppe
Houston 77093

Sunshine Country Records
P.O. Box 31351
Dallas 75231

Texas Re-Cord Company
Box 19
Bulverde 78163

Thoroughbred Records
P.O. Drawer 2176
Austin 78704

Wizard Rec./Colonel Redneck Records
1524 East Anderson
Austin 78752

Word, Inc.
4800 West Waco Dr.
Waco 76703

Wright Productions & Doggett Music
1045 Studewood
Houston 77008

Joseph Wyndell Productions
P.O. Box 31533
Dallas 75231

Yatahey Records
P.O. Box 31819
Dallas 75231

UTAH

Chase Media, Inc.
Hotel Newhouse, Suite 1204
Salt Lake City 84101

Salt City Records, Inc.
P.O. Box 162
Provo 84601

VERMONT

Philo Records, Inc.
The Barn
North Ferrisburg 05473

VIRGINIA

ASI Records, Inc.
P.O. Box 395, Hwy. 460
Oakwood 24531

American Voices Record Company
216 Applewood Ln.
Virginia Beach 23452

Blue Mace Music
Box 62263
Virginia Beach 23462

Bridge the Gap Records & Tapes
909 West Washington St.
Petersburg 23803

Country Records
Box 191
Floyd 24091

Dominion Bluegrass Recordings
P.O. Box 993
Salem 24153

Fink–Pinewood Records
P.O. Box 5241
Chesapeake 23324

Martin Gary Productions
Box 131, Rte. 4
Louisa 23093

Major Recording Company
P.O. Box 2072
Waynesboro 22980

Pesante Record Company
744 West 28th
Norfolk 23508

Richtown/Gospel Truth Records
1529 Edgelawn Circle, Apt. B
Richmond 23231

Scada Productions, Inc.
35 West Reed Ave.
Alexandria 22305

Sounds of Winchester
P.O. Box 574
Winchester 22601

Spinn Records
Box 100-N, RFD 3
Stuart 24171

Telemark Dance Records
6845 Elm St., Suite 609
McLean 22101

Times Management Corporation
1216 Granby St.
Norfolk 23510

WASHINGTON

Emcee Records
6425 Nyanza Park Dr.
Tacoma 98499

Fiddler Records
1916 Pike Pl., No. 22
Seattle 98101

Gibson Enterprises
P.O. Box 2098
Vancouver 98661

Great Northwest Music Company
300 Vine St.
Seattle 98121

Tell International Recording Company
Box 368-A, Rte. 5
Yakima 98903

Voyager Recordings
424 35th Ave.
Seattle 98122

WEST VIRGINIA

Rebel Recording Company, Inc.
Rte. 12
Asbury 24916

Scene Productions
P.O. Box 1243
Beckley 25801

Sweetsong, Inc.
P.O. Box 2041
Parkersburg 26101

Wing & A Prayer Record Company
33 Highland Ln.
Wheeling 26003

WISCONSIN

Artist Direct Records
Blue Mounds 53517

Cadet Polka Records
Box 36
Burnett 53922

Gold Records
304 North Point Dr.
Stevens Point 54481

Mountain Railroad Records, Inc.
2103 Pleasant Rd.
Cambridge 53523

Nu-Trayl Record Company
10015 West Eight Mile Rd.
Franksville 53126

  Branch:
403 Tuckahoe Dr.
Nashville, TN 37115

SPEBSQSA
6315 Third Ave.
Kenosha 53141

Tool Room Records
Box 118
Pewaukee 53072

PUERTO RICO

Alhambra Records, Inc.
611 Fernandez Juncos Ave.
Offices 2, 3 & 4 Pirada 10
Miramar, Santurce 00907

Borinquen Records, Inc.
GPO Box 4785
San Juan 00936

Casa Fragosa, Inc.
P.O. Box 2774
San Juan 00903

Marylu Records
P.O. Box 6886, Loiza Sta.
Santurce 00914

Montilla Records
P.O. Box 594, Carrera 185
Km 0.8, Canovanas 00629

MUSIC
PUBLISHERS

ALABAMA

Brownleaf Music Company (BMI)
P.O. Box 7221
Mobile 36607

Carrhorn Music Company (BMI)
111 Kentucky Ave.
Sheffield 35660

Char-Belle Music (BMI)
1150 N. Center St.
Birmingham 35204

Everlovin' Publishing (BMI)
P.O. Box 4007
Huntsville 35802

Fame Publishing Company, Inc. (BMI)
603 E. Avalon Ave.
Muscle Shoals 35660

Law Publishing Company (BMI)
305 N. Hwy. 43
Saraland 36571

McDowell Music Company (BMI)
828 S. Lawrence St.
Montgomery 36104

Muscle Shoals Sound Publishing (BMI)
3614 Jackson Hwy.
Sheffield 35660

Music Mill Publishing Co. (ASCAP)
P.O. Box 2413
Muscle Shoals 35660

Nautical Music Company (BMI)
100 Harvard Ave.
Gadsden 35901

Round Sound Music
1924 Wise Dr.
Dothan 36301

Sheri Glen Publications (BMI)
1316 Alford Ave.
Birmingham 35226

Song Tailors Music Company (BMI)
P.O. Box 2631
Muscle Shoals 35660

Stairway Music Publishing (BMI)
6 Freeland Ave.
Grand Bay 36541

Tidewater Music Company
P.O. Box 4192
Huntsville 35802

Top Drawer Music (BMI)
P.O. Box 8011
Mobile 36608

Widget Publishing (BMI)
P.O. Box 2446
Muscle Shoals 35660

Woodrich Publishing Company (BMI)
Box 38
Lexington 35648

ARIZONA

Dad's Tunes (BMI)
P.O. Box 26704
Tempe 85282

Debra Music Corporation (BMI)
4625 N. 50th Dr.
Phoenix 85031

Golden Guitar Music (BMI)
P.O. Box 4364
Tucson 85717

Mighty Music (BMI)
2901 W. Maryland
Phoenix 85017

Oahu Publishing Company
10333 Coggins Dr.
Sun City 85351

Pantheon Desert Publishing (BMI)
6325 N. Invergordon Rd.
Scottsdale 85253

Renda Music, Inc. (BMI)
3830 N. Seventh St.
Phoenix 85014

Southwest Worlds & Music (BMI)
14 E. Second St.
Tucson 85705

Twiford Music (BMI)
4640 East Lewis
Phoenix 85008

Up With People (ASCAP)
3103 N. Campbell Ave.
Tucson 85719

Wolfhound Music (ASCAP)
1706 W. Surrey
Phoenix 85029

ARKANSAS

Arkoma (BMI)
P.O. Box 34
Siloam Springs 72761

Jamdan Publishing Company (BMI)
119 E. Broadway
West Memphis 72301

Tanya Music (BMI)
9207 Malabri Dr.
Little Rock 72209

Twin Towne Music (BMI)
127 Phoenix Village
Fort Smith 72901

CALIFORNIA

ATV Music Corporation (BMI)
6255 Sunset Blvd.
Hollywood 90028

Aandika Music (BMI)
740 North Kings Rd., #103
Hollywood 90028

Abernathy & Eye Music (BMI)
10447 Glory Ave.
Tujunga 91042

Accadia Music Publishing Company
(ASCAP)
9962½ Durant Dr.
Beverly Hills 90212

Fred Ahlert Music Corporation
(ASCAP)
9165 Sunset Blvd.
Los Angeles 90069

Alanbo Music (BMI)
P.O. Box 9639
North Hollywood 91609

Alcar (BMI)
1148 Tremaine Ave.
Los Angeles 90019

Alexis Music, Inc. (ASCAP)
19657 Ventura Blvd.
Tarzana 91356

Alfa Music, Inc.
9200 Sunset Blvd., #706
Los Angeles 90069

Alfred Publishing Company, Inc.
(ASCAP)
15335 Morrison St.
Sherman Oaks 91403

Aljoni Music Company (BMI)
P.O. Box 18918
Los Angeles 90018

Alkatraz Corner Music Company (BMI)
P.O. Box 3316
San Francisco 94114

Alphan Music Publishing (ASCAP)
P.O. Box 3844
Hollywood 90038

AlRuby Music, Inc. (ASCAP)
8515 Hollywood Blvd.
Hollywood 90069

Alshire Publishing Company
P.O. Box 7107
Burbank 91502

American Broadcasting Music (ASCAP)
11538 San Vicente Blvd.
Los Angeles 90049

Amestoy Music (BMI)
117 N. Las Palmas Ave.
Los Angeles 90004

Amiron Music (ASCAP)
20531 Plummer St.
Chatsworth 91311

AnnBen Music (BMI)
P.O. Box 2388
Toluca Lake 91602

Anznote Music (ASCAP)
802 E. Ocean Ave.
Lompoc 93436

Apex Music (BMI)
Twig Lane
Cupertino 95014

April Twenty-Two Music Co. (ASCAP)
9000 Sunset Blvd., Suite 1119
Los Angeles 90069

Ardavan Music (ASCAP)
P.O. Box 2512
Hollywood 90028

Argonaut Music (BMI)
P.O. Box 32044
San Jose 95152

Ariola America, Inc. (BMI)
8671 Wilshire Blvd.
Beverly Hills 90211

Astral World Music
21 Park Way
Piedmont 94611

Audio Arts Publishing Company
(ASCAP)
5611 Melrose Ave.
Hollywood 90038

Auspex Music (ASCAP)
12188 Laurel Terrace Dr.
Studio City 91604

Average Music (ASCAP)
9155 Sunset Blvd., Suite 3
Los Angeles 90069

BRS, Inc.
15010 Ventura Blvd., #306
Sherman Oaks 91403

Bal & Bal Music Publishing (ASCAP)
P.O. Box 369
La Canada 91011

Bald Mountain Music Corporation
(ASCAP)
1474 N. Kings Rd.
Hollywood 90069

Bay-Tone Music (BMI)
1218 Hollister St.
San Francisco 94124

Beachtime Music (BMI)
715 Timor Court
San Jose 95127

Beachwood Music Corporation (BMI)
1750 N. Vine St.
Hollywood 90028

Belmont Music Publishers (ASCAP)
P.O. Box 49961
Los Angeles 90049

Berdoo Music (BMI)
P.O. Box 3851
Hollywood 90028

Berkeley Cooperative Publishers
P.O. Box 3233
Berkeley 94703

Beserkley
1199 Spruce St.
Berkeley 94707

Better-Half Music Company (ASCAP)
1894 N. Stanley Ave.
Hollywood 90046

Beverly Hills Music (BMI)
c/o Lawrence Herbst Investments
P.O. Box 1659
Beverly Hills 90213

Bicycle Music Company
8756 Holloway Dr.
Los Angeles 90067

Bifern Music Publishing (BMI)
3361 S. Blue Ridge Court
Westlake Village 91361

Big Cigar Music Company (BMI)
8033 Highland Trail
Los Angeles 90046

Big Heart Music, Inc. (BMI)
9454 Wilshire Blvd.
Beverly Hills 90212

Big Island Music, Inc. (ASCAP)
5723 Star Ln.
Woodland Hills 91364

Steve Binder Productions
9000 Sunset Blvd., Suite 705
Los Angeles 90069

Bird Song Music
2700 Benedict Canyon
Beverly Hills 90210

Birthright Music (ASCAP)
3101 S. Western Ave.
Los Angeles 90018

Bisiar Music Publishing (BMI)
P.O. Box 5631
Concord 94520

Blackhawk Music Company (BMI)
1610 N. Argyle Ave., No. 110
Hollywood 90028

Blendingwell Music, Inc. (ASCAP)
9229 Sunset Blvd., No. 718
Los Angeles 90069

Blen Music Publishing (ASCAP)
220 San Vicente Blvd.
Santa Monica 90402

Blue Book Music (BMI)
1225 N. Chester Ave.
Bakersfield 93308

Blue Canyon Music (BMI)
1000 Granville Ave.
Los Angeles 90049

Blue River Music, Inc. (BMI)
6223 Selma Ave., Suite 125
Hollywood 90028

Fred Bock Music Company (ASCAP)
Box 300
Tarzana 91356

Bonton Music (ASCAP)
10441 Santa Monica Blvd.
Los Angeles 90025

Border Star Music (BMI)
7811 Waring Ave.
Los Angeles 90046

Tommy Boyce & Melvin Powers
   Music Enterprises (ASCAP)
12015 Sherman Rd.
North Hollywood 91605

Brain Drain Music Company (ASCAP)
1046 Carol Dr.
Los Angeles 90069

Braintree Music (BMI)
1900 Ave. of the Stars, Rm. 1424
Los Angeles 90067

Bridge Music Publishing Company
   (SESAC)
1350 Villa St.
Mountain View 94042

Broadside Music, Inc. (BMI)
9100 Sunset Blvd., No. 200
Los Angeles 90069

Brother Publishing Company (BMI)
3621 Sepulveda Blvd.
Manhattan Beach 90266

Brunswick Music Publishing Company
   (BMI)
136 S. Swall Dr.
Beverly Hills 90211

Budd Music Corporation (ASCAP)
18531 Wells Dr.
Tarzana 91356

Bug Music Group
6777 Hollywood Blvd., 9th Flr.
Hollywood 90028

Burchette Brothers
P.O. Box 1363
Spring Valley 92077

Bushka Music (ASCAP)
1800 Century Park East
Los Angeles 90067

Butch Music (ASCAP)
P.O. Box 49913
Los Angeles 90049

Byrdshire Music Company (ASCAP)
1601 N. Orange Grove Ave.
Hollywood 90046

CIX Publishing (ASCAP)
1617 North El Centro, Suite 3
Hollywood 90028

Cabot Music Pubberies
P.O. Box 3901
Hollywood 90028

Caesar's Music Library (ASCAP)
1022 N. Palm Ave.
Los Angeles 90069

Calliope Records, Inc.
15910 Ventura Blvd., Suite 603
Encino 91436

Calwest Songs (BMI)
c/o Lee Anderson Enterprises
P.O. Box 4141
North Hollywood 91607

Glen Campbell Music, Inc. (BMI)
10920 Wilshire Blvd.
Los Angeles 90024

Caribou Management Corporation
8600 Melrose Ave.
Los Angeles 90069

Caseyem Music (BMI)
c/o Mike Curb Productions Inc.
280 S. Beverly Dr., Suite 311
Beverly Hills 90212

Cedar Springs Music Company
(ASCAP)
19324 East Pilario
Rowland Heights 91748

Center Music Publishing Company
(ASCAP)
256 S. Robertson Blvd.
Beverly Hills 90211

Chalice Music Group
8467 Beverly Blvd.
Los Angeles 90048

Cherrolyne Music (BMI)
P.O. Box 2144
Winnetka 91306

Chromakey Music Company (ASCAP)
8489 W. Third St., Suite 38
Los Angeles 90048

Cin-Kay Publishing Company (BMI)
15130 Ventura Blvd., Suite 202
Sherman Oaks 91403

Claridge Music (ASCAP)
6381 Hollywood Blvd., Suite 318
Hollywood 90028

Clockus Music Company (BMI)
Star Rte.
Milford 96121

Martin Cohen
6430 Sunset Blvd., Suite 1500
Los Angeles 90028

Bruce Cohn Music
P.O. Box 878
Sonoma 95476

Commander Publications (ASCAP)
1209 N. Western Ave.
Hollywood 90029

Martin Cooper Music (ASCAP)
P.O. Box 3331
Beverly Hills 90212

Don Costa Productions, Inc. (BMI)
9229 Sunset Blvd.
Los Angeles 90069

Country Road Music Inc. (ASCAP)
c/o Gelfand, Breslauer, Macnow
431 S. Palm Canyon Dr.
Palm Springs 92262

Coyote Productions, Inc.
8560 West Sunset Blvd.
Los Angeles 90046

Crab Music (ASCAP)
930 S. Genesee Ave.
Los Angeles 90036

Crabshaw Music/David Forest Music
(ASCAP)
7060 Hollywood Blvd.
Los Angeles 90028

Cream Music Publishing Group
8025 Melrose Ave.
Los Angeles 90046

Creative Concepts Publishing
Corporation
967 East Ojai Ave.
Ojai 93023

Creative World Music Publications
(BMI & ASCAP)
2340 Sawtelle Blvd.
Los Angeles 90064

Cricklewood Music Company (ASCAP)
P.O. Box 9246
Berkeley 94709

Cristeval Music (BMI)
5050 Vanalden
Tarzana 91356

Criterion Music Corporation (ASCAP)
6124 Selma Ave.
Hollywood 90028

The Crystal Jukebox (BMI)
c/o CBS Studio Center
4024 Radford Ave.
N. Hollywood 90028

Cynosure Music (ASCAP)
P.O. Box 69585
West Hollywood 90069

Daedalian Music (BMI)
5656 Lexington Ave., #16
Los Angeles 90038

Dahlhouse Publishing Company
(ASCAP)
P.O. Box 3262
Hollywood 90028

Darla Music, Inc. (ASCAP)
c/o Mike Post Productions
4507 Carpenter Ave.
N. Hollywood 91607

Davike Music Company (ASCAP)
P.O. Box 8842
Los Angeles 90008

Dawnbreaker Music Company (BMI)
6430 Sunset Blvd., Suite 716
Hollywood 90028

Daybreak Music (ASCAP)
6725 Sunset Blvd., Suite 402
Hollywood 90028

Dayton Music Company (ASCAP)
1610 North Argyle, No. 109
Hollywood 90028

Debonair Music (BMI)
721 Colman St.
Altadena 91001

Deejay Music Company (BMI)
3008 Belden Dr.
Los Angeles 90068

De Gar Music (ASCAP)
665 Harrison
San Francisco 94107

Richard Delvy Enterprise, Inc.
8127 Elrita Dr.
Los Angeles 90046

DePatie-Freleng Music Company
(ASCAP)
6859 Hayvenhurst
Van Nuys 91406

Derry Music Company (BMI)
240 Stockton St.
San Francisco 94108

Diamondback Music Company (BMI)
10 Waterville
San Francisco 94124

Dickiebird Music (BMI)
c/o Michael Rosenfeld
9665 Wilshire Blvd., Suite 340
Beverly Hills 90212

Diddem Daddum Music (BMI)
13615 Victory Blvd., Suite 216
Van Nuys 91401

Dijon Music Publications (BMI)
9033 Wilshire Blvd.
Beverly Hills 90211

Walt Disney Music Company (ASCAP)
350 South Buena Vista St.
Burbank 91521

Dogfish Music (ASCAP)
P.O. Box 278
Inverness 94937

Doheny Music (BMI)
8569 Holloway Dr., No. 2
Los Angeles 90069

Dojoda Publishing, Inc. (ASCAP)
7260 Hillside Ave.
Los Angeles 90046

Dolly Bee Music (BMI)
515 E. Racquet Club Rd.
Palm Springs 92262

Donna Lee Music (ASCAP)
1313 E. Magnolia Blvd.
Burbank 91502

Doors Music Company (ASCAP)
c/o Greene & Reynolds
1900 Ave. of the Stars, Suite 1424
Los Angeles 90067

Dozier Music, Inc. (BMI)
8467 Beverly Blvd., Suite 200
Los Angeles 90048

Draw Music Company (ASCAP)
16772 Heritage Lane
Huntington Beach 92647

Drive-In Music Company, Inc. (BMI)
7120 Sunset Blvd.
Hollywood 90046

Duane Music, Inc. (BMI)
382 Clarence Ave.
Sunnyvale 94086

Dunamis Music (ASCAP)
8319 Lankershim Blvd.
North Hollywood 91605

Early Bird Music (BMI)
2308 St. Anne Pl.
Santa Ana 92704

El Chicano Music (ASCAP)
20531 Plummer St.
Chatsworth 91311

Elizabeth Music Publishing (BMI)
515 E. Racquet Club Rd.
Palm Springs 92262

Ellis Music Enterprises, Inc. (ASCAP)
5436 Auckland Ave.
North Hollywood 91601

Elm Publishing Company (BMI)
P.O. Box 1100
Westminster 92683

Lee Elvensong Music, Ltd. (BMI)
2017 Walnut Creek Pkway.
W. Covina 91791

Emilanda Musique (BMI)
731½ North Croft
West Hollywood 90069

Equinox Music (BMI)
9220 Sunset Blvd., Suite 224
Los Angeles 90069

Evanton Music Company (BMI)
P.O. Box 2217
Inglewood 90205

Evelyn Music Company, Ltd.
1305 North Highland Ave.
Hollywood 90028

Exbrook Publishing Company (BMI)
9110 Sunset Blvd., Suite 100
Los Angeles 90069

FAA Music (BMI)
844 W. 107th St.
Los Angeles 90044

FEL Publications, Ltd. (ASCAP)
1925 S. Pontius Ave.
Los Angeles 90025

FYDAQ Music (BMI)
240 E. Radcliffe Dr.
Claremont 91711

Fairchild Music (BMI)
P.O. Box 5843
Buena Park 90620

Faro Music Publishing (BMI)
255 N. New Hampshire Ave.
Los Angeles 90004

Far Out Music, Inc. (ASCAP)
7417 Sunset Blvd.
Hollywood 90046

Wes Farrell Organization
9200 Sunset Blvd., Suite 620
Los Angeles 90069

Fermata International Melodies, Inc.
  (ASCAP)
6290 Sunset Blvd., Suite 616
Hollywood 90028

Fideree Music Company (ASCAP)
3915 Prospect Ave.
Hollywood 90027

Fiesta Music, Inc. (BMI)
P.O. Box 2450
Hollywood 90028

Fifth House Music (BMI)
105 Oak Rim Court, No. 15
Los Gatos 95030

First Artists Music Company (ASCAP)
4000 Warner Blvd.
Burbank 91522

Fishbowl Music Publishers (BMI)
4834 Bissell
Richmond 94805

The Flag & Mother Music (ASCAP)
1549 North Vine St., Suite 20
Hollywood 90028

Fog City Music Publising (BMI)
700 Jerrold Ave.
San Francisco 94124

Folklore Productions, Inc.
1671 Appian Way
Santa Monica 90401

Forest Bay Music (ASCAP)
703 Canham Rd.
Santa Cruz 95060

Four Four (BMI)
811 Point San Pedro Rd.
San Rafael 94901

Four Knights Music (BMI)
6000 Sunset Blvd.
Hollywood 90028

Four Star International, Inc. (BMI)
400 S. Beverly Dr.
Beverly Hills 90212

Fourth House Music Company
10850 Wilshire Blvd., Suite 1225
Los Angeles 90024

Fred Foxx Music Company (BMI)
15 S. Ontario
San Mateo 94401

Friendship Station (ASCAP)
9911 West Pico Blvd., Suite 660
Los Angeles 90035

Front Lawn Music (BMI)
6420 Wilshire Blvd., Suite 1400
Los Angeles 90048

Fuente Music Company (BMI)
P.O. Box 1233
Santa Monica 90406

Fullness Music Company (BMI)
6922 Hollywood Blvd., Suite 316
Hollywood 90028

GP Music Corporation (BMI)
c/o PBR Music
7033 Sunset Blvd., Suite 332
Los Angeles 90028

GTP Music (BMI)
P.O. Box 14
Hollywood 90028

Galeneye Music (BMI)
c/o Ivan Hoffman
2040 Ave. of the Stars, 4th Flr.
Los Angeles 90067

Garrett Music Enterprises
6255 Sunset Blvd., Suite 1019
Hollywood 90028

Gentle Wind Publishing Company
  (BMI)
1030 48th St.
Sacramento 95819

Golden Hill Music, Inc.
P.O. Box 3691
Van Nuys 91407

Good Changes Music Publishing
(ASCAP)
4555 Prospect Ave.
Hollywood 90027

Googles Music, Inc.
7800 Woodman Ave. No. 19A
Panorama City 91402

Gopam Enterprises, Inc. (BMI)
P.O. Box 24A53
Los Angeles 90024

Gordon Music Company, Inc. (ASCAP)
2680 Cherokee Way
Palm Springs 92262

Robert E. Gordon (ASCAP)
555 California St., #3100
San Francisco 94104

Greasy King Music, Inc. (ASCAP)
P.O. Box 9245
Berkeley 94709

Great-Honesty Music, Inc. (BMI)
916 Kearny St.
San Francisco 94133

Green Apple Music (BMI)
9229 Sunset Blvd., Suite 811
Los Angeles 90069

Greenbar Music Corporation (ASCAP)
7235 Hollywood Blvd.
Los Angeles 90046

Greeneaire Publishing (ASCAP)
6632 Bertrand Ave.
Reseda 91335

Greene & Reynolds
1900 Ave. of the Stars, Suite 1424
Los Angeles 90067

Grosvenor House Music (ASCAP)
P.O. Box 1563
Hollywood 90028

Groundhog Publishing (ASCAP)
254 East 29th St.
Los Angeles 90011

Guitar Player Books/Records
P.O. Box 615
Saratoga 95070

EJ Gurren Music (ASCAP)
3929 Kentucky Dr.
Los Angeles 90068

Hall of Fame Music Company (BMI)
P.O. Box 921
Beverly Hills 90213

Hampstead Heath Music Publishers
(ASCAP)
P.O. Box 223
Sky Forest 92385

Handsome Music Publishing Company
(BMI)
9000 Sunset Blvd., Suite 600
Los Angeles 90069

T.B. Harms Company (ASCAP)
100 Wilshire Blvd., Suite 700
Santa Monica 90401

Harrison Music Corporation (ASCAP)
6381 Hollywood Blvd.
Hollywood 90028

Hartline Music, Inc. (BMI)
1901 Ave. of the Stars, Suite 1050
Los Angeles 90067

Heavy Music, Inc. (BMI)
8776 Sunset Blvd.
Los Angeles 90069

Hero Music Publishing, Ltd.
7235 Hollywood Blvd.
Hollywood 90046

Hickory Grove Music (ASCAP)
9128 Sunset Blvd.
Los Angeles 90069

Hidle Music (BMI)
12023 Rhode Island Ave.
Los Angeles 90025

Hilmer Publishing Company (ASCAP)
c/o Michael Rosenfeld
9665 Wilshire Blvd.
Beverly Hills 90212

Hip Trip Music Inc. (BMI)
9200 Sunset Blvd.
Los Angeles 90069

The Hit Machine Music Company (BMI)
P.O. Box 20692
San Diego 92120

R.A. Hodge
273 Page St.
San Francisco 94102

Ivan Hoffman
2040 Ave. of the Stars
Los Angeles 90067

Holaster Music (BMI)
2413 Hyperion Ave.
Los Angeles 90027

Horttor Music Company (BMI)
313 El Tejon Ave.
Oildale, Bakersfield 93308

Hot Egg Music (BMI)
6515 Sunset Blvd., #309
Hollywood 90028

Houndog Music (ASCAP)
Box 531
Point Reyes Station 94956

House of Rock Music (BMI)
958 W. Edgemont Dr.
San Bernardino 92405

Ice Nine Publishing Company (ASCAP)
P.O. Box 1073
San Rafael 94901

I Love Music (BMI)
5500 W. Jefferson Blvd.
Los Angeles 90016

India Music (ASCAP)
c/o Greene & Reynolds
1900 Ave. of the Stars, Suite 1424
Los Angeles 90067

Intercontinental Music Combine (BMI)
c/o Ed Sherman
16000 Ventura Blvd., Suite 202
Encino 91436

Intermountain Music (BMI)
P.O. Box 1067
Hollywood 90028

Invador Music (BMI)
8961 Sunset Blvd.
Los Angeles 90069

J & H Publishing Company (ASCAP)
415 North Tustin Ave.
Orange 92667

Janell Music (BMI)
792 E. Julian St.
San Jose 95112

Jangar Music Publishers (BMI)
7025 Claire Ave.
Reseda 91335

Jay Music (ASCAP)
6654 Allott Ave.
Van Nuys 91401

Jeeda Music (BMI)
10894 Willow Crest Pl.
Studio City 91604

Jobete Music Company
6255 Sunset Blvd.
Hollywood 90028

Jonapooh Music, Inc. (BMI)
9460 Wilshire Blvd., Suite 624
Beverly Hills 90212

Jondora Music (BMI)
10 & Parker Sts.
Berkeley 94710

Jonvis Music Company (BMI)
2233 W. 25th St.
Los Angeles 90018

Joyfully Sad (BMI)
8560 Sunset Blvd., Suite 800
Los Angeles 90069

Jucu Music (ASCAP)
P.O. Box 2161
North Hollywood 91602

Jugumba Music (ASCAP)
c/o Jay Cooper
9465 Wilshire Blvd., Suite 820
Beverly Hills 90212

Gus Kahn Music Company (ASCAP)
6223 Selma Ave.
Hollywood 90028

Les Kangas Music Publishing (BMI)
302 E. Dewey Ave.
San Gabriel 91776

Richard Kaye Publications
2234 Laurel Canyon Blvd.
Los Angeles 90046

Keca Music, Inc. (ASCAP)
9440 Santa Monica Blvd., Suite 704
Beverly Hills 90210

Keith Music (ASCAP)
4648 Park Granada, No. 172
Calabasas 91302

Kengorus Music (ASCAP)
3033 Franklin Canyon Dr.
Beverly Hills 90210

Kentucky Colonel Music (BMI)
734 Fairview Ave.
Sierra Madre 91024

Kicking Mule Publishing (BMI)
P.O. Box 3233
Berkeley 94703

Kidada Music Company/Rashida Music
  Company (BMI)
c/o A & M Records
1416 N. La Brea Ave.
Los Angeles 90028

Koala Records, Inc.
9255 Sunset Blvd.
Los Angeles 90069

Kolber Publishing Company (BMI)
332 West 14th St.
Upland 91786

Krishane Enterprises, Inc. (ASCAP)
4601 Willis Ave., Suite 309
Sherman Oaks 91403

Lady Jane Music (BMI)
c/o Abraham Somer, Esq.
1800 Century Park East, Suite 800
Los Angeles 90067

Landers-Roberts Music (ASCAP)
8899 Beverly Blvd.
Los Angeles 90048

Stuart Lanis Music, Inc. (BMI)
1273½ N. Crescent Heights Blvd.
Los Angeles 90046

Lansdowne Music Publishers (ASCAP)
P.O. Box 2941
Escondido 92069

Latimusic (BMI)
9000 Sunset Blvd., Suite 1510
Los Angeles 90069

Laurabob Music Company (BMI)
6362 Hollywood Blvd., No. 312
Hollywood 90028

Ray Lawrence Music (ASCAP)
P.O. Box 1987
Studio City 91604

Lear Music, Inc. (ASCAP)
8899 Beverly Blvd.
Los Angeles 90048

Leivas Publishing Company (BMI)
2037 Milton St.
Riverside 92507

Len-Lon Music Publishing Company
  (BMI)
c/o Sandra Newman
1326 N. Flores St.
Los Angeles 90069

Lerobal Music (BMI)
6255 Sunset Blvd., Suite 909
Hollywood 90028

Lexicon Music, Inc. (ASCAP)
21241 Ventura Blvd., Suite 288
Woodland Hills 91364

Lichelle Music Company (ASCAP)
4215 Hood Ave.
Burbank 91508

Lion's Gate Films, Inc.
1334 Westwood Blvd.
Los Angeles 90024

Little Giant Music Publishing (BMI)
1545 North Bronson Ave.
Hollywood 90028

Loring Music Company (BMI)
1048 North Carol Dr.
Los Angeles 90069

183

Lotsa Music (BMI)
1050 Carol Dr.
Los Angeles 90069

Lucky Pork (ASCAP)
230 Montcalm
San Francisco 94110

Lu-Tal Publishing (BMI)
P.O. Box 126
Bakersfield 93302

MacArthur Music (BMI)
P.O. Box 82
Palmdale 93550

Madrid Music Company (ASCAP)
P.O. Box 504
Bonita 92002

Magic Medicine Music
17029 Chatsworth St.
Granada Hills 91344

Mainspring Watchworks Music Company
27 States St.
San Francisco 94114

Main Stave Music (ASCAP)
P.O. Box 2763
Hollywood 90028

Makemore Music Publishing Company
(BMI)
1239 Appleton Way
Venice 90291

Manna Music, Inc. (ASCAP)
2111 Kenmere
Burbank 91504

Mantra Music (BMI)
222 E. Garvey Ave.
Monterey Park 91754

Manwin Music (BMI)
c/o Chapman Distributing Company
1212 Albany St.
Los Angeles 90015

Maranatha! Music (ASCAP)
P.O. Box 1396
Costa Mesa 92626

Marshua Music Company (ASCAP)
P.O. Box 6162
Long Beach 90701

Marzique Music (BMI)
5752 Bowcroft St.
Los Angeles 90016

Ray Maxwell Music Publishing (BMI)
Box 317
Hollywood 90028

McCra/Ray (BMI)
619A Buck
Vacaville 95688

Jimmy McHugh Music (ASCAP)
9301 Wilshire Blvd., Suite 400
Beverly Hills 90210

Meadowee Music (BMI)
1727 Roanoke Ave.
Sacramento 95838

Meadowlark Music, Inc. (ASCAP)
1608 Argyle
Hollywood 90028

Megusta Music (ASCAP)
29775 Pacific Coast Hwy.
Malibu 90265

Meljean Publishing (BMI)
P.O. Box 892
Seaside 93955

Melody House Publishers (BMI)
958 West Edgemont Dr.
San Bernardino 92405

Mercantile Music (BMI)
P.O. Box 2271
Palm Springs 92262

Arnold Mills & Associates
8721 Sunset Blvd., Suite 201
Los Angeles 90069

Irving Mills Music Publishers
2373 Westwood Blvd.
Los Angeles 90064

Minta Music (BMI)
7033 Sunset Blvd., Suite 303
Los Angeles 90028

Minto Music (BMI)
5619 Lankershim Blvd.
North Hollywood 91601

Mirsong Music (BMI)
P.O. Box 946
Hollywood 90028

Mission City Records & Entertainment
P.O. Box 1110
San Fernando 91341

Missprint Music (BMI)
P.O. Box 925
Hollywood 90068

Mr. Par Music (BMI)
5143 Goodland Ave.
North Hollywood 91607

Modern Music Publishing, Inc. (BMI)
5810 S. Normandie Ave.
Los Angeles 90044

Mole Hill Music (BMI)
1722 Whitley Ave.
Hollywood 90028

Monarch Music Corporation (ASCAP)
1800 Century Park East, Suite 718
Los Angeles 90067

Morgan Manor Music, Inc. (ASCAP)
1601 North Orange Grove Ave.
Hollywood 90046

Munka Music (BMI)
4920 Maiden Lane
La Mesa 92041

Musical Illusions (BMI)
930 South Bonnie Brae, No. 319
Los Angeles 90006

Musictone Music (BMI)
P.O. Box 343
Santa Monica 90406

Musicways, Inc. (BMI)
1800 Century Park East, Suite 300
Los Angeles 90067

NR Music Company (BMI)
6232 Santa Monica Blvd.
Los Angeles 90038

Namrac Music (BMI)
15456 Cabrito Rd.
Van Nuys 91406

Natural Forest Music (BMI)
P.O. Box 1985
Crestline 92325

Neil Music, Inc. (BMI)
8560 Sunset Blvd.
Los Angeles 90069

Neuron Music (ASCAP)
P.O. Box 1594
Hollywood 90028

New Wine Productions (ASCAP)
P.O. Box 544
Lomita 90717

Nicoletti Music Company (BMI)
P.O. Box 2818
Newport Beach 92663

Nida Music Publishing (ASCAP)
4014 Murietta Ave.
Sherman Oaks 91403

Northridge Music, Inc. (ASCAP)
6290 Sunset Blvd.
Hollywood 90028

Norvik/Hauge Music Publishing
  Company
897 Walker Ave.
Oakland 94610

OMP Music Publishing (ASCAP)
11110 Los Alamitos Blvd., Suite 215
Los Alamitos 90720

Old St. Paul Publishing (ASCAP)
P.O. Box 49441
Los Angeles 90049

One Publishing Company (BMI)
243 S. Ave. 50
Los Angeles 90042

Open Channel Sound Company (BMI)
231 Emerson
Palo Alto 94301

Open End Music (BMI)
824 North Robertson Blvd.
Hollywood 90069

Origatunes Publishing Company (BMI)
8839 Walnut St.
Bellflower 90706

Pacific Challenger Music (BMI)
2572 Fender Ave., Suite F
Fullerton 92631

Pacific Coast Music (BMI)
11231 Otsego St., Suite 104
North Hollywood 91601

Pad Music (BMI)
4307 S. Broadway
Los Angeles 90037

Pal Dog Music (ASCAP)
3209 Tareco Dr.
Los Angeles 90068

Pal Publishing
P.O. Box 807
Northridge 91328

Paradise Music (ASCAP)
3300 Warner Blvd.
Burbank 91510

Paramount-West Enterprises
8010 Second St.
Paramount 91723

Pasa Alta Music (BMI)
54 E. Colorado Blvd.
Pasadena 91105

Peaceable Kingdom (ASCAP)
3525 Encinal Canyon Rd.
Malibu 90265

Peaceful Music (BMI)
P.O. Box 5547
Carmel 93921

Pee Wee Valley Music, Inc. (ASCAP)
P.O. Box 9246
Berkeley 94709

Perennial Music (BMI)
2249 Fillmore St.
San Francisco 94115

Petko Music (BMI)
6331 Santa Monica Blvd.
Hollywood 90019

Pewter Pal Music (BMI)
c/o HT Productions
1741 North Ivar St., Suite 105
Hollywood 90028

Picasso Publishing Company (ASCAP)
P.O. Box 3266
Van Nuys 91407

Pigfoot Music (ASCAP)
P.O. Box 130
Point Reyes Stations 94956

Playboy Music Publishing (ASCAP)
8560 Sunset Blvd., Suite 400
Los Angeles 90069

Plunge Publishing Company (BMI)
P.O. Box 441
Northridge 91324

Poe Publishing Company (ASCAP)
5930 Vista Ave.
Sacramento 95824

Porpete Music Publishing Co. (BMI)
P.O. Box 777
Hollywood 90028

Positive Energy Publishing (BMI)
6565 Sunset Blvd.
Los Angeles 90046

Pringle Music Publishers (BMI)
7021 Hatillo Ave.
Canoga Park 91306

Pritchett Publications (BMI)
38603 Sage Tree St.
Palmdale 93550

Proud Tunes (BMI)
1722 Redondo Blvd.
Los Angeles 90019

Quackenbuch Music, Ltd. (ASCAP)
850 Devon Ave.
Los Angeles 90024

Queen-Bishop Music, Inc. (ASCAP)
P.O. Box 9446
Berkeley 94709

Fred Raphael Music (ASCAP)
8588 Wonderland Ave.
Los Angeles 90046

Bill Rase Productions, Inc.
955 Venture Ct.
Sacramento 95825

Redbeard Music (BMI)
P.O. Box 1867
Hollywood 90028

Red River Songs, Inc. (BMI)
1001 N. Lincoln St.
Burbank 91506

Leon Rene Publications (ASCAP)
2124 West 24th St.
Los Angeles 90018

Respect Music Company (BMI)
1159 South La Jolla Ave.
Los Angeles 90035

Resurrection Music Corporation (BMI)
3175 Cadet Ct.
Hollywood 90068

Rivers Music (ASCAP)
13033 Ventura Blvd.
Studio City 91604

Robb Music (BMI)
7235 Hollywood Blvd., Suite 221
Hollywood 90046

Don Robertson Music (ASCAP)
1680 N. Vine St.
Hollywood 90028

Robin Hood Music Company (BMI)
5531 Tuxedo Terr.
Hollywood 90028

Rockmore Music (BMI)
1733 Carmona Ave.
Los Angeles 90019

Roger Music, Inc. (ASCAP)
449 S. Beverly Dr.
Beverly Hills 90212

Roger-Van Buren (BMI)
1900 Fifth Ave.
Los Angeles 90018

Rondor Music, Inc.
1416 North La Brea Ave.
Hollywood 90028

Room 7 Music (BMI)
6605 Hollywood Blvd., Suite 205
Hollywood 90028

Brian Ross Productions
3884 Franklin Ave.
Los Angeles 90027

RowChar Music (ASCAP)
716 West 33rd St.
San Pedro 90731

Royalty Control Corporation
680 Beach St.
San Francisco 94109

Rubicon Music (BMI)
8319 Lankershim Blvd.
North Hollywood 91605

David Rubinson & Friends, Inc.
827 Folsom St.
San Francisco 94107

S & R Music Publishing Company
(ASCAP)
6533 Hollywood Blvd.
Hollywood 90028

Sailor Music (ASCAP)
2029 Century Park East
Los Angeles 90067

Sashasongs Unlimited (BMI)
1800 Marcheeta Place
Los Angeles 90069

Satrycon Music (BMI)
P.O. Box 75692
Los Angeles 90075

Shiffman Music Company (BMI)
8560 Sunset Blvd.
Los Angeles 90069

Schine Music (ASCAP)
626 South Hudson Ave.
Los Angeles 90005

Schroder Music Company (ASCAP)
2027 Parker St.
Berkeley 94704

Scott Music Publications
151 North Yale
Fullerton 92631

Seafood Music (BMI)
P.O. Box 42338
San Francisco 94101

John Sebastian Music (BMI)
1800 Century Park East
Los Angeles 90067

Segel & Goldman, Inc.
9200 Sunset Blvd., Suite 1000
Los Angeles 90069

Sequel Music, Inc. (BMI)
3204 Oakley Dr.
Hollywood 90068

Shade Tree Music, Inc. (BMI)
P.O. Box 842
Bakersfield 93302

Shamga Publishing Company (BMI)
254 East 29th St., Suite 7
Los Angeles 90011

Shark Music
P.O. Box 49204, Barrington Sta.
Los Angeles, 90049

Shindig Music Publishing Company
(BMI)
1608 Argyle, Suite 107
Hollywood 90028

Shoestring Music Corporation (BMI)
P.O. Box 4009
Hollywood 90028

Silk Purse Music (BMI)
1516 Oak St.
Alameda 94501

George Simon, Inc. (ASCAP)
510 Sierra Way
Palm Springs 92262

Skinny Zach Music, Inc. (ASCAP)
6430 Sunset Blvd.
Los Angeles 90028

Skyhill Publishing Company, Inc.
(BMI)/Tarka Music Company (ASCAP)
5112 Hollywood Blvd.
Hollywood 90027

Skyway Music Publishing (BMI)
P.O. Box 133
Hollywood 90028

Solar Records, Inc.
6277 Selma Ave.
Hollywood 90028

Solo Music, Inc. (ASCAP)
4708 Van Noord Ave.
Sherman Oaks 91423

Songpower (ASCAP)
22802 Pacific Coast Hwy.
Malibu 90265

Sonlife Music Company (ASCAP)
8577 Canoga Ave.
Canoga Park 91304

Soprano Music Publishing (BMI)
4118 West 106th St.
Lennox 90304

Sound of Nolan Music (BMI)
211 South Beverly Dr., Suite 108
Beverly Hills 90212

Sound Syndicate
7769 Melrose Ave.
Los Angeles 90046

Spaceark Music (ASCAP)
P.O. Box 4523
North Hollywood 91607

Sparrow Song (BMI)
8587 Canoga Ave.
Canoga Park 91304

Spectrum Publications (SESAC)
P.O. Box 757
San Carlos 94070

Speed Music (BMI)
8465 Shirley Ave.
Northridge 91324

Spina Music (ASCAP)
2232 Vista Del Mar Pl.
Hollywood 90068

Stampede Music Company
(BMI)
830 South Live Oak Park Rd.
Fallbrook 92028

Standup Music, Inc. (ASCAP)
P.O. Box 9405
Berkeley 94709

Stanyan Music Company (ASCAP)
8440 Santa Monica Blvd.
Hollywood 90069

Star Show Music (ASCAP)
15300 Ventura Blvd., Suite 210
Sherman Oaks 91403

Startime Music (ASCAP)
P.O. Box 643
La Quinta 92253

Startingate Music (BMI)
3539 Monterosa Dr.
Altadena 91001

Stinson Music (ASCAP)
P.O. Box 3415
Granada Hills 91344

Stonbass Music Company (BMI)
163 Orizaba Ave.
San Francisco 94132

Studio 10, Inc., Ltd.
354 Shoreline Hwy.
Mill Valley 94941

Sufi Pipkin Music (BMI)
P.O. Box 3991
Hollywood 90028

Sugartree Music (BMI)
P.O. Box 4496
North Hollywood 91607

Sundaze Music (BMI)
P.O. Box 66
Manhattan Beach 90266

Surf City Music (ASCAP)
5460 White Oak Ave., Suite G–338
Encino 91316

Sutton/Miller, Ltd. (ASCAP, BMI)
8913 Sunset Blvd.
Los Angeles 90069

Sweet Earth Sound (ASCAP)
P.O. Box 1339
Downey 90240

Taeper Music (ASCAP)
15461 Springdale St.
Huntington Beach 92649

Tallyrand Music (BMI)
c/o Gelfand, Breslauer, Macnow
1880 Century Park East, Suite 415
Los Angeles 90067

Skip Taylor Productions
8743 Wonderland Park Ave.
Los Angeles 90046

Tejas Music (BMI)
8537 Sunset Blvd., No. 2
Los Angeles 90069

Peter Tevis Music (BMI)
P.O. Box 1102
Burbank 91507

Thirteenth Day Music (ASCAP)
6943 Valjean Ave.
Van Nuys 91406

Thirty Four Music Company (ASCAP)
4329 Colfax Ave.
Studio City 91604

3 H's Music (ASCAP)
1103 Neff Ave. South
West Covina 91790

Time Music Company (BMI)
449 S. Beverly Dr.
Beverly Hills 90212

Time Step Music (ASCAP)
141 N. St. Andrews Pl.
Los Angeles 90004

Tiny Tiger Music (ASCAP)
1800 Century Park East
Los Angeles 90067

Tom Thumb Music
Box 34485
Los Angeles 90034

Tonob Music (BMI)
c/o Ivan M. Hoffman
2040 Ave. of the Stars, 4th Flr.
Los Angeles 90067

Touch of Gold Music (BMI)
6255 Sunset Blvd., Suite 709
Hollywood 90028

Toulouse Music Publications (BMI)
P.O. Box 96
El Cerrito 94530

Tradition Music (BMI)
P.O. Box 9195
Berkeley 94709

Transatlantic Music (BMI)
P.O. Box 64
Davis 95616

Tridex Music Company (BMI)
P.O. Box 1646
Burbank 91507

Triple K Music, Inc. (BMI)
9200 Sunset Blvd., Penthouse 30
Los Angeles 90210

Triple Nine Music (ASCAP)
1335 North Detroit, Suite 103
Hollywood 90046

Trompas Music (BMI)
11526 Burbank Blvd., Suite 14
North Hollywood 91601

True Blue Music Publishing (ASCAP)
16027 Sunburst St.
Sepulveda 91343

Trust Music Management, Inc.
6255 Sunset Blvd.
Los Angeles 90028

20th Century Music Corporation
(ASCAP)
8544 Sunset Blvd.
Los Angeles 90069

Tymer Music (BMI)
P.O. Box 1669
Carlsbad 92008

Ultimate Record Music Publishing
(ASCAP)
7087 Bark Lane
San Jose 95129

United Artists Music Publishing
6920 Sunset Blvd.
Los Angeles 90028

VIZ Music Publishing (ASCAP)
P.O. Box 702
Glen Ellen 95442

V-Love Music (ASCAP)
1327 North Gardner St.
Los Angeles 90046

Vaam Music (BMI)
3740 Evans Ave., Suite C-114
Los Angeles 90027

Val-Dare (BMI)
P.O. Box 4234
Panorama City 91412

Rocky Valdez Music
4640 West 118th St.
Hawthorne 90250

Valgroup Music (USA) Company (BMI)
7033 Sunset Blvd.
Los Angeles 90028

Varese International
P.O. Box 148
Glendale 91209

Venice Music, Inc. (BMI)
8300 Santa Monica Blvd.
Hollywood 90069

Verde Vista Music (ASCAP)
2383 Union St., No. 4
San Francisco 94123

Very Important Publications (BMI)
8467 Beverly Blvd., Suite 200
Los Angeles 90048

Vibration Music Company (BMI)
P.O. Box 9726, West Gate Sta.
San Jose 95117

Warner Bros. Music (ASCAP)
9200 Sunset Blvd.
Hollywood 90069

Weatherly Music (BMI)
1415 North Hudson Ave.
Hollywood 90028

Sam Weiss Music, Inc. (ASCAP)
6087 Sunset Blvd.
Hollywood 90028

Wheezer Music (ASCAP)
1701 Nichols Canyon Rd., No. 204
Hollywood 90046

Whittley Publishing Company
1704 Harte Dr.
San Jose 95124

Wichub Music Company (BMI)
P.O. Box 1224
Studio City 91604

Wild Music (ASCAP)
12135 Valley Spring Lane
Studio City 91604

Wild Sanctuary (BMI)
680 Beach St., No. 411
San Francisco 94109

Wilhos Music (BMI)
P.O. Box 3443
Hollywood 90028

Dootsie Williams Publications (BMI)
800 West First St.
Los Angeles 90012

Ron Wilson Music Productions (BMI)
P.O. Box 285
Beverly Hills 90213

Wooden Nickel Music (ASCAP)
6521 Homewood Ave.
Los Angeles 90028

Ybarra Music (ASCAP)
P.O. Box 665
Lemon Grove 92045

Youngwood Publishing Company (BMI)
849 Bing Dr.
Santa Clara 95051

Yuggoth Music Company (BMI)
6521 Homewood
Los Angeles 90028

COLORADO

Band Box Music Publishing Company
(BMI)
P.O. Box 15477
Lakewood 80215

M. Bernstein Music Publishing (ASCAP)
295 Monaco Pkwy.
Denver 80220

Blanket Music Publishing Company
(BMI)
778 South Pearl St.
Denver 80209

Captain Country Music Inc./Bel-J
Productions Inc. (BMI)
1085 West Arizona Ave.
Denver 80223

Ferndock Music (ASCAP)
1540 Lehigh St.
Boulder 80303

Gramm Publishing (ASCAP)
1130 West Evans
Denver 80223

Great American Music Machine
1130 West Evans
Denver 80223

Red Rock Music Company (BMI)
P.O. Box 2671
Denver 80201

Seven Arrows Music (BMI)
P.O. Box 9716
Denver 80209

Twelve Tribes Music (BMI)
1106 E. 17th Ave.
Denver 80218

CONNECTICUT

BW Music
114 West Maiden Ln.
Monroe 06468

Bell Holding Music (ASCAP)
1260 East Main St.
Meriden 06450

Cherry Lane Music (ASCAP)
P.O. Box 4247
Greenwich 06830

Electrocord Music Company (ASCAP)
54 Main St.
Danbury 06810

Folk-Legacy Records Publishing (BMI)
Sharon Mountain Rd.
Sharon 06069

Lauren Kim Music (ASCAP)
16 Dundee Rd.
Stamford 06903

Paul Leka Music (BMI)
132 Merrimac Dr.
Trumball 06611

Mentor Music, Inc.
Broadview Dr.
Brookfield 06804

H. & G. Randall, Inc. (ASCAP)
29 Elaine Rd.
Milford 06460

Rohm Music (BMI)
10 George St.
Wallingford 06492

Rustron Music Productions (BMI)
53 Chamberlain St.
New Haven 06512

South End Music (BMI)
P.O. Box 371
Rocky Hill 06067

Story Songs, Ltd. (ASCAP)
11 Bailey Ave.
Ridgefield 06877

Surron Music (BMI)
182 Allen St.
New Britain 06053

Take Home Tunes!
Box 496
Georgetown 06829

Yellow Earl Publishing (ASCAP)
70 Turner Hill Rd.
New Canaan 06840

DELAWARE

Beth-Ann Music Company (ASCAP)
615 Baldwin Ln.
Wilmington 19803

K–D Music (BMI)
111 Valley Rd.
Richardson Park
Wilmington 19804

DISTRICT OF COLUMBIA

Double Jon Publishing Company (BMI)
1750 16th St. N.W., Suite 704
Washington, DC 20009

Gallatin Gateway Music, Inc. (ASCAP)
2000 "P" St. N.W.
Washington, DC 20036

Jac–Wana (BMI)
P.O. Box 2875
Washington, DC 20013

Little City Publishing Company (BMI)
P.O. Box 1079
Washington, DC 20013

Shekere Music (BMI)
4409 Douglas St. N.E.
Washington, DC 20019

Showtime Publishing Company (BMI)
P.O. Box 40074
Washington, DC 20016

Tal-Fran (BMI)
5333 Astor Pl. S.E.
Washington, DC 20019

FLORIDA

Acropolis Publications (BMI)
4012 Oklahoma Ave.
Tampa 33616

Affiliated Music Entertainments
 Company
P.O. Box 1929
Melbourne 32901

Artsongs Publishing (ASCAP)
P.O. Box 15032
Fort Lauderdale 33318

BLB Music Corporation (ASCAP)
2501 South Ocean Dr.
Hollywood 33022

Beantown Publishing Company (BMI)
206 East Jordan St.
Pensacola 32503

Carlson Music Company (BMI)
4625 N.W. 44th St.
Fort Lauderdale 33319

Dana Publishing Company (BMI)
1130 Stillwater Dr.
Miami Beach 33141

Demarest Music Company (ASCAP)
719 Periwinkle Way
Sanibel 33957

Four Grand Music Publishers (BMI)
P.O. Box 460
Miami 33161

Gil Gilday Publishing Company
(ASCAP)
6730 Taft St.
Hollywood 33024

Gold Coast Music Publishing Company
8268 N.E. Miami Court
Miami 33138

Harrick Music, Inc. (BMI)
P.O. Box 1780
Hialeah 33011

Jay-Jay Publishing Company (BMI)
P.O. Box 4155, Normandy Branch
Miami Beach 33141

Edwin F. Kalmus & Company (ASCAP)
P.O. Box 1007
Opa Locka 33054

Kelton, Inc. (ASCAP)
3505 South Ocean Dr., Apt. 1421
Hollywood 33019

Lantana Music, Inc. (BMI)
P.O. Box 630175
Miami 33103

Mosie Lister Publications (SESAC)
11306 Carrollwood Dr.
Tampa 33618

Little Fugitive Music (BMI)
P.O. Box 15764
Sarasota 33579

Lubrano Music Publishers (BMI)
P.O. Box 952
Tampa 33601

Michavin Music (BMI)
P.O. Box 2061
Daytona Beach 32015

Miracle Strip Music Publishing (BMI)
25 North Devilliers St.
Pensacola 32501

Palamar Music Publishers (BMI)
726 Carlson Dr.
Orlando 32804

George Paxton Corporation (ASCAP)
836 Riomar Dr.
Vero Beach 32960

Pine Island Music (BMI)
P.O. Box 630175
Miami 33163

Pinellas Music (BMI)
1374 East Cleveland St.
Clearwater 33515

Platinum Music Publishing (ASCAP)
567 N.W. 27th St.
Miami 33127

Revolver Music (ASCAP)
P.O. Box 11321
St. Petersburg 33733

Rubank Inc. (ASCAP)
16215 N.W. 15th Ave.
Miami 33169

Schabraf Music (BMI)
P.O. Box T
Winter Park 32789

Seasun Experience Music Productions
P.O. Box 41425
Jacksonville 32203

Sherlyn Publishing Company (BMI)
495 S.E. 10th Ct.
Hialeah 33010

Sound Masters Commercial Recording
4702 S.W. 75th Ave.
Miami 33155

Tight Rope Music Publishing (BMI)
P.O. Box 1924
Fort Walton Beach 32548

Tweed Music Company (ASCAP)
1913 South Ocean Dr., Apt. 230
Hallandale 33009

Velezdy Music (ASCAP)
419 Fecco St.
Cocoa 32922

Velvet Music, Inc. (BMI)
10128 N.W. 80th Ave.
Hialeah Gardens 33016

Norm Vincent Publishing (BMI)
2110 The Wood Dr.
Jacksonville 32211

Watchour Music Company (BMI)
Box 209, Rte. 3
Palatka 32077

GEORGIA

Altaview Music Co. (BMI)
P.O. Box 557
Lithia Springs 30057

Atteiram Publishing Company (BMI)
P.O. Box 418
Smyrna 30080

Azinda Publications (BMI)
230 Peachtree St. N.W., #1800
Atlanta 30303

Boogie Bear Music (BMI)
3807 Norwich St.
Brunswick 31520

Bruboon Publishing Company (BMI)
P.O. Box 3388
Albany 31701

Bullwinkle Music Company (ASCAP)
P.O. Box 557
Lithia Springs 30057

Candlestick Publishing Company (BMI)
582–584 Armour Circle N.E.
Atlanta 30324

Charlie Boy Music Company (ASCAP)
1031 Wylie Rd., Lot 48
Marietta 30060

Commercial Studios (BMI)
412 Holley Dr. S.E.
Atlanta 30354

Charlie Dee Music Publishing (BMI)
1324 Old Yatesville Rd.
Thomaston 30286

Earnest Music (BMI)
6232 Lynridge Dr.
Columbus 31904

Focal Point Music Publishing (BMI)
922 McArthur Blvd.
Warner Robbins 31093

Genelle Music Company (BMI)
Box 986, Rte. 4
Tifton, 31794

Gullah Music Company (ASCAP)
174 11th St. N.E.
Atlanta 30309

Gusman (BMI)
1201½ E. Broad St.
Savannah 31402

Hustlers, Inc. (BMI)
602 Southern Trust Bldg.
Macon 31201

Mylon LeFevre (BMI)
P.O. Box 400
Atlanta 30301

Locity Music (BMI)
6700 Peachtree Industrial Blvd., #M-8
Atlanta 30340

Lowery Group
1224 Fernwood Circle
Atlanta 30319

Lyresong, Inc. (BMI)
1227 Spring St. N.W.
Atlanta 30309

Mimic Music (BMI)
P.O. Box 201
Smyrna 30081

New Mint Legume Publications (BMI)
P.O. Box 47147
Atlanta 30340

No Exit Music Company, Inc. (BMI)
535 Cotton Ave.
Macon 31201

Nuarts Music (BMI)
Box 737, Rte. 2
Lizella 31052

Pay Dirt Music (ASCAP)
1227 Spring St. N.W.
Atlanta 30309

Ralph's Radio Music (BMI)
P.O. Box 127, Hwy. 441
Demorest 30535

Rose Music
651-F Morosgo Dr. N.E.
Atlanta 30324

Seyah Music (BMI)
1227 Spring St. N.W.
Atlanta 30309

Starfox Publishing
P.O. Box 13584
Atlanta 30324

Trager Publishing Company (BMI)
799½ Martin Luther King Dr. N.W.
Atlanta 30314

Trolley Music (ASCAP)
3759 Main St.
College Park 30337

Tumac Music Publishing (ASCAP)
P.O. Box 7729
Atlanta 30337

Utopia Music (ASCAP)
P.O. Box 5314
Macon 31204

War Bonnet Music (BMI)
1743 Warm Springs Rd.
Columbus 31904

Web IV Music Inc. (BMI)
2107 Faulkner Rd.
Atlanta 30324

HAWAII

Five & A-Half B Music (BMI)
P.O. Box 932
Honolulu 96808

Hawaiian Recording & Publishing
Company (ASCAP)
P.O. Box 2061
Honolulu 96805

Melway Music Inc. (ASCAP)
Ala Moana Blvd., Suite 919
Honolulu 96814

New Child Music Publishing (ASCAP)
P.O. Box 524
Kailua-Kona 96740

Oahu Music Publishing (BMI)
1020 Auahi St.
Honolulu 96814

Panini Music (BMI)
P.O. Box 15808
Honolulu 96815

IDAHO

American Heritage Music Corporation
1208 Everett St.
Caldwell 83605

ILLINOIS

Amalgamated Tulip Corporation (BMI)
117 West Rockland Rd.
Libertyville 60048

Angelshell Music Corporation (BMI)
P.O. Box 49606
Chicago 60649

Angot Music Publisher (BMI)
5320 South Michigan Ave.
Chicago 60615

Athon Music Company (BMI)
26 West Benton Ave.
Naperville 60540

August Day Music, Inc. (BMI)
2630 N. Mannheim Rd.
Franklin Park 60131

Aven Music Publishing Company
(ASCAP)
3250 Irving Park
Chicago 60618

Black Kat Record Company Publishing
(BMI)
542 South Dearborn
Chicago 60605

Bula Records & Publishing Company
Rte. 1
Crossville 62827

CJ Publishing (BMI)
4827 South Prairie Ave.
Chicago 60615

Cameron Organization, Inc.
320 South Waiola Ave.
La Grange 60525

Cetra Music Corporation (BMI)
5828 South University Ave.
Chicago 60637

Clark Musical Productions (BMI)
P.O. Box 299
Watseka 60970

Clear Sky Music, Inc. (BMI)
2201 Lunt Ave.
Elk Grove Village 60007

M.M. Cole Publishing Company (BMI)
251 East Grand
Chicago 60611

Content Music (BMI)
1101 North Lockwood
Chicago 60651

Cool Duck Music (ASCAP)
2058 First St.
Highland Park 60035

Crescendo Music Sales Company
P.O. Box 395
Naperville 60540

Curtom Record Company
5915 North Lincoln Ave.
Chicago 60659

Deliverance Music Publishing (BMI)
Box 576
Libertyville 60048

Denture Whistle Music Company (BMI)
2513 North Major
Chicago 60639

Bernard L. Dixon Publishing (BMI)
7212 South Wabash Ave.
Chicago 60619

Don-Del (BMI)
15041 Wabash Ave.
S. Hallard 60473

Edgewater Music Inc. (BMI)
233 East Erie St.
Chicago 60611

Eyeball Music (BMI)
P.O. Box 11741
Chicago 60611

H.T. FitzSimons Company, Inc.
(SESAC)
615 North La Salle St.
Chicago 60610

Flying Fish Music (BMI)
3320 North Halsted
Chicago 60657

Mark Foster Music Company (ASCAP,
BMI)
P.O. Box 4012
Champaign 61820

Garamoni Music Publishing Company
(BMI)
676 North La Salle St.
Chicago 60610

Heno Publishing (BMI)
8959 South Oglesby
Chicago 60617

Hope Publishing Company (ASCAP)
Carol Stream 60817

House of Hi Ho (BMI)
P.O. Box 8135
Chicago 60680

Insurance Music (BMI)
11616 South Lafayette Ave.
Chicago 60628

Interplanetary Music (BMI)
7901 South La Salle
Chicago 60620

Jen-Shem Music Publishers (BMI)
39 Holiday Dr.
Somonauk 60552

Joba Music Company (BMI)
P.O. Box 266
River Forest 60305

June MHoon & Associates (ASCAP)
10519 South Forest
Chicago 60628

KRPCO Music (BMI)
4926 West Gunnison
Chicago 60630

Kathjeannes Music Company (BMI)
P.O. Box 1218
Chicago 60690

Neil A. Kjos Music Company (SESAC)
525 Busse Hwy.
Park Ridge 60068

Legut Music
494 Gregory Ave., 1-A
Glendale Heights 60137

Media Interstellar Music (BMI)
Box 20346
Chicago 60620

Midday Music Publishing (BMI)
233 East Erie St.
Chicago 60611

Mighty Chicago Music (BMI)
7363 South Shore Blvd., Suite 207
Chicago 60649

Ovation, Inc. Group
1249 Waukegan Rd.
Glenview 60025

PA Enterprises, Inc.
875 North Michigan Ave., Suite 5404
Chicago 60611

Pel Music (BMI)
1936 North Clark St.
Chicago 60614

Planned That Way Music (BMI)
1547 North Larrabee
Chicago 60610

Raft Ventures
300 North State St., No. 4712
Chicago 60610

Rawlins Music
1757 North Mohawk
Chicago 60614

Rich-Lo Publishing Company
600 South Ninth Ave.
LaGrange 60525

Rowilco (BMI)
P.O. Box 8135
Chicago 60680

Semerak Publishing Company (BMI)
4327 South Sacramento Ave.
Chicago 60632

Shelview Publications Company (BMI)
4148 South King Dr.
Chicago 60653

The Staples Music
255 E. 103rd St.
Chicago 60628

Stone Row Music Company (BMI)
2022 Vardon Lane
Flossmoor 60422

Summy-Birchard Company (ASCAP)
1834 Ridge Ave.
Evanston 60204

3-Deal Music (BMI)
2123 North Seminary Ave.
Chicago 60614

Trice Publishing Company (BMI)
9006 South Ridgeland
Chicago 60617

Trouserworm Tunes (BMI)
P.O. Box 701
Champaign 61820

Ul-Trac Publishing Company (BMI)
10358 South Forest Ave.
Chicago 60628

Ultra-Nova Publishing (ASCAP)
501 East Providence
Palatine 60067

Vitak-Elsnic Company (SESAC)
6400A S. Woodward Ave.
Downers Grove 60515

Warus (BMI)
1410 East 72nd St.
Chicago 60619

Winner Music (BMI)
c/o International Recording Co.
1649 West Evergreen
Chicago 60622

INDIANA

Canal Publishing, Inc. (BMI)
6325 Guilford
Indianapolis 46220

Gaither Music Company, Inc. (ASCAP)
P.O. Box 300
Alexandria 46001

Hoosier Hill Publishing (BMI)
1309 Celesta Way
Sellersburg 47172

Jade Ring Publishing (BMI)
P.O. Box 561
Terre Haute 47808

Mishawaka Music (BMI)
2420 River Ave.
Mishawaka 46544

Pinpoint Publishing Company (BMI)
c/o Little Nashville Records
Box 137, Rte. 3
Nashville 47448

Rodeheaver Company (ASCAP)
P.O. Box 337
Winona Lake 46590

Seven Hills Publishing Company (BMI)
905 North Main St.
Evansville 47711

Slingshot Music (BMI)
1330 North Illinois St.
Indianapolis 46202

Studio P/R, Inc. (BMI)
224 South Lebanon St.
Lebanon 46052

IOWA

Amphora Music Corporation (BMI)
1727 Division St.
Davenport 52804

C.L. Barnhouse Company (SESAC)
110 "B" Ave.
Oskaloosa 52577

Love Street Publishing Company (BMI)
900 County Line Rd.
W. Des Moines 50265

Mamba Music (BMI)
12 Pine Ridge Court
Clinton 52732

Mid-America Music (ASCAP)
155 First St.
Carlisle 50047

Monroe-Ames Music (BMI)
Box 871
Ames 50010

Okoboji Music Publishing Company
906 Ninth St.
Milford 51351

Silvertree Music (BMI)
4015 Muskogee Ave.
Des Moines 50312

Timberland Publishing (BMI)
Forest City 50436

KANSAS

Al's Written Music Publishers (BMI)
1313 Washington
Parsons 67357

Brickbert Music (BMI)
6801 West 76th St.
Overland Park 66205

Great Leawood Music, Inc. (ASCAP)
8103 Overbrook Rd.
Leawood 66206

Inner-Glo Music Company (BMI)
15 South Washington St.
Emporia 66801

Rabbitt One Music Publishing (BMI)
P.O. Box 1997
Wichita 67201

Steve's Crusade Music Publishers (BMI)
2500 Grand Ave.
Parsons 67357

Stone Post Publishing (BMI)
P.O. Box 1213
Emporia 66801

KENTUCKY

Falls City Music (BMI)
9701 Taylorsville Rd.
Louisville 40299

Hand Made Music (BMI)
514 Apache Dr.
Hopkinsville 42240

Lemco Music Publishing Company (BMI)
P.O. Box 8013
Lexington 40503

Jimmy Price Music Publisher (BMI)
1662 Wyatt Pkwy.
Lexington 40505

Trusty Publications (BMI)
Nebo 42441

Willis Music Company (SESAC)
7380 Industrial Rd.
Florence 41042

Working Man's Music (BMI)
155 Walton-Nicholson Pike
Walton 41904

LOUISIANA

John Berthelot & Associates (ASCAP)
P.O. Box 30029
New Orleans 70190

Big Deal Music Publishing Company
(BMI)
Box 60-A
Cheneyville 71325

Cabriolet Music (BMI)
P.O. Box 7422
Shreveport 71107

Cajun Publishing Company, Inc. (BMI)
P.O. Box 1130
Shreveport 71120

Cosmic Q, Inc. (BMI)
1536 Terpsichore St.
New Orleans 70130

Days Of Old Publishing Company
3116 Metairie Rd.
Metairie 70001

Flat Town Music (BMI)
P.O. Drawer 10
Ville Platte 70586

Jake-Carl Publications (BMI)
744 North Main St.
Opelousas 70570

Jamil Music (BMI)
413 North Parkerson Ave.
Crowley 70526

Jon Music (BMI)
39 West Main
Church Point 70525

La Lou Music (BMI)
711 Stevenson St.
Lafayette 70501

Marsaint Music, Inc. (BMI)
3809 Clematis Ave.
New Orleans 70122

Matzo Ball Music (BMI)
316 Riverside Mall
Baton Rouge 70801

Nasetan Publishing Company (BMI)
P.O. Box 1485
Lake Charles 70602

Orchid Publishing (BMI)
P.O. Box 4220
Shreveport 71104

Rogan Publications
3316 Line Ave.
Shreveport 71104

Sapphire Music Publishers (BMI)
2815 Octavia St.
New Orleans 70115

Scales of Justice Music, Inc. (BMI)
P.O. Box 2609
Lafayette 70502

Sound of America (BMI)
P.O. Box 15110
New Orleans 70175

Su-Ma Publishing Company (BMI)
P.O. Box 1125
Shreveport 71163

Thistle Productions (ASCAP)
6560 Colbert St.
New Orleans 70124

TouPat Music Publishing (BMI)
402 Shotwell Ave.
Monroe 71201

Tune-Kel Publishing (BMI)
715 Camp St.
New Orleans 70130

Zora Delta (BMI)
P.O. Box 15582
New Orleans 70130

MAINE

Darleen Music Publishing Company
(BMI)
10 Hardy Rd.
Westbrook 04092

MARYLAND

Blind Basement Music (BMI)
P.O. Box 288
Silver Spring 20907

Bouldin Music Publishing (BMI)
P.O. Box 1375
Baltimore 21203

Country Showcase (BMI)
11350 Baltimore Ave.
Beltsville 20705

Dawn Productions
P.O. Box 535
Belair 21014

Dimitri Music Company (BMI)
7859 Bastille Pl.
Severn 21144

Farmer & Thomas Music (BMI)
P.O. Box 1257
Landover 20785

Folkstone Music Publishing Company
(BMI)
Box 388, Rte. 4
Deer Park 21550

Free Soul Music (BMI)
5115 Glassmanor Dr.
Oxon Hill 20021

Juldane Music Company (BMI)
8037 13th St.
Silver Spring 20910

Kaymar Music (BMI)
P.O. Box 624
Ellicott City 21043

Mag Music (BMI)
P.O. Box 1493
Landover 21285

Red Robin Records Corporation
1728 Presstman St.
Baltimore 21217

Seal Publishing Company (BMI)
13310 Collingwood Terr.
Silver Spring 20904

Henry J. Sommers (ASCAP)
P.O. Box 322
Silver Spring 20907

S'one Songs (BMI)
826 South Conkling St.
Baltimore 21224

Up Tight (BMI)
2104 Lake Ave.
Baltimore 21218

MASSACHUSETTS

Boston Music Company (ASCAP)
116 Boylston St.
Boston 02116

Castle Hill Publishing, Ltd. (ASCAP)
P.O. Box 529
Townsend 01469

Clear Light Productions, Inc. (ASCAP)
P.O. Box 391
Newton 02158

Critique Music Publishing Company
(BMI)
125 Main St.
Reading 01867

Donna Marie Music Publishing
(ASCAP)
P.O. Box 113
Woburn 01801

Drayeniv Music Publishing Company
(BMI)
P.O. Box 934
Edgartown 02539

Elf Music (BMI)
P.O. Box 404, Astor St. Sta.
Boston 02123

Happy Valley Music (BMI)
186 Willow Ave.
Somerville 02144

Hyannis Music Publications (BMI)
622 Rte. 3A
Cohasset 02025

Jay Six Publishing Company (BMI)
19 Ledge Hill Rd.
West Roxbury 02132

Long Sought After Pond Publications
P.O. Box 338, Essex Sta.
Boston 02112

Mainsail Music (BMI)
1126 Boylston St.
Boston, 02215

Newport Music Company (ASCAP)
1105 Little Bldg.
80 Boylston St.
Boston 02116

New Valley Music Press
Sage Hall, Smith College
Northampton 01063

Periscope Music Company (BMI)
129 Bishop St.
Brockton 02402

E.C. Schirmer Music Company (ASCAP)
112 South St.
Boston 02111

Standard–Colonial Music (BMI)
Bldg. 8, 6 Gill St.
Woburn 01801

MICHIGAN

Art Audio Publishing Company (BMI)
9706 Cameron St.
Detroit 48211

Big Willie Music (BMI)
5004 West Francis Rd.
Clio 48420

Birge Music (BMI)
19230 James Couzens Fwy.
Detroit 48235

Brian-James Music Company (BMI)
3100 South Airport
Bridgeport 48722

Bridgeport Music Inc. (BMI)
19631 West Eight Mile Rd.
Detroit 48219

Chetkay Music (BMI)
8880 Hubbell
Detroit 48228

Chris Music Publishing Company (BMI)
P.O. Box 207
Manistique 49854

Davida Recording & Publishing
Company
9700 Burnette
Detroit 48204

Del–Jon Music Company (ASCAP)
11478 Timken
Warren 48089

Empire Music Company (BMI)
P.O. Box 413
Port Huron 48060

Endeavor Music (ASCAP)
30064 Annapolis Circle
Inkster 48141

Ernkel Music Company (BMI)
20414 Warrington Dr.
Detroit 48221

Flem Music (BMI)
8986 Birwood
Detroit 48204

Fortune Hi-Q Records
3942 Third Ave.
Detroit 48201

Golden Dawn Music (BMI)
20855 Pickford
Detroit 48219

Groovesville Productions, Inc.
15855 Wyoming Ave.
Detroit 48238

Heavy Hank Publishing (BMI)
1644 Glynn Court
Detroit 48206

Hot Bullet Music
5629 Beech Daly Rd. North
Dearborn Heights 48127

Insanity's Music (BMI)
24548 Pierce
Southfield 48075

Jaymore Publishing Company (BMI)
6260 Meyer St.
Brighton 48116

Jibaro Music Company (BMI)
P.O. Box 424
Mt. Clements 48043

KellGriff Music Publishing, Inc. (BMI)
20021 James Couzens Fwy.
Detroit 48235

La-Car Publishers (BMI)
3150 Francis St.
Jackson 49203

Lucky's Kum-Ba-Ya Publishing
(ASCAP)
P.O. Box 6
Brohman 49312

Manfred Music (BMI)
27335 Penn St.
Inkster 48141

Muzacan Publishing Company (BMI)
44844 Michigan Ave.
Canton 48188

Neostat Music Company (BMI)
425 Bryn Mawr
Birmingham 48009

Nine Mile Music
24266 Roxana
East Detroit 48021

Olenik Records (ASCAP)
G–10282 North Saginaw Rd.
Clio 48420

Patlow Publications Company (BMI)
17429 Indian Ave.
Detroit 48240

Johnny Powers Music (BMI)
3384 West 12 Mile Rd.
Berkley 48072

Publishing People, Inc. (ASCAP)
635 Elm St.
Birmingham 48011

Reksirb Music Publishing (BMI)
10169 Violetlawn
Detroit 48204

Singspiration, Inc. (SESAC)
1415 Lake Dr. S.E.
Grand Rapids 49506

Sound, Inc. Music (BMI)
56880 North Ave.
New Haven 48048

Tru-Soul Publishing Company (BMI)
26645 West 12 Mile Rd., Suite 211
Southfield 48034

Valco Music Publishing (BMI)
1327 Cobb Ave.
Kalamazoo 49007

Villa Reserve Music (BMI)
Box 32, Rte. 2
Vandalia 49095

We Productions, Inc.
14744 Puritan
Detroit 48227

The Word of God Music
P.O. Box 87
Ann Arbor 48107

MINNESOTA

Augsburg Publishing House (SESAC)
526 South Fifth St.
Minneapolis 55415

Dawn-Glo Publishing
29 North 59th Ave. West
Duluth 55807

Front Page Music (BMI)
642 Monroe St. N.E.
Minneapolis 55413

Gentilly Music Publishing (BMI)
P.O. Box 536
Crookston 56716

Gravy Publishing Company (BMI)
2541 Nicollet Ave. South
Minneapolis 55404

Heights (BMI)
4315 University Ave. N.E.
Minneapolis 55421

Hal Leonard Publishing Corporation
(ASCAP)
960 East Mark St.
Winona 55987

Lingua–Musica (BMI)
11225 Ewing Circle
Minneapolis 55431

Linton Music Publishing (BMI)
226 Cedar Lake Rd. South
Minneapolis 55405

Minniepaul Music Publishing (BMI)
7440 Olson Hwy.
Minneapolis 55427

Portage Publishing Company (BMI)
16634 Gannon West
Rosemount 55068

Sanskrit Publishing Company (ASCAP)
7515 Wayzata Blvd., No. 110
Minneapolis 55426

Schmitt Publications (SESAC)
110 North Fifth St.
Minneapolis 55403

Spare Changes Music
Snake Trail
Cushing 56443

Starlet Music Company (ASCAP)
7129 Augsburg Ave.
Minneapolis 55423

Symposium Music Publishing, Inc.
(BMI)
204 Fifth Ave. S.E.
Minneapolis 55414

Tektra Publishing (BMI)
711 West Broadway
Minneapolis 55411

Three-Penny Music Publishing (BMI)
P.O. Box 755
Minneapolis 55440

MISSISSIPPI

Johnny Angle Publishing (BMI)
2224 Belvedere Dr.
Jackson 39204

Axent Music (ASCAP)
P.O. Box 552
Biloxi 39533

Coach & Four Music (BMI)
1024 Third Ave. North
Columbus 39701

Jamvah Music, Inc. (BMI)
P.O. Box 10530
Jackson 39203

Malaco Music Company (BMI)
3023 West Northside Dr.
Jackson 39213

Paulmond Music (BMI)
P.O. Box 67
Wesson 39191

Singing River Publishing Company (BMI)
205 Acacia St.
Biloxi 39530

Whitsett Churchill Music (BMI)
4403 Manhattan Dr.
Jackson 39206

MISSOURI

Earl Barton Music, Inc. (BMI)
1121 South Glenstone
Springfield 65804

Mel Bay Publications
Pacific 63069

Best Bet Music (ASCAP)
106 West Madison
Kirkwood 63122

Briarmeade Music Unlimited (ASCAP)
2008 South 39th St.
St. Louis 63119

Albert E. Brumley & Sons (SESAC)
Powell 65730

Clayton-Davis & Associates, Inc. (BMI)
8229 Maryland St.
St. Louis 63105

Concordia Publishing House (SESAC)
3558 South Jefferson Ave.
St. Louis 63118

Contemporary Mission Music (BMI)
P.O. Box 21
St. Louis 63166

Country Stream Music (BMI)
Box 2644
St. Louis 63116

Frandoro Music, Inc. (BMI)
8 Heather Dr.
St. Louis 63123

Joe Keene Music Company (BMI)
P.O. Box 602
Kennett 63857

Lillenas Publishing Company (SESAC)
P.O. Box 527
Kansas City 64141

Louie B. Publishing Company (BMI)
4201 Locust St., No. 404
Kansas City 64110

Masterclase Music Publications (BMI)
P.O. Box 234
St. Louis 63166

Nada Music & Records (ASCAP)
P.O. Box 248
Lutesville 63762

Palaco Musical Enterprises, Inc. (ASCAP)
4545 Van Brunt
Kansas City 64130

Peak Publishing (BMI)
12 East 39th
Kansas City 64111

Quinones Music Company (BMI)
1344 Waldron
St. Louis 63130

SAICO Publishing Company (BMI)
4521 Natural Bridge
St. Louis 63115

Starco Music Publishing (BMI)
3211 Park Ave.
St. Louis 63104

Value Music Publications (BMI)
501 West 11th St., Rm. 515
Kansas City 64105

Wyandotte Music (ASCAP)
25 East 12th St.
Kansas City 64106

NEBRASKA

Beef State Publishing Company (BMI)
Box 14267
Omaha 68114

Flin-Flon Music (BMI)
P.O. Box 103
Mullen 69152

Jim Hall Production (ASCAP)
P.O. Box 975
Norfolk 68701

Peter Jan Publishing (BMI)
2313 South 49th Ave.
Omaha 68106

Sound Packages (BMI)
2322 South 64th Ave.
Omaha 68106

NEVADA

Apocalypse Music (SESAC)
1321 Hewitt
Las Vegas 89106

Billy Bob Publishing, Inc. (BMI)
2251 Casey Ave.
Las Vegas 89119

Corda Music, Inc. (ASCAP)
3398 Nahatan Way
Las Vegas 89109

Demisole Music Publishing (ASCAP)
4139 Meadow Glen Circle
Las Vegas 89121

Derby Music (SESAC)
3977 Vegas Valley Dr.
Las Vegas 89121

Luba Music (ASCAP)
P.O. Box 42696
Las Vegas 89104

Northchester Music, Inc. (ASCAP)
1515 Westwood Dr.
Las Vegas 89102

Thackaberry Music (ASCAP)
401 East Fremont
Las Vegas 89101

Weslou Music
P.O. Box 10044
Las Vegas 89119

White Eagle Publishing (BMI)
P.O. Box 5606
Las Vegas 89102

NEW HAMPSHIRE

Jaspar Music Publishing Company (BMI)
852 Elm St.
Manchester 03101

NEW JERSEY

Andira Publishing Company (ASCAP)
41 Central Ave.
Newark 07102

Ascension Music (ASCAP)
P.O. Box 2484
Trenton 08607

Ashley Publications, Inc. (BMI)
263 Veterans Blvd.
Carlstadt 07072

Big Hurry Music Company, Inc.
(ASCAP)
321 Commercial Ave.
Palisades Park 07650

Boca Music, Inc. (ASCAP)
532 Sylvan Ave.
Englewood Cliffs 07632

Joseph Boonin, Inc. (ASCAP)
P.O. Box 2124
South Hackensack 07606

Capano Music (ASCAP)
237 Chestnut St.
Westville 08093

Ciano Publishing Company (BMI)
P.O. Box 263
Hasbrouck Heights 07604

Danmar Internations (BMI)
145 Komorn St.
Newark 07105

Dirty Martha Music Company (BMI)
6015 Pleasant ave.
Pennsauken 08110

Eden Music Corporation/Iza Music
Corporation
P.O. Box 325
Englewood 07631

Farr Music, Inc. (BMI)
Box 1098
Somerville 08876

Friday's Child Music (BMI)
38 Pelham Rd.
Marlton 08053

Glori Gospel Music (BMI)
110 Academy St.
Jersey City 07302

Goydish Music & Publishing Company
(BMI)
P.O. Box 24
Belle Mead 08502

Hot Pot Music (BMI)
327 Columbia Ave.
Stratford 08084

Joka Music (BMI)
403 Summit St.
Vineland 08360

Leigh Group, Inc.
530 James St.
Lakewood 08701

Maranta Music Publishing Company
(BMI)
P.O. Box 1005
Englewood Cliffs 07632

Bob May Publishing (BMI)
735 Lincoln Blvd.
Middlesex 08846

Miracle-Joy Publications (BMI)
425 Park St.
Hackensack 07601

Missle Music Publishing (BMI)
1933 Birchwood Park Dr.
Cherry Hill 08003

Never Ending Music (BMI)
P.O. Box 58
Glendora 08029

Package Good Music (BMI)
1145 Green St.
Manville 08835

Paganiniana Publications, Inc.
211 West Sylvania Ave.
Neptune 07753

Perla Music (ASCAP)
20 Martha St.
Woodcliff Lake 07675

Playwell Music Company, Inc.
P.O. Box 848
North Arlington 07032

Positive Productions (BMI)
P.O. Box 1405
Highland Park 08904

Jesse G. Principato Music (BMI)
124 Valley Brook Ave.
Lyndhurst 07071

Rob-Lee Music (BMI)
P.O. Box 1385
Merchantville 08109

Sandman Music Publishing (ASCAP)
6 Morris Ave.
Montville 07045

Savgos Music (BMI)
625 Pennsylvania Ave.
Elizabeth 07201

Seven of Us Music (BMI)
26 Mountain Ave.
Dover 07801

Martin Sherry Music (BMI)
467 Mundet Place
Hillside 07205

Springboard Music Publishing
947 U.S. Hwy. 1
Rahway 07065

Trajames Music (ASCAP)
11 Harrison Court
South Orange 07079

Virginia Music Company (BMI)
209 Main St.
Fort Lee 07024

Wizdom Music Company (ASCAP)
11 Harrison Court
South Orange 07079

NEW MEXICO

Astronette Publishing Company (BMI)
2037 Alvarado Dr. N.E.
Albuquerque 87110

Enchantment Music Company (BMI)
P.O. Box 998
Mesilla Park 88047

Little Richie Johnson Music Company
(BMI)
P.O. Box 3
Belen 87002

Kimkris Music (BMI)
202 Wisconsin St. N.E.
Albuquerque 87108

Stinger Music Corporation (BMI)
P.O. Box 8207
Albuquerque 87108

Striking Music Publishing (BMI)
1927 San Mateo N.E.
Albuquerque 87110

NEW YORK

Abkco Music, Inc. (BMI)
1700 Broadway
New York 10019

A Dish-A Tunes, Ltd. (BMI)
1674 Broadway, No. 603
New York 10019

Adra Music Publishing Company (BMI)
113 West 70th St., No. 5A
New York 10023

Alabaster Music, Inc. (ASCAP)
250 West 57th St.
New York 10019

J. Albert & Son Pty., Ltd.
4 East 52nd St.
New York 10022

Al-Bo Music Company (ASCAP)
37 Odell Ave.
Yonkers 10701

Al-Do (ASCAP)
37 Odell Ave.
Yonkers 10701

Allied Artists Music Company (ASCAP)
15 Columbus Circle
New York 10023

Alpha Music, Inc. (BMI)
40 East 49th St.
New York 10017

American Composers Alliance (BMI)
170 West 74th St.
New York 10023

Andustin Music (ASCAP)
P.O. Box 669
Woodstock 12498

Antisia Music, Inc. (ASCAP)
1650 Broadway, Suite 1001
New York 10019

April Blackwood Music, Inc.
1350 Ave. of the Americas, 23rd Flr.
New York 10019

Arc Music Corporation (BMI)
110 East 59th St.
New York 10022

Arista Music Publishing Group
6 West 57th St.
New York 10019

Arlo Publishing/Bearce Publishing
7653 Telephone Rd.
LeRoy 14482

Arnakata Music, Inc. (ASCAP)
c/o Kurtz & Vassallo PC
598 Madison Ave.
New York 10022

Artref Publishing
846 Seventh Ave.
New York 10019

Associated Music Publishers (BMI)
866 Third Ave.
New York 10022

Aulos Music Publishers
P.O. Box 54
Montgomery 12549

Baby Tate Music Corporation (BMI)
P.O. Drawer AB
Rosendale 12472

Bacardi Publications (ASCAP)
3235 Emmons Ave.
Brooklyn 11235

Bach-Trac Music, Inc. (ASCAP)
315 East 86th St.
New York 10028

Balanced Music (BMI)
166-26 89th Ave.
Jamaica 11432

M. Baron Company
P.O. Box 149
Oyster Bay 11771

Barton Music Corporation (ASCAP)
249 East 62nd St.
New York 10021

Beldock, Levine & Hoffman
565 Fifth Ave.
New York 10017

Belwin-Mills Publishing Corporation
16 West 61st St.
New York 10023

Benner Publishers (ASCAP)
1739 Randolph Rd.
Schenectady 12308

Phil Bennett Music Company (ASCAP)
1 East 42nd St.
New York 10017

Irving Berlin Music Corporation (ASCAP)
1290 Ave. of the Americas
New York 10019

Big Boro Publishing Corporation
1700 Broadway
New York 10019

Big Mike Music (BMI)
408 West 115th St.
New York 10025

Big Pumpkin Music (BMI)
75 Rockefeller Plaza
New York 10019

Big Seven Music Corporation (BMI)
17 West 60th St.
New York 10023

Big Sky Music (ASCAP)
P.O. Box 216, Cooper Sta.
New York 10003

Biograph Music, Inc. (ASCAP)
16 River St.
Chatham 12037

Eubie Blake Music (ASCAP)
284–A Stuyvesant Ave.
Brooklyn 11221

Blanchris Music (BMI)
160 West 71st St.
New York 10023

Eric Blau Music Inc. (BMI)
251 West 92nd St.
New York 10025

Blue Umbrella Music Publishing
(ASCAP)
3011 Beach 40 St., Sea Gate
Brooklyn 11224

BO Cult Songs, Inc. (ASCAP)
23 Green St.
Huntington 11743

Boosey & Hawkes, Inc. (ASCAP)
30 West 57th St.
New York 10019

Botanical Music (BMI)
166–26 89th Ave.
Jamaica 11432

Bourne Company (ASCAP)
1212 Ave. of the Americas
New York 10036

Tommy Boyle Music (BMI)
84A Rte. 66
East Nassau 12062

Brooklyn Heights Music (ASCAP)
124 Montague St.
Brooklyn 11201

Brookside Music Corporation (ASCAP)
159 West 53rd St.
New York 10019

Alexander Broude, Inc.
225 West 57th St.
New York 10019

Broude Brothers, Ltd. (ASCAP)
56 West 45th St.
New York 10036

Brut Music Publishing (ASCAP)
1345 Ave. of the Americas
New York 10019

Buddah Music, Inc. (ASCAP)
810 Seventh Ave.
New York 10019

Burlington Music Corporation (ASCAP)
539 West 25th St.
New York 10001

Buttermilk Sky Music Publishing (BMI)
545 Madison Ave.
New York 10022

Bygosh Music Corporation (ASCAP)
50 West 23rd St.
New York 10010

CAM Productions (BMI)
489 Fifth Ave.
New York 10017

Caligula, Inc. (ASCAP)
1 Hudson St.
New York 10013

Can't Stop Music (BMI)
65 East 55th St.
New York 10022

Capaquarius Publishing (ASCAP)
2400 Johnson Ave.
Riverdale 10463

Don Casale Music (ASCAP)
377 Plainfield St.
Westbury 11590

Catalogue Music, Inc. (BMI)
870 Seventh Ave., Suite 348
New York 10019

Ceberg Music Corporation (ASCAP)
c/o Bergen-Whitelaw Productions, Ltd.
159 West 53rd St., Suite 23A
New York 10019

Ceilidh Productions, Inc. (ASCAP)
350 West 51st St.
New York 10019

Chappell Music Company
810 Seventh Ave.
New York 10019

Charing Cross Music, Inc. (BMI)
36 East 61st St.
New York 10021

Chrysalis Music Corporation (ASCAP)
115 East 57th St.
New York 10022

Cimino Publications, Inc. (ASCAP)
P.O. Box 75
Farmingdale 11735

Clara Music Publishing Corporation
(ASCAP)
c/o Leventhal
250 West 57th St., Suite 2017
New York 10019

Clave Music Publishing, Inc. (ASCAP)
747 10th Ave.
New York 10019

Coco Music, Inc. (BMI)
1700 Broadway
New York 10019

Comreco Music, Inc. (ASCAP)
3 Kensington Oval
New Rochelle 10805

Condominium Publishing Group (BMI)
P.O. Box 5473, Grand Central Sta.
New York 10010

Controlled Sheet Music Services, Inc.
112 Hudson St.
Copiague 11726

Copyright Service Bureau, Ltd.
221 West 57th St.
New York 10019

Cotillion Music, Inc. (BMI)
75 Rockefeller Plaza
New York 10019

Cousins Music, Inc. (BMI)
382 East Fordham Rd.
Bronx 10458

Creative Funk Music, Inc. (ASCAP)
122-21 Merrick Blvd.
St. Albans 11431

Croma Music Company (ASCAP)
37 West 57th St.
New York 10019

Crushing Music (BMI)
200 W. 57th St.
New York 10019

Daksel Music Corporation (BMI)
65 West 55th St.
New York 10019

Damila Music, Inc. (ASCAP)
1650 Broadway
New York 10019

Damit Music (BMI)
108 Sherman Ave.
New York 10034

Dantroy Music (BMI)
c/o Edward Germano Productions, Inc.
353 West 48th St.
New York 10036

David Music (BMI)
1650 Broadway
New York 10019

Joe Davis (ASCAP)
70 Riverside Dr.
New York 10024

Deacon Daniel Music (ASCAP)
17 Ann
Ossining 10562

Deep Blue Music (BMI)
30 Lark Dr.
Woodbury 11797

Pietro Deiro Publications (SESAC)
113 Seventh Ave. South
New York 10014

Denton & Haskins Corporation
(ASCAP)
P.O. Box 340, Radio City Sta.
New York 10019

Dobro Publishing Company (BMI)
Box 49, Rte. 1
Utica 13502

Dunbar Music, Inc. (BMI)
1133 Ave. of the Americas
New York 10036

Dward Music (ASCAP)
P.O. Box 187, Cooper Sta.
New York 10003

Dy-Cor, Inc. (BMI)
792 Columbus Ave., Apt. 10A
New York 10025

EMP Company (BMI)
40 West 57th St.
New York 10019

Earthling Music (ASCAP)
110 West 86th St.
New York 10024

Elvee-Deekay Music, Inc. (ASCAP)
350 West 51st St.
New York 10019

Elvis Music, Inc. (BMI)
1619 Broadway
New York 10019

Emko Music Corporation (BMI)
P.O. Box 176
Monsey 10952

Erva Publishing Company, Inc. (BMI)
200 West 57th St., Suite 1404
New York 10019

Experience Group, Ltd.
P.O. Box 767
New York 10019

Fairyland Music Corporation (ASCAP)
159 West 53rd St.
New York 10019

Fallenwood Publishing Group (BMI)
470 Smith St.
Farmingdale 11735

Famous Music Corporation (ASCAP)
1 Gulf + Western Plaza
New York 10023

Fania Publishing Company, Inc. (BMI)
888 Seventh Ave.
New York 10019

Fennario Music Publishers, Inc.
(ASCAP)
71 West 23rd St.
New York 10010

Carl Fisher, Inc. (ASCAP)
62 Cooper Square
New York 10003

Fisher Music Corporation (ASCAP)
1619 Broadway
New York 10019

Fist-O-Funk, Ltd. (BMI)
293 Richard Court
Pomona 10970

Folksways Music Publishers (BMI)
10 Columbus Circle
New York 10019

Fort Knox Music Company (BMI)
1619 Broadway
New York 10019

Forum Music Publications
49 Murdock Court
Brooklyn 11223

Fourth Floor Music, Inc. (ASCAP)
75 East 55th St., Suite 404
New York 10022

Fredola Music Publishing Company
(BMI)
7–11 East Genesse St.
Auburn 13021

From Now On, Inc.
225 West 57th St., Suite 602
New York 10019

Front Line Music, Inc. (ASCAP)
43 Perry St.
New York 10014

Galaxy Music Corporation (ASCAP)
2121 Broadway
New York 10023

Al Gallico Music Corporation (BMI)
65 West 55th St.
New York 10019

Gaucho Music (BMI)
161 West 54th St.
New York 10019

General Music Publishing Company,
Inc. (ASCAP)
P.O. Box 267
Hastings-on-Hudson 10706

Gil Music Corporation (BMI)
1650 Broadway
New York 10019

Glad Hamp Music, Inc.
(ASCAP)
1995 Broadway
New York 10023

Golden West Melodies (BMI)
110 East 59th St.
New York 10022

Manny Gold Music Publishers (ASCAP)
895 McDonald Ave.
Brooklyn 11218

Gospel Birds, Inc. (BMI)
250 West 57th St.
New York 10019

Gospel Clef Publishing Company (BMI)
279 Buffalo Ave.
Brooklyn 11213

Great Metropolitan Music (BMI)
240 West 55th St.
New York 10019

Green Menu Music Company (ASCAP)
50 West 57th St.
New York 10019

Green Mountain Music Corp. (BMI)
1650 Broadway, Suite 1011
New York 10019

Gudi Music (BMI)
157 West 57th St.
New York 10019

Gunhill Road Music Corporation
(ASCAP)
149 Bleecker St.
New York 10012

Hargail Music Press (ASCAP)
28 West 38th St.
New York 10018

Lee Hazlewood Music Corporation
(ASCAP)
1501 Broadway, 30th Flr.
New York 10036

Helios Music Corporation (BMI)
1619 Broadway, Suite 603a
New York 10019

Higher Music Publishing (ASCAP)
36 East 61st St.
New York 10021

Hob & Nob Music Publishers (BMI)
158 West 15th St., Suite 2D
New York 10011

Hollie-Har Music Company (ASCAP)
42 Chapman Ave.
Auburn 13021

Hot Damn Again (ASCAP)
130 West 42nd St.
New York 10036

Tash Howard Music Group
1697 Broadway
New York 10019

Hudson Bay Music Company (BMI)
1619 Broadway
New York 10019

Integrity Music Corporation (ASCAP)
1050 Fifth Ave.
New York 10028

Intercontinental Entertainment
1650 Broadway
New York 10019

The International Music Company
(ASCAP)
214 West 96th St.
New York 10025

Interval Music (BMI)
414 East 52nd St.
New York 10022

Italian Book Corporation
1119 Shore Pkwy.
Brooklyn 11214

JBP Music Corporation (ASCAP)
c/o Pryor, Cashman & Sherman
410 Park Ave.
New York 10022

JWT-Music, Inc. (ASCAP)
420 Lexington Ave.
New York 10017

Jackelope Music, Inc.
565 Fifth Ave., Rm. 601
New York 10017

Dick James Music, Inc. (BMI)
119 West 57th St.
New York 10019

Jepalana Music (BMI)
723 Seventh Ave.
New York 10019

Jimpire Music, Inc. (BMI)
110 East 59th St.
New York 10022

Joli Music, Inc. (BMI)
1619 Broadway
New York 10019

Jomewa Music
135 East 65th St.
New York 10023

Jova Music, Inc. (ASCAP)
159 West 53rd St.
New York 10019

Kack Klick (BMI)
645 Titus Ave.
Rochester 14617

Kamakazi Music Corporation (BMI)
1650 Broadway, Suite 701
New York 10019

Bob Karcy Music (ASCAP, BMI)
437 West 16th St.
New York 10011

KasKat Music, Inc. (BMI)
323 East Shore Rd.
Great Neck 11023

Katch Nazar Music (ASCAP)
3929 New Seneca Tpke.
Marcellus 13108

Kendor Music Inc. (SESAC)
Main & Grove Sts.
Delevan 14042

Kenwood Music, Inc. (BMI)
747 Third Ave., 27th Floor
New York 10017

Kipahula Music Company (ASCAP)
c/o Colgems-EMI Music Inc.
New York 10022

Charles Kipps Music, Inc. (BMI)
1 Lincoln Plaza
New York 10023

Don Kirshner Music, Inc. (BMI)
1370 Ave. of the Americas
New York 10019

Klondike Enterprises, Ltd. (BMI)
888 Seventh Ave.
New York 10019

Knud-Feldt Music Company (BMI)
78-08 88th Ave.
Woodhaven 11421

Kool Kat Music (BMI)
39 South Main St.
Spring Valley 10977

Kropotkin (ASCAP)
273 New York Ave.
Huntington 11743

LF Music Group
c/o Famous Music
1 Gulf + Western Plaza
New York 10023

Laurel Canyon Music, Ltd. (ASCAP)
75 East 55th St.
New York 10022

Lea Pocket Scores
P.O. Box 138, Audubon Sta.
New York 10032

Cora Lee Music (BMI)
133 North St.
Rochester 14604

Lennon Music (BMI)
1370 Ave. of the Americas
New York 10019

Lou Levy Music Company (ASCAP)
35 West 53rd St.
New York 10019

Lider Music Corporation (BMI)
748 10th Ave.
New York 10019

Lisa Sue Music, Inc. (ASCAP)
750 Kappock St.
Bronx 10463

Little Night Music (BMI)
40 Hamilton St., Suite 20-B
New York 10019

Loena Music Publishing (ASCAP)
239 West 18th St.
New York 10011

Lola Publishing Corporation (BMI)
20 West End Ave.
New York 10023

Lollipop Music Corporation (BMI)
214 East 70th St.
New York 10021

Lone Lake Songs, Inc. (ASCAP)
P.O. Box 126
Elmsford 10523

Lori-Joy Music (BMI)
39 West 55th St.
New York 10019

Lovelace Music Company (ASCAP)
Island View Rd.
Cohoes 12047

Love-Zager Productions, Inc.
1697 Broadway, Suite 1209
New York 10019

Lyra Music Company (ASCAP)
133 West 69th St.
New York 10023

William Lymonlee Music (BMI)
455 Mountainview Ave.
Syracuse 13224

MBA Music, Inc.
8 East 48th St.
New York 10017

MCA Music (ASCAP)
445 Park Ave.
New York 10022

M-E Music Company (ASCAP)
1697 Broadway, Suite 1201
New York 10019

MJQ Music, Inc. (BMI)
200 West 57th St.
New York 10019

MRI Music (ASCAP)
161 West 54th St., Suite 601
New York 10019

Mainman, Ltd. (ASCAP)
200 Central Park South
New York 10019

Myrna March Music (ASCAP)
25 Central Park West
New York 10023

Marielle Music Publishing Corporation
(BMI)
P.O. Box 842, Radio City Sta.
New York 10019

Edward B. Marks Music (BMI)
1790 Broadway
New York 10019

Masada Music
888 Eighth Ave.
New York 10019

Mayflower Music Corporation
(ASCAP)
20 West 64th St.
New York 10023

McAfee Music Corporation
(ASCAP)
300 East 59th St.
New York 10022

McGinnis & Marx Music Publishers
(BMI)
201 West 86th St., Apt. 706
New York 10024

McRon Music Company (ASCAP)
521 Fifth Ave.
New York 10017

Robert Mellin Music (BMI)
1841 Broadway
New York 10023

Memnon, Ltd. (ASCAP)
P.O. Box 84
Glen Cove 11542

Merrimac Music Corporation (BMI)
110 East 59th St.
New York 10022

Merry Sounds (ASCAP)
P.O. Box 313, Kingsbridge Sta.
Bronx 10463

Meshugah Music (BMI)
3242 Irwin Ave.
Kingsbridge 10463

Metorion Music Corporation (ASCAP)
19 West 44th St.
New York 10036

Mexican Music Centre (ASCAP)
345 West 58th St., Suite 2-P
New York 10019

Michlin & Hill, Inc.
40 West 55th St.
New York 10019

Midsong Music International (ASCAP)
1650 Broadway
New York 10019

Mietus Copyright Management
527 Madison Ave., Suite 317
New York 10022

Miracle Records Publishing Company
(ASCAP)
170-30 103th Ave.
Jamaica 11434

Ivan Mogul Music Corporation (ASCAP)
40 East 49th St.
New York 10017

Morley Music Company (ASCAP)
c/o Eastman & Eastman
39 West 54th St.
New York 10019

Edwin H. Morris & Company
(ASCAP)
810 Seventh Ave.
New York 10019

Mother Bertha Music (BMI)
c/o Machat & Kronfeld
1501 Broadway, 30th Flr.
New York 10036

Mounted Music
888 Eighth Ave.
New York 10019

Musicanza Corporation (ASCAP)
2878 Bayview Ave.
Wantagh 11793

Music for Percussion (BMI)
17 West 60th St.
New York 10023

Music in General (BMI)
c/o Michael Tannen, Esq.
36 East 61st St.
New York 10021

Musicmaster Publications (ASCAP)
1650 Broadway
New York 10019

Music Minus One Music Group
43 West 61st St.
New York 10023

Music Music Music, Inc. (ASCAP)
157 West 57th St.
New York 10019

Music Sales Corporation (ASCAP)
33 West 60th St.
New York 10023

Music Treasure Publications
620 Forth Washington Ave., #1-F
New York 10040

Mustevic Sound Publishing (BMI)
193–18 120th Ave.
New York 11412

NRP Music Group
385 Grand St.
New York 10002

Near East Music Associates (BMI)
191 Atlantic Ave.
Brooklyn 11201

Neptune Music Publishers (BMI)
82 Aldine St.
Rochester 14619

Nick-O-Val Music
332 West 71st St.
New York 10023

Nic-Lyn Music Company
101 North Hamilton Ave.
Lindenhurst 11757

Night Time (BMI)
c/o Martin J. Machat
1501 Broadway, 30th Flr.
New York 10036

Notable Music Company, Inc.
  (ASCAP)
161 West 54th St.
New York 10019

Novello Publications (ASCAP)
145 Palisade St.
Dobbs Ferry 10522

Oneida Music Publishing Company
(BMI)
760 Blanding St.
Utica 13501

Oneira Music Publishing (BMI)
760 Blanding St.
Utica 13501

Organic Management
745 Fifth Ave.
New York 10022

Oxford University Press, Inc.
  (ASCAP)
200 Madison Ave.
New York 10016

PPX Publishers (BMI)
301 West 54th St.
New York 10019

PR Dynamics (ASCAP)
1697 Broadway, Suite 701
New York 10019

Pablo Music (BMI)
26 Jane St.
New York 10014

O. Pagani & Bro., Inc. (SESAC)
289 Bleecker St.
New York 10014

Pambar Music, Ltd. (BMI)
150 West 55th St.
New York 10019

Joseph Patelson Music House (ASCAP)
160 West 56th St.
New York 10019

Pecan Pie Music, Inc.
300 East 74th St., Apt. 32C
New York 10021

Peer-Southern Organization
1740 Broadway
New York 10019

Pellegrino Music Company, Inc.
(ASCAP)
311 Brook Ave.
Bayshore 11706

Pelton Publishing Company (BMI)
P.O. Box 182, Midwood Sta.
Brooklyn 11230

Periterra Music (BMI)
45-15 21st St.
Long Island City 11101

C.F. Peters Corporation (BMI)
373 Park Ave. South
New York 10016

Pickwick International, Inc.
135 Crossways Park Dr.
Woodbury 11797

Pinent Music Company (BMI)
P.O. Box 197
Wampsville 13163

Placid Music Corporation (BMI)
c/o A. Halsey Cowan
1350 Ave. of the Americas
New York 10019

Playnote Music Publishing (BMI)
P.O. Box 219, Radio City Sta.
New York 10019

Plibby Music (BMI)
c/o Stoy, Inc.
279 East 44th St.
New York 10017

Polka Towne Music (BMI)
211 Post Ave.
Wesbury 11590

Portnow Miller Company
107 East 35th St.
New York 10016

Publishers' Licensing Corporation
488 Madison Ave.
New York 10022

Gerald W. Purcell Associates (ASCAP)
133 Fifth Ave.
New York 10003

RSO
135 Central Park West, Suite 1NE
New York 10023

Rae-Cox & Cooke Music (ASCAP)
1674 Broadway
New York 10019

Ragmar Music Corporation (BMI)
200 West 57th St.
New York 10019

Ragmop Music Corporation (BMI)
850 Seventh Ave.
New York 10019

Ram's Horn Music (ASCAP)
P.O. Box 289, Cooper Sta.
New York 10003

Rayven Music Company (BMI)
157 West 57th St.
New York 10019

Red Giant, Inc. (ASCAP)
130 Beach 137 St.
Belle Harbor 11694

Red Greg Enterprises
1650 Broadway, Suite 714
New York 10019

Redplow (BMI)
1458 Buffalo Rd.
Rochester 14624

Herb Reis Music Corporation (BMI)
15 East 48th St., Rm. 801
New York 10017

Ren-Maur Music Corporation (BMI)
663 Fifth Ave.
New York 10022

William Rezey Music Company (BMI)
P.O. Box 1257
Albany 12201

Rockford Music Company (BMI)
150 West End. Ave., Apt. 6–D
New York 10023

Rockmasters, Inc. (BMI)
177 Rt. 304
New City 10956

Rock & Roll Music
60–23 Marathon Pkwy.
Little Neck 11362

Roncom Music Company (ASCAP)
305 Northern Blvd.
Great Neck 11021

Roseville Music, Inc. (BMI)
77 St. Marks Place
New York 10003

Royal Spin Music, Inc. (BMI)
26 Cass Place
Brooklyn 11235

SVG (ASCAP)
3725 Crescent St.
Long Island City 11101

Sagittarius Entertainment, Inc.
375 Park Ave.
New York 10022

St. Nathanson Music (ASCAP)
c/o Brighton Towers
50 Brighton First Rd.
Brooklyn 11235

St. Nicholas Music, Inc. (ASCAP)
1619 Broadway
New York 10019

Salabert Music Publisher (ASCAP)
575 Madison Ave.
New York 10022

Salsoul Music Publishing (ASCAP)
240 Madison Ave.
New York 10016

Sanga Music, Inc. (BMI)
250 West 57th St., Suite 2017
New York 10019

San-Lyn Music (BMI)
P.O. Box 46
Syracuse 13025

G. Schirmer, Inc. (ASCAP)
866 Third Ave.
New York 10022

Schlok Publishing
411 Milton Rd.
Rye 10580

A. Schroeder International, Ltd.
25 West 56th St.
New York 10019

Schwartz Music Company (ASCAP)
20–F Robert Pitt Dr.
Monsey 10952

Screen Gems–EMI Music, Inc. (BMI)
1370 Ave. of the Americas
New York 10019

Seaside Publishing Company (BMI)
1697 Broadway
New York 10019

Sebiniano Music (ASCAP)
285 East 49th St.
Brooklyn 11203

Neil Sedaka Music Publishing
1370 Ave. of the Americas
New York 10019

Seesaw Music Corporation (ASCAP)
1966 Broadway
New York 10023

Sidney A. Seidenberg, Inc.
1414 Ave. of the Americas
New York 10019

Seldak Music Corporation
(ASCAP)
65 West 55th St.
New York 10019

September Music Corporation
(ASCAP)
161 West 54th St.
New York 10019

Septima Music, Inc. (BMI)
424 Madison Ave., Suite 1401
New York 10017

Shada Music, Inc. (ASCAP)
1650 Broadway
New York 10019

Shapiro, Bernstein & Company
10 East 53rd St.
New York 10022

Sheila Music Corporation (BMI)
130 West 57st St.
New York 10019

Sheral Productions
132 East 35th St.
New York 10016

Shotgun Music Company (BMI)
22 Pine St.
Freeport 11520

Showpiece Productions (BMI)
P.O. Box 79
Yonkers 10702

Silver Blue Music, Ltd. (ASCAP)
220 Central Park South
New York 10019

Paul Simon (BMI)
c/o Michael Tannen
36 East 61st St.
New York 10021

Siri Music, Inc. (BMI)
30 Marksman Lane
Levittown 11756

SkyHigh Publishing (BMI)
111 East Ave., Suite 228
Rochester 14604

Harrison Smith (BMI)
254 New York Ave.
Brooklyn 11216

Solar Systems Music (ASCAP)
441 East 20th St.
New York 10010

Solar Wind Music
157-52 196th St.
Howard Beach 11414

Son-Deane Publishers (ASCAP)
Hartsdale 10530

Sophisticate Music, Inc. (BMI)
1619 Broadway
New York 10019

Sorority Fraternity Record Publications
(ASCAP)
135 Hamilton Pl., Suite 6B
New York 10026

Sounds Music Company (ASCAP)
663 Fifth Ave.
New York 10022

Space Angel Music Company (BMI)
555 Kappock St.
Riverdale 10463

Space Potato Music (ASCAP)
150 East 58th St.
New York 10022

Spencer Music Company (ASCAP)
507 Fifth Ave.
New York 10017

Larry Spier, Inc. (ASCAP)
240 Madison Ave.
New York 10016

Spiral Record Corporation (ASCAP)
17 West 60th St.
New York 10023

Stallman Records (BMI)
333 East 70th St.
New York 10021

Star Spangled Music (ASCAP)
405 Park Ave.
New York 10022

Georgg Stephens Music, Inc.
c/o Prager & Fenton
444 Madison Ave.
New York 10022

Miriam Rose Stern Agency
301 East 69th St.
New York 10021

Sudden Rush Music (BMI)
750 Kappock St.
Riverdale 10463

Sugar 'n Soul Music, Inc. (ASCAP)
3929 Carpenter Ave.
Bronx 10466

Sun Bear Corporation
1650 Broadway, Rm. 202
New York 10019

Sweet Cherry Music (ASCAP)
850 Seventh Ave., Suite 705
New York 10019

Sweet Swamp Music (BMI)
The Gables, Halcott Rd.
Fleischmanns 12430

System Four Artist
655 Madison Ave.
New York 10021

TRO
10 Columbus Circle
New York 10019

TWC Music (SESAC)
GPO Box 2021
New York 10001

Takya Music, Inc. (ASCAP)
265 West 20th St.
New York 10011

Creed Taylor, Inc.
1 Rockefeller Plaza
New York 10020

Tempi Music Company (BMI)
133 West 87th St.
New York 10024

Terry Music Company (ASCAP)
157 West 57th St.
New York 10019

Tinker Street Tunes (BMI)
36 East 61st St.
New York 10021

Tintagel Music Company
(ASCAP)
75 East 55th St., Suite 404
New York 10022

Tobill Music (ASCAP)
107 Delaware Ave.
Buffalo 14202

Tom-Tom Publishing (BMI)
Andrew Street Rd.
Massena 13662

Track Music, Inc. (BMI)
200 West 57th St.
New York 10019

Transaction Music, Ltd.
225 E. 57th St.
New York 10022

Transcontinental Music Publications
1674 Broadway
New York 10019

Trina Jill Music (ASCAP)
240 Madison Ave.
New York 10016

Trio Music Company (BMI)
1619 Broadway
New York 10019

Triumph Publications, Inc. (BMI)
30 West 60th St.
New York 10023

Twin Music, Inc. (BMI)
41–45 39th St.
Long Island City 11104

Ucronia Music Company (ASCAP)
505 Park Ave.
New York 10022

United International Copyright Reps
5 Riverside Dr.
New York 10023

Vado Music Company (ASCAP)
2226 McDonald Ave.
Brooklyn 11223

Tommy Valando Publishing Corporation
1270 Ave. of the Americas, #2110
New York 10020

Thomas J. Valentino (ASCAP)
151 West 46th St.
New York 10036

Vanguard Music Corporation (ASCAP)
250 West 57th St.
New York 10019

Van Heusen Music Corporation
(ASCAP)
301 East 69th St.
New York 10021

Van-Jak Music (ASCAP)
221 West 57th St.
New York 10019

Stan Vincent Music (BMI)
337 East 54th St.
New York 10022

Vin-Joy Music (ASCAP)
2805 Creston Ave.
Bronx 10468

Jerry Vogel Music Company (ASCAP)
121 West 45th St.
New York 10036

WPN Music Company (ASCAP)
10 Swirl Lane
Levittown 11756

Wanessa Music, Inc. (BMI)
P.O. Box 387, Radio City Sta.
New York 10019

Watt Works, Inc. (BMI)
6 West 95th St.
New York 10025

H.B. Webman & Co.
1650 Broadway, Suite 701
New York 10019

Weintraub Music Company
33 West 60th St.
New York 10023

Steven H. Weiss
444 Madison Ave.
New York 10022

Western Hemisphere Music (BMI)
252 Robby Lane
New Hyde Park 11040

Westwall Publishing Company
21 Meadow Lane
Lawrence 11559

Wherefore Music, Inc. (BMI)
441 West 49th St.
New York 10019

White Haven Music, Inc. (ASCAP)
1619 Broadway
New York 10019

White Way Music Company
(ASCAP)
65 West 55th St., Suite 11G
New York 10019

Wild Indigo Music (BMI)
56 Irving Place
New York 10003

Will-Du Music Publishing Company/
Deliver Music Publishing Company
18 28th Ave.
Brooklyn 11214

Words & Music, Inc. (ASCAP)
17 West 60th St.
New York 10023

World Jazz
1619 Broadway
New York 10019

World Music, Inc. (ASCAP)
18 East 48th St.
New York 10017

Worldwide Music Publishers
1966 Broadway
New York 10023

Worthy Music Company
1909 Ave. K
Brooklyn 11230

Yellow Bee Music (BMI)
245 Waverly Place
New York 10014

Vincent Youmans Company (ASCAP)
8 East 77th St.
New York 10021

NORTH CAROLINA

Border Brigands Music
1101 East Morehead St., No. 5
Charlotte 28204

Brodt Music Company (ASCAP)
P.O. Box 1207
Charlotte 28231

Charmack Publishing (BMI)
120 York Ave.
Kannapolis 28081

Clay Music Corporation (BMI)
5457 Old Monroe Rd.
Charlotte 28211

Elvitrue Recording Music Publishing
(BMI)
P.O. Box 3022
Wilmington 28401

Existential Music (BMI)
118 Fifth St.
Taylorsville 28681

Great Escape Music (ASCAP)
P.O. Box 15021
Winston-Salem 27103

Jeneret Music (BMI)
1417 Montford Dr.
Charlotte 28209

Live-Wire Music Publishers (BMI)
P.O. Box 824
Gibsonville 27249

Madonna Music
103 Mimosa Dr.
Chapel Hill 27514

Metorlina Publishing Company (BMI)
2624 Chesterfield Ave.
Charlotte 28205

Old Sparta Music Corporation (BMI)
Box 638
Bailey 27807

Old Statesville Town Publishing (BMI)
218 West Broad St.
Statesville 28677

Parchment Publishing Corporation
(ASCAP)
P.O. Box 22106
Greensboro 27420

People Pleaser Music (BMI)
1018 Central Ave.
Charlotte 28204

Songs of Bobby & Ginny Music (BMI)
P.O. Box 302
Wilmington 28401

Sueno Publishing Company (BMI)
Rte. 2
Troutman 28166

Tompaul Music Company (BMI)
628 South St.
Mount Airy 27030

OHIO

Aesthetic Artist Records (ASCAP)
P.O. Box 144, Mid-City Sta.
Dayton 45402

American Mutual (SESAC)
Carew Tower, Lower Arcade
Cincinnati 45202

Astral 7 Publishing (BMI)
1514 West Dorothy Ln.
Dayton 45409

Beckenhorst Press (ASCAP)
P.O. Box 14273
Columbus 43214

Canyon Press, Inc.
P.O. Box 1235
Cincinnati 45201

Cara Publications (ASCAP)
2000 West Devon Rd.
Columbus 43212

Carwin Publishing Company (BMI)
3728 West 130th St.
Cleveland 44111

Chantry Music Press, Inc. (SESAC)
Box 1101
Springfield 45501

Cifi Publishing Company (BMI)
3966 Standish Ave.
Cincinnati 45213

Cincinnati Music Company (BMI)
906 Main St., Rm. 405
Cincinnati 45202

Coberly Music
53 Tamiami Terrace
Lexington 44904

Counterpart Music (BMI)
3744 Applegate Ave.
Cincinnati 45211

Danielle Music Company (ASCAP)
P.O. Box 315
Cleveland 44127

Deborah Productions (BMI)
5758 Rhode Island Ave.
Cincinnati 45237

Delgay International Music Publishers
(BMI)
1584 East 31st St.
Cleveland 44114

Ekco Music, Inc. (ASCAP)
791 East Third Ave.
Columbus 43201

Fairweather Publishing (BMI)
P.O. Box 435
Cambridge 43725

Galactic Enterprises
1285 Parkamo Ave.
Hamilton 45011

Gallery Square Publishing Company
(BMI)
4524 283rd St.
Toledo 43611

Grenoble Songs (BMI)
Box 222
Groveport 43125

Hal Bernard Enterprises, Inc.
P.O. Box 6507
Cincinnati 45206

Halnat Publishing Company (BMI)
1527 Beaverton Ave.
Cincinnati 45237

Hedge Apple Music (BMI)
2551 Sunbury Rd.
Columbus 43219

Jaclyn Music (BMI)
1806 Brown St.
Dayton 45409

Jevert Music (BMI)
639 Bulen Ave.
Columbus 43205

Lorenz Industries (ASCAP)
501 East Third St.
Dayton 45401

Loving & Loving Music Company (BMI)
6701 Hope Ave.
Cleveland 44102

Monologg (BMI)
1391 Oakland Park
Columbus 43224

Omega Century Music Company (BMI)
3291 East 119th St.
Cleveland 44120

Pamlyn Music Company (BMI)
P.O. Box 6211
Cleveland 44101

Paubil Music Publishing (BMI)
3518 Champlain Ave.
Youngstown 44502

QCA Music, Inc. (ASCAP)
2832 Spring Grove Ave.
Cincinnati 45225

Rite Music (BMI)
9745 Lockland Rd.
Cincinnati 45215

Robadon Music (BMI)
P.O. Box 2094
Sheffield Lake 44054

Jimmie Skinner Music Publishing
(BMI)
5825 Vine St.
Cincinnati 45216

Skudrin Music Company (BMI)
5417 Fleet Ave.
Cleveland 44105

Sokit Music (BMI)
455 North Snyder Rd.
Dayton 45427

Stone-Rap Music Company (BMI)
28001 Chagrin Blvd., No. 205
Cleveland 44122

Sugar Bear Music (BMI)
1044 Lilly
Canton 44730

Tema Music (ASCAP)
10104 Plymouth Ave.
Garfield Heights 44125

Termyra Music Publishing Company
(BMI)
909 Keil Rd.
Toledo 43607

Tomlew Publishing (BMI)
12202 Union Ave.
Cleveland 44105

True Music Publishing (BMI, ASCAP)
9902 Adams Ave.
Cleveland 44108

Wel Dee Music (BMI)
Box 561
Wooster 44691

World Library Publications (SESAC)
2145 Central Pkwy.
Cincinnati 45214

Rusty York Music (BMI)
1594 Kinney Ave.
Cincinnati 45231

OKLAHOMA

Alvera Publishing Company (BMI)
P.O. Box 9304
Tulsa 74107

Big Diamond Publishing (BMI)
P.O. Box 15018
Tulsa 74115

Bullshoot Publishing Company (BMI)
P.O. Box 193
Shawnee 74801

Catalpa Publishing Company (BMI)
2609 N.W. 36th St.
Oklahoma City 73112

Nitfol Music (BMI)
1502 South Boulder
Tulsa 74119

Payline Publishing Company (BMI)
4449 Woodedge Dr.
Del City 73115

Sunny Lane Music (ASCAP)
105 Burk Dr.
Oklahoma City 73115

OREGON

Klickitat Music (BMI)
122 S.W. Third
Portland 97204

Moon June Music (BMI)
4647 S.W. Pendleton
Portland 97221

Mygar Publishing Company (BMI)
565 Rose St. N.E.
Salem 97301

PENNSYLVANIA

Amigo Music & Record Company
  (ASCAP)
6137 North Sixth St.
Philadelphia 19120

Andrea Music Company (SESAC)
925 North Third St.
Philadelphia 19123

Annuit Music, Ltd. (ASCAP)
2933 River Rd.
Croydon 19020

Bacone & Sons Music (BMI)
2600 North Corlies St.
Philadelphia 19132

Best Shot (BMI)
71 Smithbridge Rd.
Glen Mills 19342

Brigantine Music (BMI)
1445 North Hills Ave.
Willow Grove 19090

Bynum Music Publishing Company
  (BMI)
8227 Williams Ave.
Philadelphia 19150

Charter Publications, Inc. (ASCAP)
P.O. Box 850
Valley Forge 19482

Country Star Music (ASCAP)
439 Wiley Ave.
Franklin 16323

Crimson Dynasty (ASCAP)
P.O. Box 271
Jenkintown 19046

Darkhorse Productions
64 Carol Dr.
Carnegie 15160

Delev Music Company (BMI)
7231 Mansfield Ave.
Philadelphia 19138

Drucker Publishing Company (BMI)
234 West Green St.
West Hazleton 18201

East Coast Records Inc.
P.O. Box 5363
Philadelphia 19142

Eastwick Music Publishing Company
(BMI)
1314–24 South Howard St.
Philadelphia 19147

Henri Elkan Music Publisher (ASCAP)
1316 Walnut St.
Philadelphia 19107

Fee Bee Music Company (BMI)
4517 Wainwright Ave.
Pittsburgh 15227

Ferncliff Music (BMI)
4905 Parkside Ave.
Philadelphia 19131

Fortress Press (ASCAP)
2900 Queen Lane
Philadelphia 19129

Sam Fox Publishing Company (ASCAP)
P.O. Box 850
Valley Forge 19482

Galanco Music (BMI)
726 Elgin Rd.
Newtown Square 19073

Gold Clef (BMI)
P.O. Box 43
Chester 19016

Goosepimple Music (BMI)
RD 4
Myerstown 17067

Gravenhurst Music (BMI)
105 Park Lane
Beaver Falls 15010

Grubbs Brothers Music (BMI)
2429 West Thompson St.
Philadelphia 19121

Eddie Holman, Inc. (BMI)
905 Robinson Bldg., 42 South 15th St.
Philadelphia 19102

JJ Jules Enterprises
485 Fort Couch Rd.
Pittsburgh 15241

James Boy Publishing Company
(BMI)
P.O. Box 128
Worcester 19490

Jamie Music Publishing Company
(BMI)
919 North Broad St.
Philadelphia 19123

JoCher Music Company (BMI)
Box 102C, RD 1, Chubbic Rd.
Canonsburg 15317

Jo-Renee Music (BMI)
P.O. Box 32
Minersville 17954

Kalmann Music Inc. (ASCAP)
Hilltop Rd.
Birchrunville 19421

King Henry Music (BMI)
1851 Lehigh St.
Easton 18042

Ladd Music Company (BMI)
401 Wintermantle Ave.
Scranton 18505

Little Joe Music
604 Broad St.
Johnstown 15906

Masterview Music Publishing (BMI)
Ridge Rd. and Rte. 563
Perkasie 18944

Metronome Music Publishing
Corporation
400 West Glenwood Ave.
Philadelphia 19140

Mighty Three Music (BMI)
309 South Broad St.
Philadelphia 19107

Mom Bell Music Publishing (BMI)
c/o David J. Steinberg, Esq.
818 Widener Bldg., 1339 Chestnut
Philadelphia 19107

Moon Lake Publishing (BMI)
5007 "F" St.
Philadelphia 19124

James E. Myers Enterprises
(ASCAP)
1607 East Cheltenham Ave.
Philadelphia 19124

New Chatham Music (ASCAP)
P.O. Box 11
Pittsburgh 15230

New Outlook Music, Inc. (BMI)
c/o David J. Steinberg
818 Widener Bldg., 1339 Chestnut
Philadelphia 19107

Nise Productions, Inc. (BMI)
P.O. Box 5132
Philadelphia 19141

Omnivox (BMI)
P.O. Box 5363
Philadelphia 19142

Len Pakula & Associates (BMI)
P.O. Box 548
Feasterville 19047

Theodore Presser Company (ASCAP)
Presser Place
Bryn Mawr 19010

Regal Music Publications (ASCAP)
1429 Hawthorne St.
Pittsburgh 15201

Lloyd Zane Remick
1529 Walnut St., 6th Flr.
Philadelphia 19102

Roaring Flame Publishing Company
(BMI)
907 North Front St.
Harrisburg 17102

Robin Sean Music Publishing (BMI)
5635 Verona Rd.
Verona 15147

Scully Music Company (ASCAP)
800 South Fourth St.
Philadelphia 19147

Shawnee Press, Inc. (ASCAP)
Delaware Water Gap 18327

Shelton Associate (BMI)
2250 Bryn Mawr Ave.
Philadelphia 19131

Six Strings Music (BMI)
2201 North 54th St.
Philadelphia 19131

Sky Rock Music, Inc. (ASCAP)
1651 Broadway Ave.
Pittsburgh 15216

Slide Music Publishing (ASCAP)
P.O. Box 691
Reading 19601

Sulzer Music (BMI)
4073 Higbee St.
Philadelphia 19135

Sure Music & Record Company
P.O. Box 94
Brookmall 19008

Tom Cabin Music (BMI)
RD 2
Honesdale 18431

Twin Tail Music (BMI)
8809-11 Rising Sun Ave.
Philadelphia 19115

Tymena Music (BMI)
430 Pearce Rd.
Pittsburgh 15234

Vokes Music Publishing Company
(BMI)
P.O. Box 12
New Kensington 15068

Volkwein Brothers, Inc. (ASCAP)
117 Sandusky St.
Pittsburgh, 15212

Don White Publishing (ASCAP)
2020 Ridge Ave.
Philadelphia 19121

Rex Zario Music (BMI)
3010 North Front St.
Philadelphia 19133

SOUTH CAROLINA

The Herald Association
P.O. Drawer 218, Wellman Heights
Johnsonville 29555

Jack Redick Music (BMI)
Box 266, Rte. 1
Georgetown 29440

Sivatt Music (BMI)
P.O. Box 1079
Easley 29640

Sweet Polly Music (BMI)
P.O. Box 521
Newberry 29108

Township Group, Inc.
P.O. Box 7084
Greenville 29610

Wejac Music (BMI)
P.O. Box 743
Lake City 29560

TENNESSEE

Abingdon Press
201 Eighth Ave. South
Nashville 37202

Above Music Publications (ASCAP)
P.O. Box 110765
Nashville 37211

Acoustic Music, Inc. (BMI)
5304 Camelot C.
Brentwood 37027

Acuff-Rose Publications, Inc. (BMI)
2510 Franklin Rd.
Nashville 37204

Adventure Music Company (ASCAP)
1201 16th Ave. South
Nashville 37212

Ahab Music Company, Inc. (BMI)
1707 Grand Ave.
Nashville 37212

Aletha Jane Music (ASCAP)
P.O. Box 4796
Nashville 37216

Rex Allen, Jr.
357 Cedarmont Dr.
Nashville 37211

American Cowboy Music Company
(BMI)
11 Music Circle South
Nashville 37203

American Cowboy Songs
The Homeplace
Mount Juliet 37122

American Music (ASCAP)
44 Music Square East, #107
Nashville 37203

Ash Valley Music, Inc. (ASCAP)
1609 Hawkins St.
Nashville 37203

Audigram Music (BMI)
P.O. Box 22635
Nashville 37202

Aunt Polly's Publishing Company
(BMI)
P.O. Box 12647
Nashville 37212

BC Enterprises of Memphis
(BMI)
726 East McLemore
Memphis 38106

Bacchanalia Music Company
(BMI)
P.O. Box 3201
Oak Ridge 37830

Barlow Music (ASCAP)
c/o Jack Butcher
3706-D Hillsboro Rd.
Nashville 37215

Baron Music Publishing Company
(BMI)
916 19th Ave. South
Nashville 37212

BeniBob Music (BMI)
115 Airfloat Dr.
Hendersonville 37075

John T. Benson Publishing Company
(ASCAP)
365 Great Circle Rd.
Nashville 37228

Black Sheep Music (BMI)
P.O. Box 22635
Nashville 37202

Bloc-6, Inc. (BMI)
3749 Maple Leaf Cove
Memphis 38118

Blue Creek Music (BMI)
11 Music Circle South
Nashville 37203

Bocephus Music Company (BMI)
815 18th Ave. South
Nashville 37203

Boxer Music (BMI)
Box 12501
Nashville 37212

Brass Press (BMI)
148 Eighth Ave. North
Nashville 37203

Brite Country (SESAC)
728 16th Ave. South
Nashville 37203

Brougham Hall Music Company, Inc.
(BMI)
50 Music Square West
Nashville 37203

Bryte (ASCAP)
728 16th Ave. South
Nashville 37203

Buckhorn Music Publishers, Inc. (BMI)
1007 17th Ave. South
Nashville 37212

By-Nash of Nashville (BMI)
P.O. Box 22701
Nashville 37202

Cape Ann Music Inc. (BMI)
P.O. Box 6128
Nashville 37212

Captive Music (BMI)
2407 12th Ave. South
Nashville 37204

Carry & Mr. Wilson Music Inc. (BMI)
700-B 18th Ave. South
Nashville 37203

Cedarwood Publishing Company, Inc.
(BMI)
39 Music Square East
Nashville 37203

Channel Music Company
(ASCAP)
1300 Division St., Suite 100
Nashville 37203

Cherritown Publishing (BMI)
161 Jefferson Ave., Suite 1200
Memphis 38102

Jerry Chestnut Music, Inc. (BMI)
40 Music Square East
Nashville 37203

Coal Miners Music, Inc. (BMI)
7 Music Circle North
Nashville 37203

Combine Music Group (BMI)
35 Music Square East
Nashville 37203

Con Brio Music (BMI)
P.O. Box 196
Nashville 37202

Contention Music (SESAC)
P.O. Box 824
Nashville 37202

Copper Music, Inc. (ASCAP)
50 Music Square West
Nashville 37203

Danor Music, Inc. (BMI)
1802 Grand Ave.
Nashville 37212

Debdave Music, Inc. (BMI)
P.O. Box 2154
Nashville 37214

Depot Music, Inc. (ASCAP)
1013 16th Ave. South
Nashville 37212

Division Publishing
107 Music City Circle
Nashville 37214

Sounds of Memphis
P.O. Box 16676
Memphis 38116

Soundstage Studios, Inc.
Box 23618
Nashville 37202

Southern Writers Group
Box 40764
Nashville 37204

Stafree Publishing Company (BMI)
3114 Radford Rd.
Memphis 38111

Starburst Music (ASCAP)
50 Music Square West, Suite 901
Nashville 37203

Stonehill Music Company (BMI)
Box 5766
Nashville 37218

Stuckey Publishing Company (BMI)
P.O. Box 102
Brentwood 37027

Stylecraft Music Company (BMI)
P.O. Box 11522
Memphis 38111

Su-Ann Publishing Company
(SESAC)
1707 Church St.
Nashville 37203

Sugarplum Music Company (BMI)
1006 17th Ave. South
Nashville 37212

John L. Sullivan Enterprises
130 17th Ave. South
Nashville 37212

SuLyn Publishing, Inc. (BMI)
P.O. Box 28835
Memphis 38128

Sure-Fire Music Company (BMI)
60 Music Square West
Nashville 37212

Sword & Shield Music (SESAC)
P.O. Box 50
Nashville 37203

Tackhammer (BMI)
1300 Division St., Suite 201
Nashville 37203

Tannen Music, Inc. (BMI)
1207 16th Ave. South
Nashville 37212

Joe Taylor Music (ASCAP)
2401 Granny White Pike
Nashville 37204

Teardrop Music (ASCAP)
P.O. Box 40001
Nashville 37204

Tiffin Music International
P.O. Box 12741
Nashville 37212

Tippetoe Music Publishing (BMI)
306 Cumberland Plaza
Crossville 38555

Top Five Songs (BMI)
20 Music Square West
Nashville 37203

Tree Publishing Company, Inc. (BMI)
P.O. Box 1273
Nashville 37202

Triunz Music, Inc. (ASCAP)
824 19th Ave. South
Nashville 37203

True Artist Music (ASCAP)
Box 4690
Nashville 37216

Twitty Bird Publishing Company
(BMI)
8 Music Square West
Nashville 37203

Two Rivers Music (ASCAP)
21 Music Circle East
Nashville 37203

Harrison Tyner Productions
38 Music Square East
Nashville 37203

Universal Entertainment Corporation
120 Hickory St.
Madison 37115

Vector Music (BMI)
1107 18th Ave. South
Nashville 37212

Wal-Fran Music Company (BMI)
P.O. Box 75
Gatlinburg 37738

Hank Williams, Jr. Music (BMI)
50 Music Square
Nashville 37203

Windchime Music, Inc. (BMI)
1201 16th Ave. South
Nashville 37212

Window Music Publishing (BMI)
809 18th Ave. South
Nashville 37203

Curtis Wood Music (ASCAP)
1108 16th Ave. South
Nashville 37212

World Wide Music, Inc.
1300 Division St.
Nashville 37203

Xenia Music Company (BMI)
1906 South St.
Nashville 37212

Faron Young Music (ASCAP)
1300 Division St., Rm. 103
Nashville 37203

TEXAS

Abnak Music Enterprises, Inc. (BMI)
825 Olive at Ross
Dallas 75201

Adams-Ethridge Publishing Company
  (BMI)
P.O. Box 434
North Galveston 77550

Alamman Music Publishing Company
551 Carroll
San Antonio 78225

Andrades Publishing Company (BMI)
P.O. Drawer 520
Stafford 77477

Arsak Music (BMI)
P.O. Box 1293
Amarillo 79105

Auburn Mae Publishing (BMI)
P.O. Box 31553
Dallas 75231

Autumn Leaves Music (ASCAP)
3810 Cavalier St.
Garland 75042

BAS Music Publishing (ASCAP)
5925 Kirby Dr., Suite 226
Houston 77005

Babcock North Music (BMI)
6835 Spring Manor
San Antonio 78249

Barrett-Hill Music Company (ASCAP)
14502 Broadgreen
Houston 77079

Beau-Jim Agency, Inc. (ASCAP)
P.O. Box 758
Lake Jackson 77566

Big State Music Publishing (BMI)
1311 Candlelight Ave.
Duncanville 75137

Brown Moon Music (ASCAP)
P.O. Box 19274
Houston 77024

Buena Vista Publishing Company (BMI)
P.O. Box 28553
Dallas 75228

Burning Rope Publishing Company
  (BMI)
137 East Sixth St.
Austin 78701

Catchup Music (BMI)
P.O. Box 9830
Fort Worth 76107

Cherie Music (BMI)
3621 Heath Lane
Mesquite 75150

Chisholm Publishing Company (BMI)
508 East Loop 340
Waco 76705

Cochise Publishing Company (BMI)
P.O. Box 1415
Athens 75751

Crazy Cajun Music (BMI)
5626 Brock
Houston 77023

DC-3 Music (ASCAP)
71 Hillside
Little Elm 75068

Demand Music (BMI)
P.O. Box 57291
Dallas 75207

Al Dexter Songs (BMI)
P.O. Box 71
Denton 76201

Earthbound Publishing Company
   (BMI)
8428 Kate St., No. 226
Dallas 75225

Don Edgar Music Company (BMI)
2312 Jasper
Fort Worth 76106

Edmark Productions (BMI)
20802 Cedar Lane
Tomball 77375

El Paso Music Company (ASCAP)
P.O. Box 9398
Fort Worth 76107

Erection Publishing (BMI)
4606 Clawson
Austin 78745

Charlie Fitch Music Company (BMI)
311 East Davis
Luling 78648

Clinton H. Forsman Publishing (BMI)
210 East Main
Robstown 78380

Glad Music Company (BMI)
316 East 11th St.
Houston 77008

Golden Sands Enterprises, Inc. (ASCAP)
602 Golfcrest Dr.
San Antonio 78239

Green Door Music (BMI)
P.O. Box 9470
Fort Worth 76107

John Hall Music (SESAC)
P.O. Box 13344
Fort Worth 76118

Hare Music Company (BMI)
P.O. Box 1209
Andrews 79714

Homebrew Music Publishing Company
   (ASCAP)
1102 S.W. Fifth Ave.
Mineral Wells 76067

Hornsby Music Company (BMI)
P.O. Box 13661
Houston 77019

House of Diamonds (BMI)
P.O. Box 449
Cleburne 76031

International Doorway Music (ASCAP)
3410 Ave. R
Lubbock 79412

JPM Music Publishers
2015 Castroville Rd.
San Antonio 78237

Lake Country Music (BMI)
P.O. Box 1073
Graham 76046

Le Bill Music, Inc. (BMI)
P.O. Box 11152
Fort Worth 76110

Foy Lee Publishing (BMI)
P.O. Box 7505
San Antonio 78207

Leonard Productions, Inc. (BMI)
P.O. Box 222
Gainesville 76240

Mactroy Music Company (BMI)
7210 Roos
Houston 77074

Main Gate Publishing (BMI)
P.O. Box 237
Lancaster 75146

A.W. Marullo Music (BMI)
1121 Market St.
Galveston 77550

Metropolitan Music Company (BMI)
4225 University Blvd.
Houston 77005

Warren R. Miller Publishing (BMI)
2302 Dunloe Dr.
Dallas 75228

Misty Haze Music (BMI)
1023 Studewood
Houston 77008

Montgomery Publishing Company
(BMI)
8914 Georgian Dr.
Austin 78753

Mulberry Square Publishing (ASCAP)
10300 North Central Expwy., No. 120
Dallas 75231

Neches Music Company (BMI)
1812 Procter
Port Arthur 77640

Oakridge Music Publishing Company
(BMI)
2001 Elton Rd.
Haltom City 76117

Mary Frances Odle (BMI)
8431 Howard Dr., Studio 2
Houston 77017

Ooga Ooga Music Company (BMI)
3941 Don Juan
Abilene 79605

Pantego Sound
2310 Raper Blvd.
Pantego 76013

Prophecy Publishing, Inc. (ASCAP)
P.O. Box 4945
Austin 78765

Publicare Publishing (ASCAP)
9717 Jensen
Houston 77093

Ramsgate Music (BMI)
Box 551
Hamilton 76531

Rhythm Valley Music (ASCAP)
1304 Blewett St.
Graham 76046

Ridge Runner Publications
3035 Townsend Dr.
Fort Worth 76110

Royalty T Music
P.O. Box 54
Mansfield 76063

Saran Music Company (BMI)
P.O. Box 17667
Dallas 75217

Sea Three Music (BMI)
1310 Tulane
Houston 77008

Silicon Music, Inc. (BMI)
222 Tulane St.
Garland 75043

Sixpence Publications (BMI)
6115 Red Bird Court
Dallas 75232

Southern Music Company (ASCAP)
Box 329
San Antonio 78292

Sprinkle Publishing Company (BMI)
P.O. Box 13464
Austin 78711

Stoneway Publishing Company
(BMI)
2817 Laura Koppe
Houston 77093

Sunnybrook Music Company (BMI)
P.O. Box 775
Tyler 75701

Sunshine Country Enterprises
(BMI)
777 South Central
Richardson 75080

Floyd Tillman Music (BMI)
412 Main St., Suite 1005
Houston 77002

Tyler Publishing (BMI)
P.O. Box 231
Tyler 75701

Wasu Music Menagerie (BMI)
P.O. Box 1206
Plano 75075

Western Head Music (ASCAP)
P.O. Box 19
Bulverde 78163

Woodglen Publications (BMI)
P.O. Box 35855
Houston 77035

Word Inc. (ASCAP)
4800 W. Waco Dr.
Waco 76710

Yatahey Music (BMI)
P.O. Box 31819
Dallas 75231

UTAH

Blanding Publishing Company (BMI)
P.O. Box 162
Provo 84601

VERMONT

Other Music, Inc. (ASCAP)
The Barn
North Ferrisburg 05473

VIRGINIA

Able Music, Inc. (BMI)
P.O. Box 306
Vansant 24656

Blue Mace Music (BMI)
P.O. Box 62263
Virginia Beach 23462

Burriesci Brothers Music Production
  (ASCAP)
5001 Bldg., #41, West Broad St.
Richmond 23230

Cottonhill Publishing Company (BMI)
Box 447, Rte. 7
Roanoke 24018

Cow Catcha Music Publishing
  Company (BMI)
909 West Washington St.
St. Petersburg 23803

Crash Music Company (BMI)
12200 Nutmeg Ln.
Reston 22091

District Music Company (BMI)
9224 Rosslyn Sta.
Arlington 22209

Dooms Publishing Company (BMI)
P.O. Box 2072
Waynesboro 22980

Dora Music
P.O. Box 5241
Chesapeake 23324

Fairystone Publishing Company
  (BMI)
P.O. Box 594
Rocky Mount 24151

Fender Bender Music (BMI)
2030 North Oakland St.
Arlington 22207

Festive Music (BMI)
12592 Warwick Blvd.
Newport News 23606

Hot Gold Music Publishing Company
P.O. Box 25654
Richmond 23260

Iffin Music Publishing Company
  (BMI)
216 Applewood Ln.
Virginia Beach 23452

Luray Music Company (BMI)
P.O. Box 62
Luray 22835

Jim McCoy Music (BMI)
P.O. Box 574
Winchester 22601

Van McCoy Music, Inc. (BMI)
6901 Old Keene Mill Rd., Suite 500
Springfield 22150

Newbag Music Company (BMI)
Box 131, Rte. 4
Louisa 23093

Perkins & Simson Publishing (BMI)
612 East Liberty St.
Norfolk 23510

Perpetual Music (BMI)
744 West 28th St.
Norfolk 23508

Perryal Publishing Company (BMI)
3307 South Stafford St.
Arlington 22206

Powahatan Music Publishing (BMI)
P.O. Box 993
Salem 24153

Reeder Music Company (BMI)
7065 Idylwood Rd.
Falls Church 22046

Short Pump Publishing
P.O. Box 11292
Richmond 23230

Summerduck Publishing Corporation
1216 Granby St.
Norfolk 23510

Sunray Music (BMI)
P.O. Box 138
Chesapeake 23321

Waterwheel Music, Inc. (BMI)
847 East Fincastle
Tazewell 24651

WilSing Music Publishers (BMI)
P.O. Box 100–N, RFD 3
Stuart 24171

James Wilson Music (BMI)
9125 Ridgely Dr.
Lorton 22079

WASHINGTON

Jerden
300 Vine St.
Seattle 98121

Kaye-Smith Productions
2212 Fourth Ave.
Seattle 98121

Kiner Music Company
P.O. Box 724
Redmond 98052

Lamplighter (BMI)
2227 Fifth Ave.
Seattle 98121

Merritt & Norman Music (BMI)
Box 368–A, Rte, 5
Yakima 98903

Northwest (BMI)
911 East Fourth Ave.
Olympia 98506

Otherworld Music (BMI)
615 East Pike St.
Seattle 98122

Raven Music (BMI)
4107 Woodland Park Ave. North
Seattle 98103

Ripcord Music (BMI)
P.O. Box 2098
Vancouver 98661

Soul West Music (BMI)
319 North 85th St.
Seattle 98103

Mike Wing Music Publishing (BMI)
P.O. Box 171
Bellevue 98009

WEST VIRGINIA

Bo-Gal Music (BMI)
P.O. Box 6687
Wheeling 26003

Mordick Music (BMI)
P.O. Box 2041
Parkersburg 26101

Mount Rainier Music (BMI)
Rte. 12
Asbury 24916

Purple Haze Music (BMI)
P.O. Box 1243
Beckley 25801

WISCONSIN

California's Blue-Rose (BMI)
P.O. Box 483, Shadow Ln.
Fontana 53125

Chicorel Music Corporation, Inc.
P.O. Box 17827
Whitefish Bay, 53217

Hilaria Music, Inc. (ASCAP)
520 University Ave., #125
Madison 53703

Jennie John Music (BMI)
4123 North 44th St.
Milwaukee 53216

Montello Music (BMI)
5709 Hempstead Rd.
Madison 53711

Nu-Trayl Publishing (ASCAP)
10015 West Eight Mile Rd.
Franksville 53126

Sight & Sound International, Inc.
600 Larry Court
Waukesha 53186

Summerhome Music (ASCAP)
Box 118
Pewaukee 53072

WYOMING

Breeze Publishing Company (BMI)
Box 1354A, Rte. 2
Cheyenne 82001

FORMS OF AGREEMENT, WITH REVISIONS

In using this section, note that the revisions suggested for the various contracts appear in the outer column. Lines and paragraphs which are crossed out in the contract text are also suggested revisions.

ARTIST'S CONTRACT

XYZ RECORDS, INC.
Beverly Hills, California

Date_____

Dear Artist:

This will confirm our understanding and agreement with you with reference to your exclusive services for us as a recording artist as follows:

1. The term of this Agreement shall commence as of the date hereof and shall continue for an initial period of one (1) year. During such initial period, you shall record for us a minimum of selections (hereinafter sometimes called "Masters"), plus additional Masters at our election. The

sufficient in number to comprise one normal-length single disc, 12″, 33⅓ rpm, long-playing album ("LP"),

as you and we shall mutually agree.

mutually	recording of Masters shall be on dates and at studios or other locations to be designated ~~by us upon reasonable notice to you.~~ The selections to be recorded shall be
mutually	designated ~~by us,~~ and each Master shall be subject to
technically	our approval as ~~commercially~~ satisfactory for manufacture and sale. Upon our request, you shall re-record any
technically	Master until a recording ~~commercially~~ satisfactory to us shall have been obtained.

2. For your services hereunder, we will pay the appropriate union scale in accordance with the applicable collective bargaining agreement. All such payments as well as payments to the musicians (including, without limitation, instrumentalists, leaders, arrangers, orchestrators, copyists and contractors) and vocalists rendering services in connection with any recordings hereunder, payments based on payroll to any labor organization or designee thereof, costs of cartage and instrument hire, studio or hall rentals, editing costs and payroll taxes (but excluding payroll taxes for you), and all other costs incurred in producing or acquiring completed Masters hereunder, shall be charged against the royalties earned by you under this Agreement ~~or any other Agreement between~~

within your control ~~you and us.~~ If you shall for any reason whatsoever delay the commencement or completion of, or be unavailable for, any recording session scheduled by us hereunder, then you shall pay all expenses and charges actually incurred or paid by us by reason thereof.

3. Conditioned upon your full and faithful performance of all of the terms hereof, we will pay to you in respect of recordings made hereunder the following royalty upon the terms hereinafter set forth:

ten percent (10%)   (a) On our sales in the United States of records in the form of discs, a royalty of ~~eight percent (8%)~~ of the suggested retail list price of each such record.

equal to   (b) On the sale of records in the United States in the form of prerecorded tapes, in any configuration, a royalty ~~of one-half (½)~~ the rate set forth in subparagraph (a) above, based upon the suggested retail list price of each such tape.

five percent (5%)   (c) On the sale of records outside of the United States, a royalty of ~~four percent (4%)~~ of the suggested retail list price of the records in the country of manufacture, the United States, or the country of sale, as we shall be paid. Such royalties shall be computed in the national currency of the applicable country and shall be credited to your royalty account hereunder at the same rate of exchange as we are paid.

(d) Notwithstanding any of the foregoing, on records sold in the United States through record clubs, direct-mail-order operations, or similar sales plans or distribution methods, a royalty of ~~four percent (4%),~~ based on [five percent (5%)] the price to club members or direct-mail purchasers. The royalty on records sold outside the United States through such methods shall be computed at one-half (½) of the royalty rate provided for in the preceding sentence. No royalties shall be payable on records furnished as free or bonus records to members, applicants or other participants in any record club, or as free or bonus records to purchasers through any direct mail distribution method. Notwithstanding the foregoing, you shall be paid royalties on not less than 50% of the aggregate number of records distributed by the applicable record club, direct-mail operation, or similar sales plan or distribution method. In the event that we manufacture and sell records hereunder by means of a record club, direct-mail operation, or similar sales plan or distribution method which is owned or controlled by us, we shall pay you your full royalty rate on such sales.

(e) On records sold in the United States as "premiums" (i.e., sold in connection with the sales of any other product, commodity or service), or as "budget" records, a royalty rate of one-half (½) of the rate set forth in (a) above, based upon the price received by us as to "premiums," and upon the suggested retail list price as to "budget" records. On records sold outside the United States as "premiums," a royalty rate of one-half (½) of the royalty rate set forth in (c) above, based upon the amount received by us. On records sold outside the United States as so-called "mid-price," "low-price," or "budget" records, the royalty rate shall be ~~one-half (½)~~ of the rate [three-fourths (¾)] set forth in (c) above, based upon the suggested retail list price of the particular record as we shall be paid.

(f) On sales or exploitation of the Masters by means or methods not otherwise provided for in subparagraphs (a) through (e) above (including, without limitation, "key outlet marketing," flat-fee licensing and licensing of individual Masters), the royalty shall be ~~the royalty rate~~ [fifty percent (50%) of] ~~set forth in (a) above, based upon the amount received by~~ [the royalty we receive] ~~us.~~ [from such sales.]

(g) No royalty shall be payable on records distributed for promotional purposes, including, without limitation, "sampler" records; on records sold for scrap or as "cut-outs"; records shipped on a no-charge or "freebie" basis, or sold at less than fifty percent (50%) of our full wholesale price. (Any discounts granted by us to our customers may be applied to us, proportionately, in computing the royalties payable under this Agreement.)

Notwithstanding the foregoing, you shall be paid royalties on not less than eight albums for each ten albums distributed and on not less than seven "singles" for each ten "singles" distributed.

(h) Notwithstanding any of the foregoing,

(i) for purposes of computing royalties, any excise, sales or comparable or similar taxes shall be excluded from the price;

(ii) for purposes of computing royalties, we may exclude from the retail price, as applicable, as an allowance for packaging, an amount equal to ten percent (10%) of such price with respect to "single-fold" album jackets or covers; twelve and one-half percent (12-½%) of such price with respect to "double-fold" album jackets or covers; and twenty- *twenty percent (20%)* ~~five percent (25%)~~ of such price with respect to tape-device containers or boxes or any other form of package, container or box not described herein; and

(iii) royalties shall be computed and paid upon ~~ninety-percent (90%)~~ *one hundred percent (100%)* of sales (less returns) for which payment has been received, except that royalties with ~~respect to licensee~~ see sales shall be computed and *or for which our account has been credited,* paid upon that number of sales as such licensee computes and pays us.

(i) No royalties shall be payable to you on sales by any of our licensees until payment on such sales has been received by us. In the event that we shall not receive payment in United States dollars in the United States from any foreign licensee, and we shall accept payment in foreign currency, we may deposit to your credit in foreign currency, we may deposit to your credit (and at your expense), such foreign currency, in a depository selected by us, any payments so received as royalties applicable to this Agreement which are then payable to you, and we shall notify you thereof promptly. Deposit as aforesaid shall fulfill our obligations hereunder as to record sales to which such royalty payments are applicable.

recordings with your consent (except for the release by us of so-called "Best of" or "sampler" type albums embodying not more than two Masters per year hereunder),

(j) If any Master is coupled on a record with other ~~recordings,~~ *recordings with your consent* the royalty hereunder shall be prorated based upon the number of Masters on such record compared to the aggregate number of all recordings embodied on such record.

with your consent

(k) If any Master is recorded hereunder by you jointly with another artist or musician to whom we are obligated to pay a royalty in respect thereof, the royalties payable to you applicable to records produced therefrom shall be reduced proportionately, and only the proportionate share of the applicable costs set forth in Paragraph 2 above shall be charged against your royalties.

(l) Statements shall be sent to you by September 30 for the semiannual period ending the preceding June 30, and by March 31 for the semiannual period ending the preceding December 31, together with payment of accrued royalties, if any, earned by you during the preceding semiannual period, less all advances and charges under this Agreement or any other agreement between you and us. Upon the submission of each statement, we shall have the right to retain as reserve against subsequent charges, credits or returns, such portion of payable royalties as shall be necessary and appropriate in our best business judgment. ^You shall be deemed to have consented to all royalty statements and all other accounts rendered by us to you, and said statements and other accounts shall be binding upon you and not subject to any objection by you for any reason, unless specific objection in writing, stating the basis thereof, is given by you to us within ~~one (1) year~~ from the date rendered. We shall maintain books of account concerning the sale, distribution and exploitation of records made hereunder. You or a certified public accountant in your behalf may, at your expense, at reasonable intervals, examine our books pertaining to the records made hereunder during our usual business hours and upon reasonable notice. Our books relating to activities during any accounting period may only be examined as aforesaid during the ~~one (1) year~~ period following service by us of the statement for said accounting period. The right to audit shall be accorded to a certified public accountant ("CPA") only, which CPA shall be subject to our reasonable approval. Further, no such examination shall be conducted, the payment for which is based on a contingent-fee arrangement. We may, at any time, elect to utilize a different method of computing royalties so long as such method does not materially alter the net monies due you.

(m) You agree and acknowledge that we shall have the right to withhold from the royalties payable to you hereunder, such amount, if any, as may be required under the applicable provisions of the California [or other state] Revenue and Taxation Code, and you agree to execute such forms and other documents as may be required in connection therewith.

~~4. Nothing herein contained shall obligate us to have you in fact record the minimum number of Masters speci~~

which reserves shall be liquidated within three accounting periods following the date of first withhold thereof.

two (2) years

two (2) year

~~fied—it being agreed that our sole obligation to you as to~~ unrecorded Masters shall be to pay to you the minimum applicable union scale for the Masters not recorded. Nothing hereincontained shall obligate us to make or sell ~~records from Masters made hereunder.~~

5. During the term of this Agreement you will not perform for the purpose of making phonograph records for any person, firm or corporation other than us. During a period of ~~five (5) years~~ after the expiration or termination of this Agreement, you will not perform any selection recorded hereunder for any other person, firm, or corporation for the purpose of making phonograph records.

three (3) years

6. You will not, at any time, manufacture, distribute, or sell, or authorize, or knowingly permit the manufacture, distribution, or sale by any person, firm, or corporation, other than us, of phonograph records embodying (a) any performance rendered by you during the term of this Agreement, or (b) any performance rendered by you within ~~five (5) years~~ after the expiration or termination of this Agreement of a selection which shall have been recorded hereunder. You will not record or authorize or knowingly permit to be recorded for any purpose any such performance without, in each case, taking reasonable measures to prevent the manufacture, distribution and sale at any time, by any person, firm, or corporation other than us, of phonograph records embodying such performance. Specifically, without limiting the generality of the foregoing, you agree that if, during the term of this Agreement, you perform any selection for the purpose of making transcription for radio or television or sound tracks for motion-picture films, or if, within ~~five (5) years~~ after the expiration or termination of this Agreement you perform for any purpose any selection which shall have been recorded hereunder, you will do so only pursuant to a written contract containing an express provision that neither such performance nor any recording thereof will be used directly or indirectly for the purpose of making phonograph records. You will promptly deliver to us a copy of the pertinent provisions of each such contract and will cooperate fully with us in any controversy which may arise or litigation which may be brought relating to our rights under this paragraph.

three (3) years

three (3) years

7. All Masters made hereunder and all reproductions made therefrom, the performances emboided therein and the copyrights therein and thereto (including any renewals and/or extensions thereof), shall be entirely our property, free of any claims whatsoever by you or any person, firm or corporation deriving any rights or interest through or from you. Without limitation of the foregoing, we and/or our designees shall have the worldwide right in perpetuity to manufacture, sell, distribute and advertise records or other reproductions (visual and nonvisual), embodying such Masters; to lease, license, convey or otherwise use or dispose of the Masters by any method now or hereafter known, in any field of use; to release records under any trademarks, trade names or labels; to perform the records or other reproductions publicly and to permit the public performance thereof by radio broadcast, television, or any other method now or hereafter known; all upon such terms and conditions as we may approve, and to permit others to do any or all of the foregoing, or we may, at our election, refrain from any or all of the foregoing. *provided the initial release of each record hereunder shall be on our "top-line" label;*

8. We shall have the worldwide right in perpetuity to use, and to permit others to use, your name (both legal and professional), and likeness and biographical material concerning you for advertising and purposes of trade and otherwise, without restriction, in connection with ~~our business and products.~~ We shall have the further right to refer to you by your legal or professional name as our exclusive artist, and you shall, in your activities in the entertainment field, use your best efforts to be billed and advertised as our exclusive artist. During the term of this Agreement, you shall not authorize your legal or professional name, or your likeness, to be used in connection with the advertising or sale of phonograph records other than those manufactured and sold by us. You hereby warrant that you are the sole owner of the professional name identified on the first page of this Agreement; and you have the sole and exclusive right to use and to permit others to use such professional name as herein permitted. *record business.*

9. You expressly acknowledge that your services hereunder are of a special, unique, and intellectual character which gives them peculiar value, the loss of which cannot be reasonably or adequately determined at law, and that in the event of a breach by you of any term, condition, or covenant hereof, we ~~will~~ be caused irreparable injury. You expressly agree that in the event you shall breach any provision of this Agreement, we shall be entitled to injunctive and other equitable relief and/or damages, as we may deem appropriate, in addition to any other rights or remedies available to us, and we shall have the right to recoup any damages from any sums which may thereafter become due and payable to you hereunder, including *may* *seek* sums otherwise payable to you after the expiration or termination of this Agreement.

10. You warrant and represent that you are under no disability, restriction, or prohibition, whether contractual or otherwise, with respect to your right to execute this Agreement and perform its terms and conditions, and with respect to your right to record any and all selections hereunder. You specifically warrant and represent that no selections recorded or to be recorded by you hereunder are subject to any rerecording restrictions under any previous recording contract to which you may have been a party. You agree to and do hereby indemnify, save, and hold us harmless from any and all loss and damage (including attorneys' fees), arising out of or connected with any claim by a third party which is inconsistent with any of the warranties, representations, or agreements made by you in this Agreement, and you agree to reimburse us, on demand, for any payment made by us at any time after the date hereof with respect to any liability or claim to which the foregoing indemnity applies. Pending the determination of any such claim, we may withhold payment of royalties or other monies hereunder.

which is reduced to judgment and

in an amount reasonably related to the amount of such claim.

11. We reserve the right, at our election, to suspend the operation of this Agreement if, for any reason whatsoever, you are unavailable and/or fail, refuse, or neglect to perform hereunder in accordance with the provisions hereof, or if, due to any labor controversy or adjustment thereof, or to any other cause not entirely within our control or which we cannot by reasonable diligence avoid, we are materially hampered in the recording, manufacture, distribution, or sale or records, or our normal business operations become commercially impractical. Such suspension shall last for the duration of any such contingency of unavailability. At our election, a period of time equal to the duration of such suspension and/or unavailability and/or failure, neglect, or refusal to perform shall be added at the end of either the then current period (whether initial or renewal), or any subsequent period for which we exercise our option, including, without limitation, the final such renewal period, and such period shall be accordingly extended.

Unless the cause for such suspension pursuant to this Paragraph 11 is due to your unavailability, failure, refusal and/or neglect to perform, or unless the cause affects the entire record industry, our right to suspend the operation of this agreement shall be limited to six months.

12. Each composition recorded hereunder and written or composed by you and/or published by you or a firm or corporation owned or controlled in whole or in part by you, shall be licensed to us, ~~at a rate of $.015~~ per composition embodied upon each record manufactured and sold. ~~Arranged versions of musical compositions in the public~~ domain, when furnished by you for recordings hereunder, shall be free of copyright royalties. Any assignment made by you or by the publishing company referred to above of the copyright or any interest in any such composition or in any such arranged version of a musical composition in the public domain, shall be made subject ~~to the provisions hereof.~~

at the current statutory rate

13. We may, at our election, and upon written notice to you, assign this Agreement, or any part hereof, to any party who shall ~~assume our obligations hereunder.~~

acquire all or a substantial portion of our stock or assets.

14. If your voice should be materially and permanently impaired, ~~or, if you should do any act offensive to decency, morality, or social propriety tending to result in public scandal, hatred, ridicule, or contempt,~~ or, if you should fail, refuse, or neglect to comply with any of your other obligations hereunder, then, in addition to any other rights or remedies which we may have, we may elect to terminate your engagement hereunder by notice in writing and shall thereby be relieved of any liability in connection with unrecorded Masters.

15. ~~You hereby grant to us all merchandising rights and~~ the sole and exclusive right to use your name (both legal and professional), likeness, picture, and portrait, in any manner whatsoever, in connection with the exercise of the merchandising rights herein granted. We shall have the right to grant to others (including companies affiliated with us), upon such terms as we shall see fit, the right to exercise or cause to be exercised, such merchandising rights. We shall pay to you, in addition to any and all net monies provided for in this Agreement, one-half (½) of all net monies received by us in connection ~~with the exercise of said merchandising rights.~~

16. You will, upon our request, appear on dates and at film studios or other locations, to be designated by us, upon reasonable notice to you, for the filming, taping, or other permanent fixation of audiovisual reproductions of performances to be rendered by you hereunder. In connection therewith, we, or our designee, will make a payment to you for the services performed by you pursuant to the terms of this paragraph, within a reasonable time after the completion thereof, at the rate of appropriate union scale.

We further agree to pay for reasonable transportation and accommodations for you if such location is more than thirty (30) miles from your place of residence, which travel and accommodation expenses shall be recoupable by us from royalties otherwise payable to you hereunder.

17. Except as otherwise provided herein, the term "records" or "phonograph records" shall include all forms of recordings (both visual and nonvisual), including, without limitation, discs of any speed or size, prerecorded tapes, cartridges, and any other recorded devices, now known or which may hereafter become known.

18. You hereby grant to us four (4) separate options, each to renew this Agreement for a one (1) year period, such renewal periods to run consecutively, beginning at the expiration of the initial period, all upon the same terms and conditions applicable to the initial period, except as otherwise specified either in the Schedule hereinbelow set forth, or elsewhere in this Agreement. Each option may be exercised only by giving you written notice at least thirty (30) days prior to the commencement of the renewal period for which the option is exercised.

SCHEDULE

Renewal Period	Minimum Number of Masters	Royalty Rate Par. 3 (a)	Royalty Rate Par. 3 (b)	Royalty Rate Par. 3 (c)
1st option	1 lp	8%	4%	4%
2nd option	1 lp	8%	4%	4%
3rd option	1 lp	8%	4%	4%
4th option	1 lp	8%	4%	4%

SCHEDULE

Renewal Period	Minimum Number of Masters	Royalty Rate Par. 3 (a)	Royalty Rate Par. 3 (b)	Royalty Rate Par. 3 (c)
1st option	2 LPs	11%	11%	5-½%
2nd option	2 LPs	12%	12%	6%
3rd option	2 LPs	13%	13%	6-½%
4th option	2 LPs	14%	14%	7%

record embodying the applicable Master was first released. The royalty rate applicable to any Master shall be the rate in effect for the period in which the ~~recording for the Master was commenced.~~

19. If you shall record more than the minimum number of Masters during any period hereof, we may, at our election, apply all or any part of the excess Masters toward the fulfillment of the minimum number of Masters specified for the next succeeding renewal period.

20. It is understood that the word "you" as used throughout this Agreement refers individually and collectively to the members of the group known as _____(name of group)_____ and that all the terms and conditions of this Agreement, including, without limitation, the restrictions imposed by Paragraphs 6, 7, and 9, shall apply to each member of the group, whether as an individual or as a member of this group, or as a member of any other group. You and we hereby mutually acknowledge that the restrictions imposed by said Paragraphs 6, 7, and 9, which are applicable to each member of the group, as aforesaid, are of the essence of this Agreement. A breach of any term of condition of this Agreement or a disaffirmance or attempted disaffirmance of this Agreement on the ground of minority by any member or members of the group, shall, at our election, be deemed a breach by the entire group. In the event of any such breach or disaffirmance by any member of the group, or in the event any member of the group is unable to render his services hereunder, then, in addition to any and all other rights which we shall have at law or in equity, we shall have the unlimited right either to utilize the services of the remaining members of the group who are available and not in default or to designate another person in place of the member of the group who is in breach or otherwise unavailable.

(a) If this Agreement is terminated as to some but not all of you;

> (i) the members of the group whose engagements are terminated shall not use the professional name of the group in any commercial or artistic endeavors;
> (ii) such professional name shall be and remain the property of those members of the group whose engagements are not terminated; and
> (iii) the persons engaged to replace the members of the group whose engagements are terminated shall be mutually agreed upon by us and the remaining members. Neither party shall unreasonably withhold agreement with regard thereto; and if agreement cannot be reached, we may terminate the engagement of the remaining members of the group, or we may require the remaining members to continue to perform their services pursuant to the terms hereof.

(b) At our election, any and all payments made to you hereunder (whether royalties, advances, or otherwise) may be made by one check, bearing the names of each of you; or we may divide each such payment into equal shares and pay each of you individually your pro rata share of such payment.

21. This Agreement shall not become effective until signed by you and countersigned by our duly authorized officer. This Agreement shall be deemed to have been made in the State of (name of applicable state) and its validity, construction and effect shall be governed by the laws of the State of (name of applicable state) applicable to agreements wholly performed therein.

22. All notices which we shall desire to give to you hereunder and all statements, royalties, and other payments which are due you hereunder, shall be addressed to you at the address set forth on Page 1 hereof, until you shall give us written notice of a new address. All notices which you shall desire to give to us hereunder shall be addressed to us at the address set forth on Page 1 hereof, until we shall give you written notice of a new address. All notices shall be delivered by hand (to an officer of our company if we shall be the addressee), or served by mail or telegraph, charges prepaid, addressed as aforesaid. The date of making personal service or of mailing or of deposit in a telegraph office, whichever shall be first, shall be deemed the date of service.

23. During the term of this Agreement, you shall become and remain a member in good standing of any appropriate labor union or unions with which we may at any time have an Agreement lawfully requiring such union membership. In particular, you represent that you are a member in good standing of the American Federation of Television and Radio Artists (AFTRA), or, if you are not now a member of said union, not later than the thirtieth (30th) day after your first recording session under this Agreement, you shall become a member, and that you shall remain a member in good standing during the term of this Agreement.

24. No failure by us to perform any of our obligations hereunder, shall be deemed a breach hereof, unless you shall have given us written notice of such failure and we
thirty (30)   have failed to cure such nonperformance within ~~sixty (60)~~ days after receipt of such notice.

25. This Agreement sets forth the entire agreement between you and us with respect to the subject matter hereof. No modification, amendment, waiver, termination, or discharge of this Agreement or any provisions hereof, shall be binding upon us unless confirmed by a written instrument signed by a duly authorized officer of our company. No waiver by us of any provision of this Agreement or of any default hereunder shall affect our rights thereafter to enforce such provision or to exercise any right or remedy in the event of any other default, whether or not similar.

26. Notwithstanding any provision in this Agreement to the contrary, it is specifically understood and agreed as follows:

(a) You and we are bound by all the terms and provisions of the AFTRA Code of Fair Practice for Phonograph Recordings.

(b) Should there be any inconsistency between this Agreement and said Code, said Code shall prevail, but nothing in this provision shall affect terms, compensation, or conditions provided in this Agreement which are more favorable to members of AFTRA than the terms, compensation and conditions provided for in said Code.

(c) If the term of this Agreement is of longer duration than the term of the Code, then from and after the expiration date of the Code: (1) the provisions of this Agreement shall be deemed modified to conform to any agreement or modifications negotiated or agreed to in a renewal or extension of the Code; and (2) while no Code is in effect, the existence of this Agreement shall not prevent you from engaging in any strike or work stoppage without penalty by way of damage or otherwise to you or AFTRA. In the event you engage in such strike or stoppage, we may suspend this Agreement for the duration of the strike or stoppage, which option must be exercised by written notice given to you within thirty (30) days after the end of the strike or stoppage.

(d) You are or will become a member of AFTRA in good standing subject to and in accordance with the union security provisions of said Code.

(e) You are covered by Paragraph 34 of said Code, entitled "AFTRA Pension and Welfare Funds."

27. You hereby grant to us an option to become obligated to pay to each of you minimum compensation in the amount of Six Thousand Dollars ($6,000.00) per year, for the then current and any remaining years of this Agreement, which sum shall include union-scale payments, advances, and royalties otherwise payable to you under this Agreement. Such option may be exercised by us at any time during the initial or any renewal period of this Agreement on written notice to you.

~~28. No payment under this Agreement shall be subject,~~ in any manner, to anticipation, alienation, sale, transfer, assignment, pledge, encumbrance, or charge, or to attachment, garnishment, or other legal process. Any attempted anticipation, alienation, sale, transfer, assignment, pledge, encumbrance, or charge of payments or subjection of payments to lien or adverse legal process of any kind, will be without force or effect and will not be recognized by us, and in such case, we may terminate your right to such payments and/or direct that they be held or ~~applied for your benefit.~~

29. Within 14 days after the commencement of the date specified in Column "A" below we shall pay you the corresponding amount set forth in Column "B" below:

Column "A"	Column "B"
First option period	$10,000.00
Second option period	$15,000.00
Third option period	$20,000.00
Fourth option period	$25,000.00

The aforesaid amounts in this Paragraph 29, shall be deemed to be advances against and shall be recoupable by us from royalties otherwise payable to you hereunder.

30. We agree to commercially release at least one album in the United States during each current period of this agreement as a condition precedent to our right to exercise our next succeeding option hereunder.

31. During the term hereof, we shall not have the right to release records in the form of "premiums" or as "budget line" without your prior consent.

32. The individual producer(s) of masters hereunder shall be subject to your and our mutual approval.

33. The preparation of art work for album covers and liners hereunder shall be mutually approved by you and us.

34. Notwithstanding anything to the contrary contained herein, this agreement shall not be cross-collateralized with any other agreement.

35. We shall not have the right to release so-called "audiovisual" records hereunder until such time as you and we have mutually agreed upon a royalty to be paid to you on sales of such audiovisual records.

36. Notwithstanding anything to the contrary contained herein, you shall have the right to make recordings for parties other than us for sound tracks of motion pictures and television provided such third party shall not have the right to release such sound-track recordings in record form unless such release by the third party is a condition precedent to your entering into an agreement with such third party and provided you have utilized your best efforts to obtain such sound-track record rights for us. In no event shall anyone but us have the right to release "single" records from such sound-track recordings.

37. We agree to spend not less than $20,000.00 per year to promote your records hereunder which amount shall not be recoupable from royalties otherwise payable to you hereunder and which amount shall be in addition to all other

amounts including, without limitation, our overhead, salaries, and administrative expenses.

38. Notwithstanding anything to the contrary contained herein, we agree not to apply a free-record policy to your records hereunder which is less favorable to you than the then current "free goods" policy in effect with respect to a majority of our other recording artists.

39. We shall not utilize your records hereunder as so-called "loss leaders" to induce the sale of records not recorded hereunder. Further, we shall pro-rate records returned hereunder in the same proportion as such records were shipped.

40. We agree to pay you fifty (50%) percent of amounts received by us with respect to records hereunder as so-called public "performance royalties."

41. You shall have the right during the term hereof to perform as a non-featured "sideman" along with other performers, provided your name shall not be utilized in a size larger than any other "sideman" on records and in no event shall your picture and/or likeness be utilized by any third party on records embodying your performances as a "sideman" during the term hereof.

If the foregoing correctly reflects your understanding and agreement with us, please so indicate by signing below.

Yours very truly,
XYZ RECORDS, INC.

By:_____

ACCEPTED AND AGREED:

_____ _____

Social Security No._____

Date of Birth_____

PRODUCTION CONTRACT

XYZ RECORDS, INC.
Beverly Hills, California

Date:_____

Artist's Recording Company

Gentlemen:

The following will confirm our understanding and Agreement with you with respect to your production, in our behalf exclusively, of master recordings featuring the recording artists, Mr. and/or Ms. Artist (jointly and severally hereinafter sometimes called "Artist"):

1. During the term hereof, you shall at our request produce master recordings featuring performances of the Artist (such master recordings being hereinafter sometimes called the "Masters").

2. Recording sessions for the Masters shall be conducted by you under your recording license, on dates and at studios or other locations to be ~~designated by us promptly upon our request.~~ *mutually designated by you and us.* We shall have the right and opportunity to have our representatives attend each such recording session. Each Master shall consist of a performance by the Artist of a selection designated by ~~us~~ *you* and shall be subject to our approval as ~~commercially~~ satisfactory for the production of records. Upon our request you shall cause the Artist to rerecord any Master until a recording *technically* commercially satisfactory ~~to us~~ shall have been obtained. You shall deliver to us a monaural tape and a two-track stereo tape for each Master, which tapes shall be fully edited, remixed, and leadered prior to delivery to us, so that they are in proper form for the production of the parts necessary for the manufacture of records. Each and every original session tape, and part thereof, and each and every mother, master, acetate copy, or other derivative shall also be delivered to us or kept available for us and subject to our control at the recording studio.

3. The term of this agreement shall commence as of the date hereof and shall continue for an initial period of one (1) year.

4. During the initial period hereof, you shall produce and deliver to us a minimum of sufficient number of Masters to constitute one single-disc 33-⅓ rpm normal length 12″ long-playing album (such album an "LP" herein), plus additional Masters at our election. ~~If more than the minimum number of Masters are produced at our~~ request during the initial period or any renewal period, we may at our election apply all or any part of the excess Masters toward the fulfillment of the minimum number of Masters ~~specified for the subsequent renewal period.~~ If you fail to deliver the minimum number of Masters for any period any later than one hundred twenty (120) days prior to the end of such period, we may terminate this agreement by notice in writing to you, and if we do not so terminate this Agreement, then such period shall automatically be extended until one hundred twenty (120) days after the delivery of such minimum number of Masters.

5. You hereby warrant and represent that you now have the exclusive right to the Artist's recording services under a valid and binding recording contract, that you shall continue to have such exclusive right during the term hereof (including any renewals or extensions), that you shall not offer, convey or deliver any Masters or other recordings featuring the Artist to any party other than us, and that you shall not release the Artist from any term or provision of said recording contract, agree to any termination of said contract, fail to exercise any renewal or extension option with respect thereto, breach, or cause a breach of said contract, permit any such breach by the Artist, or cause, authorize, or knowingly permit the Artist to perform for the purpose of making phonograph records for any party other than us, all during the term hereof (including any renewals or extensions). You are delivering to us simultaneously herewith a signed copy or a photocopy of your recording contract with the Artist.

6. All Masters made hereunder, all reproductions made therefrom, the performances embodied therein, and the worldwide copyrights in and to the Masters (including any renewals and extensions), shall be entirely our property free of any claims whatsoever by you, the Artist, or any party deriving any rights or interests through or from you or the Artist. Without limitation of the foregoing, we and/or our designees shall have the worldwide right in perpetuity to manufacture, sell, distribute and advertise records or other reproductions (visual or nonvisual), embodying such recordings, to lease, license, convey or otherwise use or dispose of the recordings by any method now or hereafter known, in any field of use, to release ⋏records under any trademarks, trade names, or labels, to perform the records or other reproductions publicly and to permit the public performance thereof by radio broadcast, television, or any other method now or hereafter known, all upon such terms and conditions as we may approve, and to permit others to do any or all of the foregoing, or we may at our election refrain from any or all of the foregoing.

provided the initial release of each record hereunder shall be on our "top-line" label,

We shall have the worldwide right in perpetuity to use and to permit others to use your name, the name (both legal and professional) of any other person who may produce Masters hereunder and the name (both legal and professional) and likeness of and biographical material concerning the Artist for advertising and purposes of trade and otherwise, without restriction in connection record   with our business ~~and products~~. We shall have the further right to refer to the Artist, by his legal or professional name, as our exclusive artist, and you shall cause him, in his activities in the entertainment field, to use his best efforts to be billed and advertised as our exclusive artist.

7. During the term of this agreement you will not, for phonograph record purposes, furnish the recording services of the Artist to, or permit the Artist to record for, any party other than us. During a period of ~~five (5)~~ years [three (3)] after the expiration or termination of this agreement, you will not, for phonograph record purposes, furnish the recording services of the Artist to, or permit the Artist to record for, any party other than us in the recording of any selection embodied in any Master recorded by the Artist hereunder. ~~During the term hereof and for five (5) years thereafter, you shall not produce or record a recording of any selection recorded hereunder unless with an entirely different arrangement.~~

8. You will not at any time manufacture, distribute or sell, or authorize or knowingly permit the manufacture, distribution or sale by any party other than us of phonograph records embodying (a) any performance rendered by the Artist during the term of this agreement or (b) any performance rendered by Artist within ~~five (5) years~~ [three (3) years] after the expiration or termination of this Agreement of any selection which shall have been recorded hereunder. You will not record or authorize or knowingly permit to be recorded, for any purpose, any such performance without in each case taking reasonable measures to prevent the manufacture, distribution, and sale at any time by any party other than us of phonograph records embodying such performance. Specifically, without limiting the generality of the foregoing, you agree that if, during the term of this agreement, the Artist performs any selection for the purpose of making transcriptions for radio or television or sound tracks for motion-picture films, or if, within ~~five (5) years~~ [three (3) years] after the expiration or termination of this agreement the Artist performs for any such purpose any selection which shall have been recorded hereunder, he will do so only pursuant to a written contract containing an express provision that neither such performance nor any recording thereof will be used directly or indirectly for the purpose of making phonograph records. You will promptly deliver to us a copy of the pertinent provisions of each such contract and will cooperate fully with us in any controversy which may arise or litigation which may be brought relating to our rights under this paragraph.

9. No recording sessions shall be produced or conducted by you hereunder, nor shall any musicians, vocalists, or arrangers be engaged by you hereunder, unless and until a written proposed recording budget for each such session shall have been submitted by you in writing and approved in writing by one of our officers. We shall not be obligated to reimburse you under Paragraph 11 hereof for recording fees for vocalists or musicians or for arranging fees if any such fees shall exceed union scale, unless such excess and the proposed recipient thereof are specified in said budget and approved by us. Further, the selection of the line producer for the Masters to be delivered by you hereunder shall be subject to ᶺour written approval, which approval we agree we will not withhold unreasonably.   your and

10. You shall be responsible for, and shall promptly pay when due, all recording costs with respect to the Masters, including, without limitation, the recording fees for the Artist and all other performers or persons connected with the recording (including instrumentalists, leaders, contractors, arrangers, copyists, and vocalists), studio rentals, editing and mastering costs, pension and welfare payments, costs of cartage and instrument hire, and payroll taxes. All such payments shall be in accordance with the requirements of the American Federation of Musicians ("AFM"), the American Federation of Television and Radio Artists ("AFTRA"), and all other appropriate unions.

11. Upon submission to us of Masters recorded hereunder, together with evidence of your payment of all recording costs therefor (i.e., receipted bills), we shall promptly reimburse you for such recording costs, provided, however, we shall not reimburse you for recording costs which shall exceed the approved budget. All payments made by us to you in reimbursement of recording costs shall constitute a nonreturnable advance against any and all royalties which may be earned by you under this agreement or under any other agreement between you and us relating to the Artist. It is of the essence of this agreement that we be furnished with copies of all union contract forms and report forms for recording sessions hereunder, all bills pertaining to such recording sessions and all ordinary payroll forms (including, without limitation, all W-4 and other Withholding Tax forms), pertaining to such recording sessions within forty-eight (48) hours after each recording session and in accordance with all applicable union requirements.

12. Conditioned upon your full and faithful performance of all of the terms hereof, we will pay to you in respect of recordings made hereunder the following royalty upon the terms hereinafter set forth:

(a) On our sales in the United States of records in the

fourteen percent
(14%)

form of discs, a royalty of ~~ten percent (10%)~~ of our retail price from time to time of each such record (less discounts).

(b) On sale of records outside of the United States,

seven percent (7%)

the royalty payable hereunder shall be ~~five percent (5%)~~ of the suggested retail list price of the records in the country of manufacture, the United States, England, or the country of sale, as we shall be paid. Such royalties shall be computed in the national currency of the applicable country and shall be credited to your royalty account hereunder at the same rate of exchange as we are paid.

(c) Royalties with respect to records in the form of prerecorded tapes, in any configuration ("tape"), sold by us or our licensees, shall by payable at ~~one-half (½) the~~

the same

~~applicable~~ royalty rates set forth in subparagraphs (a) or (b) above.

(d) Notwithstanding any of the foregoing, the royalty on records sold by us in the United States through any direct mail or mail-order distribution method, or by us or our licensees through record-club distribution, shall be one-half (½) that royalty set forth in Paragraph (b) above based on the price to club members or direct-mail purchasers; and the royalty on records sold outside of the United States through any direct-mail distribution or

one-half (½)

record-club method shall be ~~one-fourth (¼)~~ of the royalty rate provided for in (b) above and shall be based upon the price to the club members of direct-mail purchasers. Notwithstanding the foregoing, you shall be paid royalties on not less than 50% of the aggregate number of records distributed by the applicable record club, direct-mail operation, or similar sales plan or distribution method. In the event that we manufacture and sell records hereunder by means of a record club, direct-mail operation, or similar sales plan or distribution method which is owned or controlled by us, we shall pay you your full royalty rate on such sales.

(e) No royalties shall be payable on records furnished as free or bonus records to members, applicants or other participants in any record club or as free or bonus records to purchasers through any direct-mail distribution method; on records distributed for promotional purposes, including, without limitation, "sampler" records; on records sold for scrap or as cut-outs; records shipped on a no-charge or "freebie" basis, or sold at less than fifty percent (50%) of our full wholesale price. (Any discounts granted by us to our customers may be applied by us, porportionately in computing the royalties payable hereunder.)

Notwithstanding the foregoing you shall be paid royalties on not less than eight (8) albums for each ten (10) albums distributed hereunder and on not less than seven (7) "singles" for each ten (10) "singles" distributed.

(f) The royalty rate on records sold for use as premiums or promotional merchandise or sold on a "budget" or less than full-price label, shall be one-half (½) of the royalty rate provided for in (a) or (b) above, as applicable, and shall be based upon the price received by us for such records.

(g) On our sales by our licensees throughout the world by means or media other than those specifically provided in Paragraphs (a) through (f) above (including, without limitation, those sales on a flat-fee basis), whether visual or nonvisual, we shall credit your royalty account with that percentage of the net sum received by us from such sales which percentage shall be ~~that royalty rate set forth in Paragraph (a) above.~~ fifty percent (50%) of the royalty received by us from such sales.

(h) Notwithstanding any of the foregoing,

(i) for purposes of computing royalties, any excise, sales, or comparable or similar taxes shall be excluded from the price;

(ii) for purposes of computing royalties, we may exclude from the wholesale or retail price, as applicable, as an allowance for packaging, an amount equal to ten percent (10%) of such price with respect to "single-fold" album jackets or covers; twelve and one-half percent (12-½%) of such price with respect to "double-fold" album jackets or covers; and ~~twenty-five percent (25%)~~ twenty percent (20%) of such price with respect to tape-device containers or boxes or any other form of package, container, or box not described herein; and

(iii) royalties shall be computed and paid upon ~~ninety percent (90%)~~ one hundred percent (100%) of sales (less returns) for which payment has been received, except that royalties with respect to licensee sales shall be computed and paid upon that number of sales as such licensee computes and pays us.

(i) No royalties shall be payable to you on sales by any of our licensees until payment on such sales has been received by us. In the event we shall not receive payment in United States dollars in the United States from any foreign licensee, and we shall accept payment in foreign currency, we may deposit to your credit (and at your expense), such foreign currency, in a depository selected by ~~us,~~ any payments so received as royalties applicable to this Agreement which are then payable to **you,** and we shall notify you thereof promptly. Deposit as aforesaid shall fulfill our obligations hereunder as to record sales to which such royalty payments are applicable.

(j) If any Master is coupled on a record with other recordings, the royalty hereunder shall be pro-rated based upon the portion the number of Masters bears to the aggregate number of all recordings embodied on such record.

(k) If any Master is recorded hereunder by Artist jointly with another artist or musician to whom we are obliged to pay a royalty in respect thereof, the royalties payable to you applicable to records produced therefrom shall be reduced proportionately, and only the proportionate share of the applicable costs set forth in Paragraph 2 above shall be charged against your royalties.

(l) Statements as to royalties payable hereunder shall be sent by us to you on or before September 30 for the semiannual period ending the preceding June 30 and on or before March 31 for the semiannual period ending the preceding December 31, together with payment of accrued royalties, if any, earned by you during the preceding semiannual period less all advances and charges under this Agreement or any other Agreement between you and us. Upon submission of each statement, we shall have the right to retain as reserve against subsequent charges, credits, or returns, such portion of payable royalties as shall be necessary and appropriate in our best business judgment. You shall be deemed to have consented to all royalty statements and all other accounts rendered by us to you, and said statements and other accounts shall be binding upon you and not subject to any objection by you for any reason, unless specific objection in writing, stating the basis thereof, is given by you to us within ~~one (1) year~~ from the date rendered. We shall maintain books of account concerning the sale, distribution, and exploitation of records made hereunder. You or a certified public accountant ("CPA") in your behalf may, at your expense, at reasonable intervals, examine our books pertaining to the records made hereunder during our usual business hours and upon reasonable notice. Our books relating to activities during

Margin annotations (left column):

you,

with your consent (except for the release by us of so-called "Best of" or "sampler" type albums embodying not more than two Masters per year hereunder),

with your consent

which reserves shall be liquidated within three accounting periods following the date of first withhold thereof.

two (2) years

any accounting period may be examined only as afore-
said during the ~~one (1) year~~ period following service by   two (2) year
us of the statement for said accounting period. The right
to audit shall be accorded to a CPA only, which CPA shall
be subject to our reasonable approval, acting under a
Letter of Confidentiality which shall provide that any
information derived from such audit or examination shall
not be knowingly released, divulged, or published to any
person, firm, or corporation other than one directly related
to you or to a body having jurisdiction over such audit
or examination. Further, no such examination shall be
conducted the payment for which is based on a contingent-fee arrangement.

   (m) You agree and acknowledge that we shall have
the right to withhold from the royalties payable to you
hereunder such amount, if any, as may be required under
the applicable provisions of the California Revenue and
Taxation Code, and you agree to execute such forms and
other documents as may be required in connection
therewith.

13. You shall be solely responsible for and shall pay to
the Artist and any individual producer and any other
profit participant any and all royalties which may be payable to each of them by reason of the manufacture and
sale throughout the world of records embodying Masters
recorded hereunder or by reason of any other exploitation
of the Masters.

14. You expressly acknowledge that the Masters and the
recording services and other rights granted hereunder
are of a special, unique, and intellectual character which
gives them peculiar value, the loss of which cannot be
reasonably or adequately determined at law, and that in
the event of a breach by you or the Artist of any term,
condition or covenant hereof, we ~~will~~ be caused irreparable   may
injury. You expressly agree that in the event you or the
Artist shall breach any provision of this agreement, we
shall be entitled to injunctive and other equitable relief   seek
                     ^
and/or damages, in addition to any other rights or remedies
available to us, and we shall have the right to recoup
any damages from any sums which may thereafter become
due and payable to you hereunder, including sums otherwise payable to you after the expiration or termination
of this agreement.

15. You warrant and represent that you are under no
disability, restriction, or prohibition, whether contractual
or otherwise, with respect to your right to execute this

contract, grant the rights herein granted and perform its terms and conditions, and with respect to the Artist's right to record any and all selections hereunder. You specifically warrant and represent that no selections recorded or to be recorded by the Artist hereunder are subject to any rerecording restriction under any previous recording contract to which the Artist may have been a party. You further warrant and represent that none of the Masters nor any of the contents thereof, nor the manufacture and sale of records made therefrom, nor any other exploitation or use thereof, will violate or infringe upon any common-law or statutory rights of any party, including, without limitation, contractual rights, copyrights, and rights of privacy. You agree to and do hereby indemnify, save, and hold us harmless from any and all loss and damage (including reasonable attorneys' fees) *which is reduced to* arising out of or connected with any claim by a third *judgment and* party which is inconsistent with any of the warranties, representations, or agreements made by you in this Agreement, and you agree to reimburse us, on demand, for any payment made by us at any time after the date *in an amount* hereof with respect to any liability or claim to which the *reasonably related to* foregoing indemnity applies. Pending the determination *the amount of such* of any such claim, we may withhold payment of royalties *claim.* or other monies hereunder.

16. We reserve the right, at our election, to suspend the operation of this Agreement if, for any reason whatsoever, *and/or Artist* you are unavailable and/or fail, refuse, or neglect to perform hereunder in accordance with the provisions hereof, or if, due to any labor controversy or adjustment thereof, or to any other cause not entirely within our control or which we cannot by reasonable diligence avoid, we are materially hampered in the recording, manufacture, distribution or sale of records, or our normal business operations become commercially impractical. Such suspension shall last for the duration of any such contingency or unavailability. At our election, a period of time equal to the duration of such suspension and/or unavailability and/or failure, neglect, or refusal to perform shall be added at the end of either the then current period (whether initial or renewal), or any subsequent period for which we exercise our option, including, without limitation, the final such renewal period, and such period shall be accordingly extended.

Unless cause for such suspension pursuant to this Paragraph 16 is due to your and/or Artist's unavailability, failure, refusal, and/or neglect to perform, or unless the cause affects the entire record industry, our right to suspend the operation of this agreement shall be limited to six (6) months.

17. We may, at our election, and upon written notice to you, assign this Agreement or any part hereof to any party who shall assume our obligations hereunder.

18. ~~Nothing herein contained shall obligate us to have~~ you produce the minimum number of Mas~~ters specified~~ for any term hereof, it being agr~~eed that~~ the sole obligation to you as to unr~~ecorded~~ Masters shall be to pay to you the A~~rtist's~~ union minimum-scale recording fee for ~~each such unrecorded Master~~. This Agreement sets forth the entire agreement between you and us with respect to the subject matter hereof. No modification, amendment, waiver, termination, or discharge of this Agreement or any provisions hereof shall be binding upon us unless confirmed by a written instrument signed by a duly authorized officer of our company. No waiver by us of any provisions of this Agreement or of any default hereunder shall affect our rights thereafter to enforce such provision or to exercise any right or remedy in the event of any other default, whether or not similar.

19. If the voice of the Artist should be materially and permanently impaired, ~~or if the Artist should do any act~~ offensive to decency, morality, or social prop~~riety tending~~ to result in public scandal, hatre~~d, ridicule~~, or contempt, or if the Artist shoul~~d violate~~ or be charged with a violation of ~~any law~~ which tends to subject him or us to any ~~scandal, hatred, ridicule, or contempt,~~ or if the Artist should fail, refuse, or neglect to comply with any obligations under his recording contract, then in addition to any other rights or remedies which we may have, we may elect to terminate our obligations hereunder by notice in writing and shall thereby be relieved of any liability in connection with unrecorded Masters.

20. This Agreement shall be deemed to have been made in the State of (name of applicable state) and its validity, construction, and effect shall be governed by the laws of the State of (name of applicable state) applicable to agreements wholly performed therein. If any provision of this Agreement shall be declared invalid, same shall not affect the validity of the remaining provisions hereof.

21. All notices which we shall desire to give to you hereunder, and all statements, royalties, and other payments which are due you hereunder, shall be addressed to you at the address set forth on Page 1 hereof until you shall give us written notice of a new address. All notices which you shall desire to give to us hereunder shall be addressed to us at the address set forth on Page 1 hereof until we shall give you written notice of a new address. All notices shall be in writing and shall be delivered personally (to an officer if the addressee is a corporation), or served by mail or telegraph, postal or telegraph charges prepaid, addressed as aforesaid. The date of making personal service, of depositing said notice in the mails or of depositing same in a telegraph office, whichever shall be first, shall be deemed the date of service.

22. Nothing herein shall create any association, partnership, joint venture, or the relation of principal and agent between the parties hereto. You and we are, with respect to each other, independent contractors, and neither party shall bind the other in any way.

23. Except as otherwise provided herein, the term "records" or "phonograph records" shall include all forms of recordings (both visual and nonvisual), including, without limitation, discs of any speed or size, prerecorded tapes, cartridges, and any other recorded devices now known or which may hereafter become known.

24. This Agreement shall not be binding upon us until signed by you and countersigned by our duly authorized officer.

25. Each selection embodied in a Master recorded hereunder and published or copublished by you or a person, firm or corporation affiliated or connected with you directly or indirectly, or by the Artist, or written by the Artist, shall by licensed to us, at our election, ~~at a royalty~~ at the statutory rate per selection current at the time of licensing. ~~of $.015 per record side on the basis of ninety percent (90%) of records manufactured and sold. Arranged ver~~sions of musical compositions in the public domain, when furnished by you for recordings hereunder, shall be free of copyright royalties. Any assignment made by you or by the publishing company referred to above of the copyright or any interest in any such selection or in any such arranged version of a musical composition in the public domain shall be made subject to the provisions ~~hereof.~~

26. You hereby warrant, represent, and agree that:

(a) You are or, prior to the recording of the first Master hereunder, will become a signatory to the 1975 AFM Record Labor Agreement and Special Payments Funds Agreement, the 1975 AFM Music Performance Trust Agreement and the 1975 AFTRA Code for the Phonograph Record Industry and that you will, during the term hereof, become a signatory to any AFM or AFTRA agreements which shall succeed the foregoing Agreements and Code.

(b) All of the Masters shall be recorded in all respects in accordance with the then current AFM and AFTRA agreements and in accordance with agreements with all other unions having jurisdiction.

(c) You shall cause the Artist to become and remain a member in good standing of any appropriate union or unions with which you or we may at any time have an agreement lawfully requiring such union membership.

~~27. You hereby grant to us all merchandising rights and~~ the sole and exclusive right to use the name of Artist (both legal and professional), Artist's likeness, picture, and portrait in any manner whatsoever in connection with the exercise of the merchandising rights herein granted. We shall have the right to grant to others (including companies affiliated with us), upon such terms as we shall see fit, the right to exercise or cause to be exercised such merchandising rights. We shall credit to your royalty account in addition to any and all monies provided for in this contract, one-half (½) of all net monies received by us in connection with the exercise of said merchandis- ~~ing rights.~~

28. You will, upon our request, furnish Artist on dates and at film studios or other locations to be designated by us upon reasonable notice to you, for the filming, taping, or other permanent fixation of audiovisual repro- ductions or performances to be rendered by the Artist hereunder. In connection therewith, we or our designee will make a payment to the Artist for the services per- formed by him pursuant to the terms of this paragraph, within a reasonable time after the completion thereof, at the rate of appropriate union scale. We further agree to pay for reasonable transportation and accommodations for you if such location is more than thirty miles from Artist's place of residence, which travel and accommodation expenses shall be recoupable by us from royal- ties otherwise payable to you hereunder.

29. You hereby grant to us four (4) options, each to renew this contract for a one (1) year period, such renewal periods to run consecutively beginning at the expiration of the initial period, all upon the same terms and condi- tions applicable to the initial period except as otherwise specified in the schedule below and elsewhere. Each option may only be exercised by giving written notice at least thirty (30) days prior to the commencement of the renewal term for which the option is exercised. More than one (1) option may, at our election, be exercised at one time.

SCHEDULE

	Renewal Period	Minimum Number of Masters
2 LPs	1st	~~1 LP~~
2 LPs	2nd	~~1 LP~~
2 LPs	3rd	~~1 LP~~
2 LPs	4th	~~1 LP~~

30. We may secure in our own name or otherwise and at our own expense, life, accident, health, and other insurance covering Artist, either independently or together with others, and neither you nor Artist shall have any right, title, or interest in and to such insurance. You shall cause Artist to assist us to procure such insurance by timely submitting to medical examinations and by signing such applications and other instruments in writing as may be required by the insurance company involved. ~~If we are unable to obtain such insurance on Artist at standard rates without any exclusions or medical or other restrictions of any kind and without requirement of compliance with extraordinary conditions or nonstandard conditions of any kind imposed because of Artist's medical and physical condition, we shall have the right to terminate this agreement without liability by giving you written notice of termination within ten (10) days after we acquire knowledge that Artist shall fail to pass a physical examination for such insurance or otherwise qualify for such insurance on such conditions.~~

31. In the event that one or more of the Artists breach or disaffirm this Agreement, or in the event that one or more of the Artists are unable, or fails to render his services as required hereby, then, in addition to any and all other rights, we shall have at law or in equity, the unlimited right either to cause you to continue to produce the Artists who are available and not in default hereunder, or to terminate this agreement.

32. No failure by us to perform any of our obligations hereunder shall be deemed a breach hereof unless you shall have given us written notice of such failure and we shall have failed to cure such nonperformance within sixty (60) days after receipt of such notice.

33. You hereby grant to us an option to become obligated to pay to each of the Artists minimum compensation in the sum of Six Thousand Dollars ($6,000.00) each per year, for the then current and any remaining years of this agreement, which sum shall include union-scale payments, advances and royalties otherwise payable to you under this Agreement. Such option may be exercised by us at any time during the initial or any renewal period of this Agreement on written notice to you.

34. No payment under this Agreement shall be subject in any manner to anticipation, alienation, sale, transfer, assignment, pledge, encumbrance, or charge, or to attachment, garnishment, or other legal process. Any attempted anticipation, alienation, sale, transfer, assignment, pledge, encumbrance, or charge of payments or subjection of payments to lien or adverse legal process of any kind will be without force or effect and will not be recognized by us, and in such case we may terminate your right to such payments and/or direct that they be held or applied for your benefit.

35. Within 14 days after the commencement of the date specified in Column "A" below we shall pay you the corresponding amount set forth in Column "B" below:

	Column "A"	Column "B"
	First option period	$10,000.00
	Second option period	$15,000.00
	Third option period	$20,000.00
	Fourth option period	$25,000.00

The aforesaid amounts in this Paragraph 35 shall be deemed to be advances against and shall be recoupable by us from royalties otherwise payable to you hereunder.

36. We agree to commercially release at least one album in the United States during each current period of this agreement as a condition precedent to our right to exercise our next succeeding option hereunder.

37. During the term hereof, we shall not have the right to release records in the form of "premiums" or as "budget line" without your prior consent.

38. The individual producer(s) of masters hereunder shall be subject to your and our mutual approval.

39. The preparation of art work for album covers and liners hereunder shall be mutually approved by you and us.

40. Notwithstanding anything to the contrary contained herein, this Agreement shall not be cross-collateralized with any other Agreement.

41. We shall not have the right to release so-called "audiovisual" records hereunder until such time as you and we have mutually agreed upon a royalty to be paid to you on sales of such audiovisual records.

42. Notwithstanding anything to the contrary contained herein, Artist shall have the right to make recordings for parties other than us for sound tracks of motion pictures and television provided such third party shall not have the right to release such sound-track recordings in record form unless such release by the third party is a condition precedent to Artist's entering into an agreement with such

third party and provided you have utilized your best efforts to obtain such sound-track record rights for us. In no event shall anyone but us have the right to release "single" records from such sound-track recordings.

43. We agree to spend not less than $20,000.00 per year to promote records hereunder which amount shall not be recoupable from royalties otherwise payable to you hereunder and which amount shall be in addition to all other amounts including, without limitation, our overhead, salaries, and administrative expenses.

44. Notwithstanding anything to the contrary contained herein, we agree not to apply a free-record policy to records hereunder which is less favorable to you than the then current "free goods" policy in effect with respect to a majority of our other recording artists.

45. We shall not utilize records recorded hereunder as so-called "loss leaders" to induce the sale of records not recorded hereunder. Further, we shall pro-rate records returned hereunder in the same proportion as such records were shipped.

46. We agree to pay you fifty (50%) percent of amounts received by us with respect to records hereunder as so-called "public performance royalties."

47. Artist shall have the right during the term hereof to perform as a non-featured "sideman" along with other performers, provided Artist's name shall not be utilized in a size larger than any other "sideman" on records, and in no event shall Artist's picture and/or likeness be utilized by any third party on records embodying Artist's performances as a "sideman" during the term hereof.

If the foregoing correctly reflects your understanding and Agreement with us, please so indicate by signing below.

Yours very truly,
XYZ RECORDS, INC.

By:_____

ACCEPTED AND AGREED:

Artist's Recording Company

By:_____

PERSONAL MANAGEMENT CONTRACT

Date:_____

To: Mr. Personal Manager
     Beverly Hills, California

I desire to obtain your advice, counsel, and direction in the development and enhancement of my artistic and

theatrical career. The nature and extent of the success
or failure of my career cannot be predetermined, and it is
therefore my desire that your compensation be determined
in such manner as will permit you to accept the risk of
failure and likewise benefit to the extent of my success.
In view of the foregoing, we have agreed as follows:

I do hereby engage you as my PERSONAL MANAGER
for a period of ~~five years from date.~~
one year. I grant you four options each to renew this contract for a one year period,
such renewal periods to run consecutively beginning at the expiration of the initial period except as otherwise specified herein. Each option may only be exercised by giving written notice to me at least thirty (30) days prior to the commencement of the renewal term for which the option is exercised. Notwithstanding anything to the contrary contained herein, a condition precedent to your right to exercise your next option hereunder shall be the receipt by me of at least $20,000 in the then current period hereof as compensation for my services as a recording and performing artist and the appearance of at least one record embodying my performances in the Top 20 of the Top 100 charts of "Billboard," "Cashbox," or "Record World" during the then current period.

As and when requested by me during and throughout
the term hereof, you agree to perform for me one or more
of the services as follows: advise and counsel in the
selection of literary, artistic, and musical material; advise and counsel in any and all matters pertaining to
publicity, public relations, and advertising; advise and
counsel with relation to the adaption of proper format
for presentation of my artistic talents and in the determination of proper style, mood, setting, business, and
characterization in keeping with my talents; advise,
counsel, and direct in the selection of artistic talent to
assist, accompany, or embellish my artistic presentation;
advise and counsel with regard to general practices in
the entertainment and amusement industries and with
respect to such matters of which you may have knowledge
concerning compensation and privileges extended for
similar artistic values; advise and counsel concerning
the selection of theatrical agencies, artists' managers,
and persons, firms and corporations who will counsel,
advise, seek, and procure employment and engagements
for me.

You are authorized and empowered for me and in my
behalf and in your discretion to do the following: approve
and permit any and all publicity and advertising; approve
and permit the use of my name, photograph, likeness,
voice, sound effects, caricatures, literary, artistic, and
musical materials for purposes of advertising and publicity
and in the promotion and advertising of any and all

products and services; execute for me in my name and/or in my behalf any and all agreements, documents, and contracts for my services, talents, and/or artistic, literary, and musical materials; collect and receive sums as well as endorse my name upon and cash any and all checks payable to me for my services, talents, and literary and artistic materials and retain therefrom all sums owing to you; engage as well as discharge and/or direct for me, and in my name theatrical agents, artists' managers, and employment agencies as well as other persons, firms, and corporations who may be retained to obtain contracts, engagements, or employment for me. You are not required to make any loans or advances to me or for my account, but in the event you do so, I shall repay them promptly, and I hereby authorize you to deduct the amount of any such loans or advances from any sums you may receive for my account. The authority herein granted to you is coupled with an interest and shall be irrevocable during the term hereof.

I agree at all times to devote myself to my career and to do all things necessary and desirable to promote my career and earnings therefrom. I shall at all times engage and utilize proper theatrical agents, employment agencies, or artists' managers to obtain engagements and employment for me, but I shall not engage any theatrical agents, employment services, or artists' managers of which you may disapprove. I shall advise you of all offers of employment submitted to me and will refer any inquiries concerning my services to you, in order that you may determine whether the same are compatible with my career. I shall instruct any theatrical agency or artists' manager engaged by me to remit to you all monies that may become due me and may be received by it. (IT IS CLEARLY UNDERSTOOD THAT YOU ARE NOT AN EMPLOYMENT AGENT OR THEATRICAL AGENT OR ARTISTS' MANAGER, THAT YOU HAVE NOT OFFERED OR ATTEMPTED OR PROMISED TO OBTAIN, SEEK OR PROCURE EMPLOYMENT OR ENGAGEMENTS FOR ME, AND THAT YOU ARE NOT OBLIGATED, AUTHORIZED, LICENSED, OR EXPECTED TO DO SO.)

This Agreement shall not be construed to create a partnership between us. It is specifically understood that you are acting hereunder as an independent contractor and you may appoint or engage any and all other persons, firms, and corporations throughout the world in your discretion to perform any or all of the services which you have agreed to perform hereunder. Your services hereunder are not exclusive and you shall at all times be free to perform the same or similar services for others as well as engage in any and all other business activities. You shall be required only to render reasonable services which are called for by this Agreement as and when reasonably requested by me. Due to the difficulty which we may have in determining the amount of services to which I may be entitled, it is agreed that you shall not be deemed to be in default hereunder until and unless I shall first give to you written notice by Certified Mail, describing the exact service which I require on your part and then only in the event that you shall thereafter fail for a period of fifteen consecutive days to commence the rendition of the particular service required. You shall not be required to travel or to meet with me at any particular place or places except in your discretion and following arrangements for costs and expenses of such travel.

In compensation for your services, I agree to pay to you, as and when received by me, and during and throughout the term thereof, a sum equal to twenty percent (20%) of any and all gross monies or other considerations which I may receive as a result of my activities in and throughout the entertainment, amusement, music, recording, and publishing industries, including any and all sums resulting from the use of my artistic talents and the results and proceeds thereof and, without in any manner limiting the foregoing, the matters upon which your compensation shall be computed shall include any and all of my activities in connection with matters as follows: motion pictures, television, radio, music, literary, theatrical engagements, personal appearances, public appearances in places of amusement, and entertainment, records, and recordings, publications, and the use of my name, likeness, and talents for purposes of advertising and trade. I likewise agree to pay you a similar sum following the expiration of the term hereof upon and with respect to any and all engagements, contracts, and agreements entered into during the term hereof relating to any of the foregoing and upon any and all extensions, renewals, and substitutions thereof and upon any resumptions of such engagements, contracts, and agreements which may have been discontinued during the term hereof and resumed within a year thereafter. The term "gross monies or other considerations" shall include, without limitation, salaries, earnings, fees, royalties, gifts, bonuses, shares of profit, shares of stock, partnership interest, percentages, and the total amount paid for a package television or radio program (live or recorded), motion-picture or other entertainment packages, earned or received directly or indirectly by me or my heirs, executors, administrators, or assigns, or by any other person, firm, or corporation on my behalf. In the event that I receive, as all or part of my compensation for activities hereunder, stock or the right to buy stock in any corporation or that I become the packager or owner of all or part of an entertainment property, whether as individual proprietor, stockholder, partner, joint venturer, or otherwise, your percentage shall apply to my said stock, right to buy stock, individual proprietorship, partnership, joint venture, or other form of interest, and you shall be entitled to your percentage share thereof. Should I be required to make any payment for your interest, you will pay your percentage share of such payment, unless you do not want your percentage share thereof.

In the event of any dispute under or relating to the terms of this Agreement, or the breach, validity, or legality thereof, it is agreed that the same shall be submitted to arbitration to the American Arbitration Association in (insert New York City or Los Angeles)_____, and in accordance with the rules promulgated by the said association, and judgment upon the award rendered by the arbitrator(s) may be entered in any court having jurisdiction thereof. In the event of litigation or arbitration, the prevailing party shall be entitled to recover any and all reasonable attorney's fees and other costs incurred in the enforcement of the terms of this Agreement or for the breach thereof. This arbitration provision shall remain in full force and effect notwithstanding the nature of any claim or defense hereunder.

If this Agreement is with an individual, you shall have the right to assign it to any corporation or partnership in which you are a stockholder or partner or by which you may be employed, or to an individual by whom you may be employed. If this Agreement is with a partnership, you shall have the right to assign it to a corporation in which any of the partners is a stockholder or by which any of the partners is employed, to another partnership consisting of one or more of the same partners, or to one or more of the partners. If this Agreement is with a corporation, you shall have the right to assign it to an individual who is a stockholder or to a partnership at least one of whose partners is a stockholder, or to another corporation which acquires all or substantially all of your assets.

This Agreement shall be deemed to be executed in the State of (applicable state), and shall be construed in accordance with the laws of said State. In the event that any provision hereof shall for any reason be illegal or unenforceable, then and in any such event, the same shall not affect the validity of the remaining portion and provisions hereof.

This Agreement is the only agreement of the parties, and there is no other or collateral agreement (oral or written) between the parties in any manner relating to the subject matter hereof.

YOU HAVE ADVISED ME THAT YOU ARE NOT AN "AR-TISTS' MANAGER," BUT ACTIVE SOLELY AS A PER-SONAL MANAGER, THAT YOU ARE NOT LICENSED AS AN "ARTISTS' MANAGER" UNDER THE LABOR CODE OF THE STATE OF CALIFORNIA OR AS A THEATRICAL EMPLOYMENT AGENCY UNDER THE GENERAL BUSI-NESS LAW OF THE STATE OF NEW YORK: YOU HAVE AT ALL TIMES ADVISED ME THAT YOU ARE NOT LI-CENSED TO SEEK OR OBTAIN EMPLOYMENT OR ENGAGEMENTS FOR ME AND THAT YOU DO NOT AGREE TO DO SO, AND YOU HAVE MADE NO REPRE-SENTATIONS TO ME, EITHER ORAL OR WRITTEN, TO THE CONTRARY.

As used in this agreement the terms "I" and/or "we" shall mean all of the members of the group jointly and severally, and as individual members of the group.

Notwithstanding anything to the contrary contained in this Agreement:

1. You shall not be entitled to any amounts hereunder from any events or agreements relating to me which occurred prior to the date of this Agreement.

2. In the event of any disagreement with respect to any agreements or arrangements relating to my career as an entertainer, my decision shall be final.

3. I shall have the right of approval of any person to whom you may assign your duties hereunder, and if I object to such person, I shall advise you of such objection. If you and I cannot agree on such assignment withint fourteen (14) business days following my written objection, I shall have the right to terminate the term of this Agreement by notice in writing to you.

If the foregoing meets with your approval please indicate your acceptance and agreement by signing in the space herein below provided.

Very truly yours,

_____
(Artists' Signature)

I DO HEREBY AGREE TO THE FOREGOING:

_____

(Personal Manager)

_____

EXCLUSIVE SONGWRITER'S AND COMPOSER'S AGREEMENT

THIS AGREEMENT made and entered into as of the____ day of_____, 19_____, by and between XYZ Music, Inc. (hereinafter referred to as "Publisher"), and Mr. and/or Ms. Songwriter (hereinafter referred to as "Writer"). For and in consideration of the mutual covenants herein set forth, the parties do hereby agree as follows:

1. *Employment.* Publisher hereby employs Writer to render his services as a songwriter and composer and otherwise as may hereinafter be set forth. Writer hereby accepts such employment and agrees to render such services exclusively for Publisher during the term hereof, upon the terms and conditions set forth herein.

2. *Term.* The term of this Agreement shall commence with the date hereof and shall continue in force for a period of six (6) months from said date.

3. *Grant of Rights.* Writer hereby irrevocably and absolutely assigns, transfers, sets over and grants to Publisher, its successors, and assigns, each and every and all rights and interests of every kind, nature, and description in and to the results and proceeds of Writer's services hereunder, including, but not limited to, the titles, words, and music of and all original musical compositions in any and all forms and original arrangements of musical compositions in the public domain in any and all forms, and/or all rights and interests existing under all agreements and licenses relating thereto together with all worldwide copyrights and renewals and extensions thereof, which musical works have been written, composed, created, or conceived, in whole or in part, by Writer alone or in collaboration with another or others, and which may hereafter, during the term hereof, be written, composed, created, or conceived by Writer, in whole or in part, alone or in collaboration with another or others, ~~and which are now owned or controlled~~ and which may, during the term hereof, be owned or controlled, directly or indirectly, by Writer, alone or with others, or as the employer or transferee, directly or indirectly, of the writers or composers thereof, including the title, words, and music of each such composition, and all worldwide copyrights and renewals and extensions thereof, all of which Writer does hereby represent are and shall at all times be Publisher's sole and exclusive property as the sole owner thereof, free from any adverse claims or rights therein by any other person, firm, or corporation. Writer acknowledges that included within the rights and interest hereinabove referred to, but without limiting the generality of the foregoing, is Writer's irrevocable grant to Publisher, its successors, licensees, sublicensees, and assigns, of the sole and exclusive right, license, and privilege and authority throughout the entire world with respect to the said original musical compositions and original arrangements of compositions in the public domain, whether now in existence or hereafter created during the term hereof, as follows:

(a) To perform said musical compositions publicly for profit by means of public and private performance, radio broadcasting, television, or any and all other means, whether now known or which may hereafter come into existence.

(b) To substitute a new title or titles for said compositions and to make any arrangement, adaptation, translation, dramatization and transposition of said compositions, in whole or in part, and in connection with any other musical, literary or dramatic material as Publisher may deem expedient or desirable.

(c) To secure copyright registration and protection of said compositions in Publisher's name, or otherwise, as Publisher may desire, at Publisher's own cost and expense and at Publisher's election, including any and all renewals and extensions of copyrights, and to have and to hold said copyrights, renewals, extensions, and all rights of whatsoever nature thereunder existing, for and during the full term of all said copyrights and all renewals and extensions thereof.

(d) To make or cause to be made master records, transcriptions, sound tracks, pressings, and any other mechanical, electrical, or other reproductions of said compositions, in whole or in part, in such form or manner and as frequently as publisher's sole and uncontrolled discretion shall determine, including the right to synchronize the same with sound motion pictures and the right to manufacture, advertise, license, or sell such reproductions for any and all purposes, including, but not limited to, private performances and public performances by broadcasting, television, sound motion pictures, wired radio, and any and all other means or devices, whether now known or which may hereafter come into existence.

(e) To print, publish, and sell sheet music, orchestrations, arrangements, and other editions of said compositions in all forms, including the right to include any or all of said compositions in song folios or lyric magazines with or without music, and the right to license others to include any or all of said compositions in song folios or lyric magazines with or without music.

(f) Any and all other rights of every and any nature, now or hereafter existing under and by virtue of any common-law rights, and any copyrights and renewals and extensions thereof, in any and all of such compositions. Writer grants to Publisher, without any compensation other than as specified herein, the perpetual right to use and publish and to permit others to use and publish Writer's name (including any professional name heretofore or hereafter adopted by Writer), likeness, voice, and sound effects and biographical material, or any reproduction or simulation thereof and titles of all compositions hereunder in connection with the printing, sale, advertising, distribution, and exploitation of music, folios, recordings, performances, player rolls, and otherwise concerning any of the compositions hereunder, and for any other purpose related to the business of Publisher, its affiliated and related companies, or to refrain therefrom. This right shall be exclusive during the term hereof and nonexclusive thereafter. Writer will not authorize or permit the use of his name, likeness, biographical material concerning Writer, or other identification of Writer, or any reproduction or simulation thereof, for or in connection with any musical composition or works, in any manner or for any purpose, other than by or for Publisher. Writer further grants to Publisher the right to refer to Writer as a "Publisher Exclusive Songwriter and Composer," or other similar appropriate appellation.

4. *Exclusivity.* From the date hereof and during the term of this Agreement, Writer will not write or compose, or furnish or dispose of, any musical compositions, titles,

lyrics, or music, or any rights or interests therein whatsoever, nor participate in any manner with regard to the
same for any person, firm or corporation other than
Publisher, nor permit the use of his name or likeness as
the writer or co-writer of any musical composition by any
person, firm or corporation other than Publisher.

5. *Warranties.* Writer hereby warrants and represents to
Publisher that Writer has the full right, power, and
authority to enter into and perform this Agreement, and
to grant to and vest in Publisher all the rights herein set
forth, free and clear of any and all claims, rights, and
obligations whatsoever; all the results and proceeds of
the services of Writer hereunder, including all of the titles,
lyrics, music, and musical compositions, and each and
every part thereof, delivered and to be delivered by Writer
hereunder are and shall be new and original and capable
of copyright protection throughout the entire world, and
that no part thereof shall be an imitation or copy of, or
shall infringe any other original material, and that Writer
has not and will not sell, assign, lease, license, or in any
other way dispose of or encumber the rights herein
granted to Publisher.

6. *Power of Attorney.* Writer does hereby irrevocably
constitute, authorize, empower, and appoint Publisher,
or any of its officers, Writer's true and lawful attorney
(with full power of substitution and delegation), in Writer's
name, place, and stead, or in Publisher's name to take
and do such action, and to make sign, execute, acknowledge, and deliver any and all instruments or documents which Publisher, from time to time, may deem
desirable or necessary to vest in Publisher, its successors, assigns, and licensees, any of the rights or interests
granted by Writer hereunder, including, but not limited to,
such documents required to secure to Publisher the renewals and extensions of copyrights throughout the
world of musical compositions written or composed by
Writer and owned by Publisher, and also such documents
necessary to assign to Publisher, its successors, and
assigns, such renewal copyrights and all rights therein
for the terms of such renewals and extensions for the
use and benefit of Publisher, its successors, and assigns.

7. *Compensation.* Provided that Writer shall faithfully
and completely perform the terms, covenants and conditions of this Agreement, Publisher hereby agrees to pay
Writer for the services to be rendered by Writer under
this Agreement and for the rights acquired and to be ac-

quired hereunder, the following compensation on the musical compositions which are the subject hereof:

(a) Five cents (5¢) per copy for each and every regular piano copy and for each and every dance orchestration sold and paid for to Publisher, after deduction of each and every return, in the United States and Canada.

(b) Ten percent (10%) of the wholesale selling price upon each and every printed copy of each and every other arrangement and edition thereof printed, published and sold and paid for to Publisher, after deduction of each and every return, in the United States, except that in the event such compensation shall be used or caused to be used in whole or in part, in conjunction with one or more other musical compositions in a folio or album, Writer shall be entitled to receive that proportion of said ten percent (10%) which the subject musical composition shall bear to the total number of musical compositions contained in such folio or album.

(c) Fifty percent (50%) of any and all net royalties actually earned and received (less any costs for collection) by Publisher from mechanical rights, electrical transcription, and reproducing rights and all other rights (except public performing rights) therein.

(d) Writer shall receive his public-performance royalties throughout the world directly from his own affiliated performing-rights society and shall have no claim whatsoever against Publisher for any royalties received by Publisher from any performing-rights society which makes payment directly (or indirectly, other than through Publisher) to writers, authors, and composers.

(e) Fifty percent (50%) of any and all net royalties actually earned and received (less any costs for collection) by Publisher from sales and uses directly related to subject musical compositions in countries outside of the United States [other than public performance royalties as hereinabove mentioned in Paragraph 7 (d)].

(f) Publisher shall not be required to pay any royalties on professional or complimentary copies or any copies or mechanical derivatives which are distributed gratuitously to performing artists, orchestra leaders, disc jockeys, or for advertising or exploitation purposes. Furthermore, no royalties shall be payable to Writer on consigned copies unless paid for, and not until such time as an accounting therefore can properly be made.

(g) Royalties as specified hereinabove shall be payable solely to Writer in instances where Writer is the sole author of the entire composition, including the words and music thereof. However, in the event that one or more other songwriters are authors along with Writer on any compositions, then the foregoing royalties shall be divided equally between Writer and the other songwriters of such composition, unless another division of royalties is agreed upon in writing between the parties concerned.

(h) Except as herein expressly provided, no other royalties or monies shall be paid to Writer.

8. *Accounting.* Publisher will compute the total composite royalties earned by Writer pursuant to this Agreement and pursuant to any other agreement, previous, simultaneous or subsequent hereto between Writer and Publisher, within ninety (90) days after the first day of January and the first day of July of each year for the preceding six (6) month period, and will remit to Writer the net amount of such royalties, if any, after deducting any and all unrecouped advances and chargeable costs under this Agreement or any other agreement between Writer and Publisher, together with the detailed royalty statement, within such ninety (90) days. All royalty statements rendered by Publisher to Writer shall be binding upon Writer and not subject to any objection by Writer for any reason unless specific objection is made, in writing stating the basis thereof, to Publisher within one (1) year from the date rendered. Writer shall have the right, upon the giving of at least thirty (30) days' written notice to Publisher, to inspect the books and records of Publisher, insofar as the same concerns Writer, at the expense of Writer, at reasonable times during normal business hours, for the purpose of verifying the accuracy of any royalty statement rendered to Writer hereunder.

9. *Collaboration with Other Writers.* Whenever Writer shall collaborate with any other person in the creation of any musical composition, any such musical composition shall be subject to the terms and conditions of this Agreement, and Writer warrants and represents that prior to the collaboration with any other person, such other person shall be advised of this exclusive agreement and that all such compositions must be published by Publisher. In the event of such collaboration with any other person, Writer shall notify Publisher of the extent of interest that such other person may have in such musical composition, and Writer shall use his reasonable efforts to cause such other person to execute a separate Songwriter's Agreement with respect thereto, which Agreement shall set forth the division of the Songwriter's share of income between

Writer and such other person, and Publisher shall make payment accordingly. If Publisher so desires, Publisher may request Writer to execute a separate agreement in Publisher's customary form with respect to each musical composition hereunder. Upon such request, Writer will promptly execute such Agreement. Publisher shall have the right, pursuant to the terms and conditions hereof, to execute such agreement in behalf of Writer hereunder. Such agreement shall supplement and not supersede this Agreement. In the event of any conflict between the provisions of such agreement and this agreement, whether requested by Publisher or not, shall not affect the rights of each of the parties hereunder, including, but not limited to, the rights of Publisher to all of the musical compositions written and composed by Writer.

10. *Writer's Services.* Writer agrees to perform the services required hereunder conscientiously and solely and exclusively for and as requested by Publisher. Writer is deemed to be a "writer for hire" hereunder, with full rights of copyright renewal vested in Publisher. Writer further agrees to promptly and faithfully comply with all requirements and requests made by Publisher in connection with its business as set forth herein. Writer will deliver to Publisher a manuscript copy of each musical composition hereunder immediately upon completion of acquisition of such musical composition. Nothing contained in this Agreement shall obligate Publisher to exploit in any manner any of the rights granted to Publisher hereunder. Publisher, at its sole discretion, shall reasonably make studio facilities available for Writer so that Writer, subject to the supervision and control of Publisher, may make demonstration records of the musical compositions hereunder and also for Writer to perform at such recording sessions. Writer shall not incur any liability for which Publisher may be responsible in connection with any demonstration record session without having first obtained Publisher's written approval as to the nature, extent and limit of such liability. In no event shall Writer incur any expense whatsoever in behalf of Publisher without first having received written authorization from Publisher. Writer shall not be entitled to any compensation (in addition to such compensation as may be otherwise provided for herein), with respect to services rendered in connection with such demonstration record recording sessions. Publisher shall advance the costs for the production of demonstration records, and one-half (½) of such costs shall be deemed additional nonreturnable advances to Writer and shall be deducted from royalties payable to Writer by Publisher under this or any other Agreement between the parties. All recordings and reproductions made at demonstration recording sessions hereunder shall become the sole and exclusive property of Publisher, free of any claims whatsoever by writer or any person deriving any rights from Writer.

Writer will, from time to time, at Publisher's request, whenever the same will not unreasonably interfere with other professional engagements of Writer, appear for photography, art work, and other similar reasons under the direction of Publisher or its duly authorized agent, appear for interviews with such representatives of newspapers, magazines, and other publications, confer and consult with Publisher regarding Writer's services hereunder and other matters which may concern the parties hereto. Writer will also cooperate with Publisher in promoting, publicizing, and exploiting musical compositions written or composed by Writer hereunder, and for any other purpose related to the business of Publisher, its affiliated and related companies. Writer shall not be entitled to any compensation (other than as may be specified herein) for rendering such services.

11. *Unique Services.* Writer acknowledges that the services to be rendered hereunder are of a special, unique, unusual, extraordinary, and intellectual character which gives them a peculiar value, the loss of which cannot be reasonably or adequately compensated in damages in an action at law, and that a breach by Writer of any of the provisions of this Agreement will cause Publisher great and irreparable injury and damage. Writer expressly agrees that Publisher shall be entitled to the remedies of injunction and other equitable relief to prevent a breach of this Agreement or any provision hereof, which relief shall be in addition to any other remedies, for damages or otherwise, which may be available to Publisher.

12. *Actions.* Publisher may take such action as it deems necessary, either in Writer's name or in its own name, against any person to protect all rights and interests acquired by Publisher hereunder. Writer will, at Publisher's request, cooperate fully with Publisher in any controversy which may arise or litigation which may be brought concerning Publisher's rights and interests obtained hereunder. Publisher shall have the right, in its absolute discretion, to employ attorneys and to institute or defend any action or proceeding and to take any other proper steps to protect the right, title, and interest of Publisher in and to each musical composition hereunder and every portion thereof and in that connection, to settle, compromise, or in any other manner dispose of any matter, claim, action, or proceeding and to satisfy any judgment that may be rendered, in any manner as Publisher, in its sole discretion, may determine. Any legal action brought by Publisher against any alleged infringer of any musical composition hereunder shall be initiated and prosecuted by Publisher, and, if there is any recovery made by Publisher as a result thereof, after deduction of the expense of litigation, including, but not limited to, reasonable attorneys' fees and court costs, a sum equal to fifty percent (50%) of such net proceeds shall be paid to writer. If a claim is presented against Publisher in respect of any musical composition hereunder, and because thereof Publisher is jeopardized, Publisher shall have the right thereafter, until said claim has been finally adjudicated or settled, to withhold ~~any and all~~ royalties that may be or become due with respect to such disputed compositions pending the final adjudication or settlement of such claim. ~~Publisher, in addition, may withhold other royalties to be earned pursuant to this Agreement or any other Agreement between Writer and Publisher, and its affiliated or related companies, sufficient in the opinion of Publisher to reimburse Publisher for any contemplated damages, including court costs and reasonable attorneys' fees and costs resulting therefrom.~~ Publisher shall advance the costs of litigation, if any, including court costs and attorneys' fees, together with any damages which may be paid as a result of the settlement or adjudication of a claim in connection with a musical composition written or composed by Writer. All such costs and damages shall be deemed an advance against any royalties payable to Writer under this or any other Agreement between Writer and Publisher. Upon the final adjudication or settlement of each and every claim hereunder, all moneys withheld shall then be disbursed in accordance with the rights of the parties as provided hereinabove.

13. *Notices.* Any written notice, statement, payment, or matter required or desired to be given to Publisher or Writer pursuant to this Agreement shall be given by addressing the same to the addresses of the respective parties referred to above, or to such other address as either party may hereafter designate, in writing, to the other party and on the date when same shall be deposited, so addressed, postage prepaid, in the United States mail, or on the date when delivered, so addressed, toll prepaid, to a telegraph or cable office, or on the date when same shall be delivered to the other party personally or to his duly authorized agent (as designated in writing), such notice shall be deemed to have been duly made pursuant hereto.

14. *Entire Agreement.* This Agreement supersedes any and all prior negotiations, understandings, and agreements between the parties hereto with respect to the subject matter hereof. Each of the parties acknowledges and agrees that neither party has made any representations or promises in connection with this Agreement or the subject matter hereof not contained herein.

15. *Modification, Waiver, Illegality.* This Agreement may not be cancelled, altered, modified, amended, or waived, in whole or in part, in any way, except by an instrument in writing signed by both Publisher and Writer. The waiver by Publisher of any breach of this Agreement in any one or more instances shall in no way be construed as a waiver of any subsequent breach (whether or not of a similar nature) of this Agreement by Writer. If any part of this Agreement shall be held to be void, invalid, or unenforceable, it shall not affect the validity of the balance of this Agreement. This Agreement shall be governed by and construed under the laws and judicial decisions of the State of California [or other state].

16. *Assignment.* Publisher shall have the right to assign this agreement or any of its rights hereunder to any party.ʌ who acquires all or a substantial portion of Publisher's stock or assets. This agreement shall inure to the benefit of and be binding upon each of the parties hereto and their respective successors, assigns, heirs, executors, administrators, and legal and personal representatives.

17. *Termination.* ~~Publisher shall have the right to terminate this Agreement upon thirty (30) days' prior written notice to Writer.~~

18. *Options.* Writer hereby grants to Publisher three (3) separate, consecutive, and irrevocable options to renew the term of this Agreement, each to run consecutively, beginning at the expiration of the initial term, upon all the same terms and conditions applicable to the initial term, except as may be provided to the contrary herein. The first such renewal term shall be for a period of six (6) months, and the remaining two (2) renewal terms shall be for periods of one (1) year each. Each option may be exercised by giving Writer written notice at least thirty (30) days prior to the commencement of the renewal term for which the option is exercised. More than one (1) option may, at Publisher's election, be exercised at one time.

19. *Definitions.* For purposes of this Agreement, the word "person" means and refers to any individual, corporation, partnership, association, or any other organized group of persons or legal successors or representatives of the foregoing. Whenever the expressions "the term of this agreement" or "period hereof", or words of similar connotation, are included herein, they shall be deemed to mean and refer to the original period of this Agreement and the periods of any renewals, extensions, substitutions, or replacements of this Agreement, whether expressly indicated or otherwise.

Two Thousand Dollars ($2,000.00),

Seventy-Six Dollars and Ninety-Two Cents ($76.92)

Three Thousand Dollars ($3,000.00),

One Hundred Fifteen Dollars ($115.00)

Eight Thousand Dollars ($8,000.00),

One Hundred Fifty-Three Dollars and Eighty-Four Cents ($153.84) per week;

Ten Thousand Dollars ($10,000.00),

One Hundred Ninety-Two Dollars and Thirty Cents ($192.30)

20. Conditioned upon Writer's full and faithful performance of all of the terms and provisions hereof, Publisher agrees to pay Writer the following sums, which sums shall be deemed to be advances against and recoupable by Publisher from royalties otherwise payable to Writer hereunder and/or pursuant to any other Agreement between Publisher and Writer:

(a) Initial six (6) month period: ~~One Thousand Dollars ($1,000.00)~~ payable at the rate of ~~Thirty Eight Dollars and Forty Six Cents ($38.46)~~ per week;

(b) First option period (if exercised): ~~Two Thousand Dollars ($2,000.00)~~, payable at the rate of ~~Seventy Six Dollars and Ninety Two Cents ($76.92)~~ per week;

~~(c) Second option period (if exercised): Four Thousand Dollars ($4,000.00),~~ payable at the rate of ~~Seventy Six Dollars and Ninety Two Cents ($76.92) per week;~~

(d) Third option period (if exercised): ~~Four Thousand Dollars ($4,000.00),~~ payable at the rate of ~~Seventy Six Dollars and Ninety Two Cents ($76.92) per week.~~

21. For the purposes of obtaining injunctive relief, Writer hereby grants to Publisher an option to become obligated to Writer to pay to Writer the sum of Six Thousand Dollars ($6,000.00) for the then current and any remaining years of this contract, which sum shall include any royalties and other amounts which may otherwise be payable to Writer under this contract. Such option may be exercised by Publisher at any time during the initial or any renewal term of this contract on written notice to Writer.

22. Notwithstanding anything to the contrary contained herein, all of the copyright rights shall revert to Writer with respect to each musical composition hereunder that has not been commercially released in recorded form in the United

States within one (1) year following the submission of such applicable musical composition to Publisher hereunder.

23. Notwithstanding anything to the contrary contained herein, Publisher agrees to pay Writer a sum equal to fifty percent (50%) of any advances received by or credited to Publisher with respect to musical compositions hereunder as well as fifty percent (50%) of all amounts received by or credited to Publisher resulting from the exploitation of any musical composition hereunder for which there is no provision for payment hereunder.

24. Notwithstanding anything to the contrary contained herein, Publisher shall have no rights whatsoever with respect to musical compositions written by Writer prior to the date of this Agreement.

25. Notwithstanding anything to the contrary contained herein, this Agreement shall not be cross-collateralized with any other agreement.

IN WITNESS WHEREOF, the parties hereto have executed this Agreement as of the day and year first above written.

XYZ MUSIC, INC.

By:_____

_____
(Writer's Signature)

S.S. #_____

Date of Birth:_____

SYNCHRONIZATION LICENSE

THIS AGREEMENT, made and entered into this _____ day of_____,
19 _____ by and between LICENSOR RECORDS, INC. (hereinafter referred to as "LICENSOR") and LICENSEE COMPANY (hereinafter referred to as "LICENSEE").

1. LICENSOR is primarily engaged in producing, manufacturing, distributing and selling sound phonograph records, and has recorded the performances of Mr. and/or Ms. Artist (hereinafter referred to as "ARTIST") of the musical composition "ROCK AND ROLL" (hereinafter referred to as "Said Master Recording").

2. LICENSEE is engaged in the business of production of films and, in particular, in the production of a film entitled "LIFE AND TIMES OF THE ANT" (hereinafter referred to as "Said Film").

3. It is the desire of LICENSEE to utilize Said Master Recording in connection with Said Film.

NOW, THEREFORE, pursuant to the above facts and in consideration of the payment of monies described below and of the mutual covenants and conditions herein set forth, the parties do hereby agree as follows:

1. LICENSOR does hereby grant to LICENSEE the nonexclusive right in perpetuity to use up to three minutes in the aggregate of Said Master Recording on the sound track of Said Film provided that the performances of ARTIST are not used nor permitted to be used for release on phonograph records or tapes or other types of sound reproduction (except for use in Said Film for motion-picture purposes only).

2. LICENSEE shall obtain AFM and any governing union clearances and copyright synchronization licenses if necessary or required, and approvals from the ARTIST, and LICENSEE shall indemnify and hold LICENSOR free and harmless from any and all claims, liabilities, costs, losses, damages, or expenses, including attorneys' fees, arising out of or in any way connected with LICENSEE's use of Said Master Recording hereunder, including but not limited to the claims of unions, union members and publishers. LICENSOR warrants it has the right to grant this license, and that it will pay all royalty monies due ARTIST (if any) provided that in no event shall LICENSOR's liability pursuant to this warranty exceed the consideration paid LICENSEE pursuant to Paragraph 5, hereinafter.

3. In consideration of the granting of such right, LICENSEE agrees to give LICENSOR credit in connection with the performance of Said Film in substantially the following manner on all positive prints of Said Film: ROCK AND ROLL by Mr. and/or Ms. ARTIST courtesy of LICENSOR RECORDS, INC.

4. LICENSOR agrees to supply LICENSEE with a tape copy for use as specified herein for which LICENSEE agrees to reimburse LICENSOR the costs in connection with making and delivering such copy.

5. LICENSEE agrees to pay LICENSOR the sum of $200.00 upon the execution hereof as consideration for the LICENSEE herein granted.

6. This instrument constitutes the entire agreement between the parties and cannot be modified except by written instrument signed by the parties hereto. This Agreement shall be governed by and interpreted in accordance with the laws and judicial decisions of the laws of the State of (applicable state).

IN WITNESS WHEREOF, the parties hereto have executed this agreement on the day and year first above written.

LICENSOR RECORDS, INC.

By:_____

LICENSEE COMPANY

By:_____

SPECIAL LICENSE AGREEMENT

LICENSOR RECORDS, INC.
Beverly Hills, California

Date:_____

LICENSEE Company

Gentlemen:

The following, when signed by you and by us, will constitute our agreement.

1. *Definitions*

(a) "Master recordings" shall mean such original recordings or duplicates of original recordings, set forth on Exhibit "A," owned or controlled by us during the period of this Agreement.

(b) "Phonograph record(s)" or "record(s)" shall mean disc records of normal sizes and speeds by which sounds may be recorded and reproduced for later listening only.

(c) "Tapes" shall mean eight-track cartridges and cassettes but does not include any other tape configuration or any hereafter discovered method of magnetic tape reproduction or audiovisual reproductions.

(d) "Term of This agreement" shall mean the two-year period beginning as of the date above.

(e) "Territory" shall mean the United States of America and Canada only.

2. *Grant of Rights*

We hereby grant to you the nonexclusive right, privilege, and license during the term of this Agreement, in the Territory, to manufacture, advertise, distribute and sell or authorize the manufacture, advertisement, distribution and sale of records and tapes subject to the following sentence, manufactured from the master recordings in an album entitled "THE BIG HITS," primarily for the purpose of sale or distribution of such records and tapes through direct mail-order solicitation by means of television advertising and radio only and not by means of or through any retail channels whatsoever including without limitation so-called "key outlets."

3. *Termination*

(a) Upon conclusion of the term of this Agreement, you shall cease the manufacture of records embodying the master recordings and shall place the applicable master-tape recordings received from us and any and all other reproducing devices such as matrices, mothers, and stampers which are capable of reproducing the performances embodied upon the master recordings at our disposal, or at our option destroy such master recordings or other reproducing devices, in which event you shall furnish to us an affidavit that such destruction has been effected.

(b) Notwithstanding anything to the contrary contained in subparagraph 3 (a) hereof, or elsewhere in This agreement, we agree that during a period of six (6) months subsequent to the expiration or termination of the term of this Agreement, you may advertise, distribute, and sell and authorize the advertisement, distribution, and sale through subsidiaries or affiliates by means of the merchandising methods authorized by paragraph 2 above, of phonograph records only manufactured from the master recordings prior to the expiration or termintion of the term of this Agreement. You will not press during the six (6) month period immediately preceding the expiration or termination hereof, more records than you may reasonably be expected to sell prior to the termination or expiration hereof. At expiration or termination, you will provide us a detailed and complete list of your inventory on hand. In the event you fail to do so, you shall have no so-called "sell-off" rights under the terms hereof. We shall be paid royalties and rendered statements with respect to such sell-off sales in the same manner and at the same rates as during the term hereof.

4. *AFM and Copyright Payments*
You agree to pay and be solely responsible for (i) the so-called Per-Record Royalty Payments which may be required to be paid to the Music Performance Trust Fund and the Special Fund established under the 1972 AFM Phonograph Record Labor Agreement (presently known as the Phonograph Record Manufacturer's Special Payments Fund) and any successor agreements in effect during the term hereof, in connection with your manufacture and sale of records (and tapes, if applicable) from the master recordings hereunder, (ii) all fees or royalties which may be required to be paid to the copyright owners in connection with the manufacture, distribution, and sale of records (and tapes, if applicable) from the master recordings hereunder, (iii) all excise or other taxes (as fixed by law), if any, for all records (and tapes, if applicable) manufactured hereunder, and (iv) the AFTRA Pension and Welfare Fund to the extent that we may be additionally liable therefor as a result of sales pursuant to this Agreement. You agree to supply us with copies of statements and checks relating to the items set forth in (i) and (iv) above at our request if you make such payments direct.

5. *Names and Likenesses*
We warrant and agree that you shall have the right to use and allow your subsidiaries and affiliates to use the names and likenesses of all persons whose performances are embodied on the master recordings and biographical material concerning them, for advertising and purposes of trade in connection with the phonograph records manufactured and sold or distributed pursuant to this Agreement. The rights referred to in this paragraph shall be limited to advertising and trade purposes concerning the sale of records hereunder and no such use shall be in the nature of an endorsement, commercial tie-up, or association.

6. *Royalties and Advances*
(a) As to all sales of records embodying the masters set forth in Exhibit "A" hereto, made hereunder from and after the commencement date hereof, and subject to the other provisions of this Agreement, you will pay us a royalty of $.03 cents per selection per disc package for each selection listed on Exhibit "A."
(b) As to all sales of tapes embodying the masters set forth in Exhibit "A" hereto, made hereunder from and after the commencement date hereof, and sub-

ject to the other provisions of this Agreement, you will pay us a royalty of $.03 cents per selection per tape package for each selection listed on Exhibit "A."

(c) You shall not have the right to distribute any records hereunder free of charge.

(d) You will pay to us, upon execution of this Agreement, the sum of One Thousand Dollars ($1,000.00), at the rate of Five Hundred Dollars ($500.00) per master leased. This sum shall be deemed a nonreturnable advance, recoupable by you from royalties otherwise payable to us under this instant Agreement only.

7. *Statements and Payments*

(a) You will maintain accurate records with respect to all records (and tapes, if applicable) manufactured and sold from the master recordings licensed hereunder and will furnish us with an accurate statement of the number of records (and tapes, if applicable) manufactured and sold within forty-five (45) days after March 31st, June 30th, September 30th, and December 31st of each year during which records made from the master recordings are sold, such statements to be accompanied by payment of any royalties due as a result of such sales.

(b) You will permit us, upon reasonable notice to you, to audit all your applicable books and records at the place where they are customarily maintained, for the purpose of verifying your royalty payments, at reasonable times during regular business hours. In the event that the calculation of royalty payments is determined by a computer-based system, then we can examine the machine-sensible data utilized by such system and the related documentation describing such system and you agree to retain such data during the entire term hereof. Such audit shall be at Licensor's expense, except that if a substantial error [in excess of ten percent (10%) of the royalties earned up to the closing date of the period for which the audit is being conducted] shall be determined, the reasonable expense of such audit shall be borne by you.

8. *Warranties and Representations by Licensor Records, Inc.*

We warrant, represent, covenant and agree that with respect to the master recordings in the Territory:

(a) We are under no liability, restriction, or prohibition in respect to our rights to execute this Agreement, to perform its terms, and to grant all of the rights granted herein to you.

(b) We are the owner of all rights granted herein with respect to the master recordings, and we now have or shall acquire all rights necessary to the manufacture, advertisement, sale, and distribution by direct mail or mail order of phonograph records manufactured from such master recordings subject to the terms hereof.

(c) The master recordings were recorded in all respects in accordance with the rules and regulations of all unions having jurisdiction and all persons whose performances appear thereon and other persons whose rights may be involved have been, or will be by us fully and completely paid (except for royalties), or have or will have in writing waived such payment, in connection with the rendering of such performances and their embodiment on the master recordings and the manufacture, advertisement, sale, or distribution of phonograph records to be made therefrom. Any royalty payments to all of such persons (except the items set forth in paragraph 4 hereof) in respect to the manufacture, advertisement, sale, or distribution of records to be manufactured from master recordings shall be borne entirely by us.

(d) You shall be under no liability, prohibition, restriction, or obligation whatsoever with respect to your manufacture, advertisement, distribution, or sale of phonograph records in the Territory manufactured from the master recordings, except as specifically provided in this Agreement.

9. *Warranties and Representations by Licensee Company*

You warrant, represent, covenant and agree that:

(a) You are under no liability, restriction, or prohibition in respect of your rights to execute this Agreement and to fully perform its provisions.

(b) You shall not sell or otherwise distribute any of the master recordings except pursuant to the terms of this agreement. It is specifically understood by you that your rights hereunder are limited to a one-time use of the masters hereunder and you shall not have the right to recoup, repackage or utilize the masters in any other way whatsoever.

(c) You will make the required payment to either us or the Musicians Performance Trust Fund, the Special Payments Fund of the American Federation of Musicians and AFTRA Pension and Welfare Funds and the appropriate copyright proprietors as are necessary by the terms of this Agreement.

(d) You shall cause the materials, component parts, technical, and pressing quality of records to be made from the master recordings to be of at least the same excellent quality as that of our regular commercial records. In order to allow us to verify the quality of the pressings, you agree to ship to us, free of charge, at least six (6) copies of each and every record which contains a master recording.

(e) You shall use all reasonable efforts to promote the sale and distribution of records embodying the master recordings.

10. *Indemnification*

You and we each agree to and do hereby indemnify, save, and hold the other harmless from loss or damage (including reasonable attorneys' fees) arising out of or connected with any claim by a third party which is inconsistent with any of the warranties, representations, or agreements made by you or us respectively in this Agreement. You or we (as the case may be) will reimburse the other on demand for any payment made by the demanding party at any time after the date hereof in respect of any liability or claim to which the foregoing indemnity relates, which has resulted in an adverse judgment against the demanding party, or which is settled with the consent of the indemnifying party. Prompt notice will be given to the indemnifying party of any claim to which this indemnity relates, and such indemnifying party shall have the right, at its own expense, to participate in the defense thereof with counsel of its choice.

11. *Assignment*

We may at our election assign this Agreement or any of the rights hereunder to any other division of our company, or to any subsidiary in which we now have or may hereafter obtain a controlling interest, or to any parent corporation which may have a substantial interest in us; provided however, that no such assignment shall relieve us of any of our obligations hereunder.

12. *Construction and Application of Law*

This Agreement sets forth the entire agreement between the parties with respect to the subject matter hereof, and no modification, amendment, waiver, termination, or discharge of this Agreement or any provision hereof shall be binding upon either party hereto unless confirmed by a written instrument signed by the party against whom any such modification, amendment, waiver, termination, or discharge is sought to be enforced. No waiver of any provision of or default under this Agreement shall affect your or our right thereafter to enforce such provision or to exercise any right or remedy in the event of any other default, whether or not similar. This Agreement, its validity, construction, and effect shall be governed by the laws of the State of (applicable state), applicable to contracts to be performed entirely therein.

13. *Album Containers, Masters, Et Cetera*

You shall be responsible for the creation, payment for, and production of album containers such as jackets, sleeves, cartridges, cassettes, slipcases, or other such similar type containers for the phonograph records (and tapes, if applicable) made from the master recordings. We shall deliver the master recordings to you hereunder promptly after your request therefor, and the master recordings shall be considered on loan pursuant to the terms hereof. You shall pay all costs and expenses of reproduction from the master recordings and shall pay all of our costs and expenses, including packing and shipping incurred in supplying you with duplicate masters, mothers, and/or stampers; all charges incurred shall be billed directly to you for your account and shall be paid promptly on receipt.

14. *Force Majeure*

If, due wholly or partly to any labor controversy or adjustment thereof or to any cause not entirely within your control or which you could not by reasonable diligence have avoided, you are materially hampered in the distribution or sale of records produced from master recordings, then, for the duration of such contingency, you may suspend the term hereof by written notice to us to such effect. If such impossibility to perform continues for ninety (90) days, then we may terminate this Agreement by thirty (30) days' written notice to you. Nothing contained herein shall affect your obligation under this Agreement to pay royalties due to you after the termination of this Agreement.

15. *Default by Licensee Company*

The occurrence of the following event shall be deemed material breaches and defaults by you under this Agreement:

(a) If you fail to account and make payments of any amounts owing on the dates due hereunder and such failure is not cured within ten (10) business days; or

(b) If you fail to perform any other material obligations required of you hereunder and such failure is not cured within thirty (30) business days after delivery to you of written notice thereof; or

(c) If you apply for, consent to, or acquiesce in the appointment of a Trustee or Receiver for you or a substantial part of your assets or in absence of such application, consent or acquiesce, a Trustee or Receiver is appointed for you or a substantial part of your assets and same is not discharged within thirty (30) days; or any bankruptcy, reorganization, debt arrangements, or other proceeding under any insolvency law, or any dissolution or liquidation proceeding is instituted by or against you, and if instituted against you, consented to or acquiesced in by you, or if not dismissed within thirty (30) days; or any final adjudication in bankruptcy or made against you; or

(d) If you distribute and sell records (or tapes, if applicable) through any distribution channels than those set forth in paragraph 2 above, or beyond the dates for which the rights herein are granted to you.

If any such events occur, then we, in addition to such other rights and remedies which we may have at law or otherwise under this Agreement, may cancel or terminate this Agreement without prejudice to any rights or claims we may have and all rights hereunder shall forthwith revert to us, and you may not thereafter manufacture records from master recordings furnished by us, nor sell such records.

16. *Credits*

You agree to give us credit with reference to said master recordings on the record or in the album liner notes substantially as follows:

"L.A. Yesterday" and "Rock and Roll" by Mr. and/or Ms. Artist courtesy of Licensor Records, Inc.

17. *Copyright Notice*

You shall place or cause to be placed upon the album cover, liner, and/or labels of each disc and tape record manufactured and sold hereunder a copyright notice with respect to the masters as follows:

"L.A. Yesterday"(P)1977, Licensor Records, Inc.
"Rock and Roll"(P)1978, Licensor Records, Inc.

Very truly yours,
LICENSOR RECORDS, INC.

_____

Agreed and accepted:
LICENSEE COMPANY

By:_____

EXHIBIT "A"   _____

TITLE	ARTIST
"Rock and Roll"	Mr. and/or Ms. Artist
"L.A. Yesterday"	Mr. and/or Ms. Artist

INDIVIDUAL PRODUCER'S CONTRACT

XYZ RECORDS, INC.
Beverly Hills, California

Date:_____

Dear Mr. Producer:

This will confirm our understanding and agreement with you with reference to your production of phonograph record master recordings embodying the performances of our recording artist Mr. and/or Ms. Artist ("Artist").

1. The term of this Contract shall commence as of the date hereof and shall continue until such time as you shall have completed all of your obligations hereunder in respect of the Masters (as hereinafter defined).

2. During the term hereof, you shall produce sufficient recordings embodying Artist's performances to constitute one (1) 33-$\frac{1}{3}$ rpm long-playing phonograph record album of customary playing time (hereinafter referred to as the "LP"). Such recordings as may be produced by you hereunder are hereinafter referred to as the "Masters."

3. Recording sessions for the Masters produced hereunder shall be conducted by you under our recording license, at times and places to be mutually designated by you and us. Each Master shall consist of a performance by us of a selection designated by us, and shall be subject to our approval as technically satisfactory for the commercial production of records.

4. You agree that you shall submit to us all union contract forms and report forms for recording sessions hereunder, all bills pertaining to such recording sessions, and all necessary payroll forms (including, without limitation, all necessary Withholding Tax forms) pertaining to such recording sessions within forty-eight (48) hours after each recording session and in accordance with all applicable union requirements.

5. It is agreed and understood that the approved recording budget for all recording costs for all of the Masters shall be (applicable dollar amount). As used herein, the term "recording costs" shall mean and include all payments to musicians, vocalists, arrangers, engineers, leaders, copyists, contractors, and all other individuals rendering services in connection with the recording of the Masters (but excluding any amounts payable to you pursuant to paragraph 19 hereof), payments to union pension and welfare funds, costs of cartage and instrument hire, studio or hall rentals, editing costs, mastering costs, and such other costs as are customarily recognized as recording costs in the record industry. In the event that the aggregate recording costs for the Masters shall exceed the amount of the aforesaid approved budget, we shall have the right to deduct an amount equal to such excess from the advance otherwise payable to you pursuant to paragraph 19 hereof, and the full amount of such excess shall be recoupable from any royalties payable to you hereunder.

6. You shall deliver to us a monaural tape and a two-track stereo tape for each Master, which tapes shall be fully edited, remixed, and leadered prior to delivery to us, so that they are in proper form for the production of the parts necessary for the manufacture of records. Each and every original session tape and part thereof, and each and every mother, master, acetate copy, or other derivative shall also be delivered to us or kept available for us and subject to our control at the recording studio.

7. We shall have the worldwide right in perpetuity to use and to permit others to use your name and likeness and biographical material concerning you on labels and jackets of phonograph records embodying the recordings made hereunder and for advertising and purposes of trade in connection with such records. We shall accord you appropriate production credit on record labels and jacket-liner notes and in trade paper advertisements under our control.

8. Conditioned upon your full and faithful performance of all of the material terms hereof, we will pay to you in respect of recordings made hereunder the following royalties upon the terms hereinafter set forth:

(a) In respect of records sold in the United States in the form of discs, and in respect of records sold in the United States in the form of prerecorded tapes (including reel-to-reel tapes, cartridges, and cassettes) or other recorded devices (other than discs) which are actually manufactured, distributed, and sold by us, we shall pay you a royalty at the rate of three percent (3%) of the suggested retail list price from time to time of such records.

(b) In respect of records sold outside of the United States, we shall pay you a royalty at the rate of one and one-half percent (1-½%) of the suggested retail list price from time to time of such records. As to sales outside of the United States, the suggested retail list price hereunder shall be the suggested retail list price in the country of manufacture, the country of sale, the country of import, or the country of export, as we shall be paid. If there are no suggested retail list prices of records in any particular country, then for the purposes of computing royalties hereunder, the prices of records in such country generally regarded as the equivalent thereof shall be deemed the suggested retail list prices of such records.

(c) Notwithstanding any of the foregoing:

(i) the royalty rate in respect of records sold through any direct-mail or mail-order distribution method (including, without limitation, record-club distribution), and/or sold through retail stores in conjunction with special radio or television advertisements (including, without limitation, records of the type referred to as "special markets" sales) shall be one-half (½) of the net royalty (as opposed to a so-called "advance" of which you shall not be entitled to receive all or any portion) which we shall receive from any licensee distributing such records.

(ii) the royalty rate in respect of the sale of mid-priced records shall be three-fourths (¾) of the otherwise applicable royalty rate as calculated in accordance with the foregoing provisions and the royalty rate in respect of the sale of budget or low-priced records shall be one-half (½) of the otherwise applicable royalty rate as calculated in accordance with the foregoing provisions;

(iii) the royalty rate in respect of records sold for use as premiums or in connection with the sale, advertising, or promotion of any other product or service shall be one-half (½) of the otherwise applicable royalty rate as calculated in accordance with the foregoing provisions and shall be based upon the price received by us for such records as to those sold by us and upon the price utilized by our licensees in accounting to us as to those sold by our licensees;

(iv) the royalty rate in respect of records sold to the United States Government, its subdivisions, departments, or agencies (including records sold for resale through military facilities), and in respect of records sold to educational institutions or libraries, shall be one-half (½) of the otherwise applicable royalty rate as calculated in accordance with the foregoing provisions;

(v) the royalty rate in respect of Masters licensed by us for phonograph record use on a flat-fee basis and for all other types of use (other than phonograph record use) on a flat-fee or royalty basis shall be an amount equal to fifty percent (50%) of the net flat fee or net royalty, as the case may be, received by us in respect of each such use.

(d) Notwithstanding any of the foregoing, no royalties shall be payable on records furnished as free or bonus records to members,applicants, or other participants in any record club or other direct-mail distribution method; on records distributed for promotional purposes to radio stations, television stations, or networks, record reviewers, or other customary recipients of promotional records; on so-called "promotional sampler" albums; on records sold as scrap, or "cutouts"; on records furnished on a so-called "no-charge" basis to distributors, subdistributors, dealers, or others, whether or not the recipients thereof are affiliated with us; and on records sold at less than fifty percent (50%) of their regular wholesale price.

(e) Notwithstanding any of the foregoing, royalties in respect of records sold at a discount to distributors, subdistributors, dealers, or others, whether or not affiliated with us, shall be reduced in the same proportion as the regular wholesale price of such records is reduced on such sales; provided that no such discount shall reduce the royalties payable to you below those which would have been payable had this subparagraph (e) not been applicable and had we shipped records as "free goods."

(f) Notwithstanding any of the foregoing:

(i) for purposes of computing royalties, there shall be deducted from the suggested retail list price (or other applicable price, if any, upon which royalties are calculated) of phonograph records hereunder an amount equal to any excise, sales, value added, or comparable or similar taxes;

(ii) for purposes of computing royalties there shall be deducted from the suggested retail list price (or other applicable price, if any, upon which royalties are calculated) of phonograph records hereunder, an amount equal to ten percent (10%) thereof for long-playing or extended-playing disc records which are packaged in our standard "single-fold" album jackets; twelve and one-half percent (12-½%) thereof for all other long-playing or extended-playing disc records; and twenty percent (20%) thereof for reel-to-reel tapes, cartridges, cassettes, or other recorded devices (other than discs);

(iii) except as expressly provided otherwise herein, royalties shall be computed and paid upon one hundred percent (100%) of net sales for which payment has been received; provided, however, that if any licensee distributing records hereunder through record clubs or other methods of mail-order distribution shall compute and pay royalties to us in respect of such records on less than one hundred percent (100%) of net sales, your royalties hereunder with respect to such records shall be computed and paid on the same percentage of sales as such licensee shall utilize in computing and paying to us royalties in respect of such records; and

(g) Notwithstanding any of the foregoing, the royalty payable to you hereunder with respect to any phonograph record embodying Masters hereunder together with other master recordings shall be computed by multiplying the otherwise applicable royalty rate by a fraction, the numerator of which shall be the number of selections contained on the Masters hereunder which are embodied on such phonograph record and the denominator of which shall be the total number of selections embodied on such phonograph record.

9. (a) Statements as to royalties payable hereunder shall be sent by us to you on or before the thirtieth day of September for the semiannual period ending the preceding June 30th, and on or before the 31st day of March for the semiannual period ending the preceding December 31st, together with payment of accrued royalties, if any, earned by you hereunder during the preceding semiannual period, less all advances and charges under this Contract. We shall have the right to retain, as a reasonable reserve against subsequent charges, credits, or returns, such portion of payable royalties as shall be reasonable in our best business judgment. Returns shall be liquidated within three (3) semiannual accounting periods following the close of the accounting period in which such reserves were originally held.

(b) No royalties shall be payable to you in respect of sales of records by any of our licensees until payment therefor has been received by us. All such sales by any such licensees shall be deemed to have occurred in the same semiannual accounting period during which our licensees shall have rendered to us accounting statements therefor.

(c) Royalties in respect of the sale of records outside the United States shall be computed in the national currency in which we are paid by our licensees and shall be credited to your royalty account hereunder at the same rate of exchange as we are paid. In the event that we shall not receive payment in United States dollars in the United States in respect of any such sales, royalties in respect thereof shall not be credited to your royalty account hereunder. We shall, however, if we are able to do so, accept such payments in foreign currency and deposit in a foreign bank or other depository, at your expense, in such foreign currency, such portion thereof, if any, as shall equal the royalties which would have actually been payable to you hereunder in respect of such sales had such payments been made to us in United States dollars in the United States and we shall notify you thereof promptly. Deposit as aforesaid shall fulfill our royalty obligations hereunder as to such record sales.

(d) You shall be deemed to have consented to all royalty statements and all other accountings rendered by us hereunder and each such royalty statement or other accounting shall be conclusive, final, and binding, shall constitute an account stated, and shall not be subject to any objection for any reason whatsoever unless specific objection in writing, stating the basis thereof, is given by you to us within two (2) years after the date rendered. No action, suit, or proceeding of any nature in respect of any royalty statement or other accounting rendered by us hereunder may be maintained against us unless such action, suit or proceeding is commenced against us in a court of competent jurisdiction within two (2) years after the date rendered.

(e) We shall maintain books of account concerning the sale of phonograph records hereunder. You, or a certified public accountant, in your behalf, may, at your sole expense, examine our said books relating to the sale of records hereunder solely for the purpose of verifying the accuracy thereof, only during our normal business hours and upon reasonable written notice. Our such books relating to any particular royalty statement may be examined as aforesaid only within two (2) years after the date rendered and we shall have no obligation to permit you to so examine our such books relating to any particular royalty statement more than once. The rights hereinabove granted to you shall constitute your sole and exclusive rights to examine our books and records.

10. All Masters produced by you hereunder and all reproductions made therefrom, the performances embodied therein and all copyrights therein and thereto, together with all renewals and extensions thereof, shall be entirely our property, free of any claims whatsoever by you or any person, firm or corporation deriving any rights or interests through or from you. Without limitation of the foregoing, we and/or our designees shall have the worldwide rights in perpetuity to manufacture, sell, distribute, and advertise records or other reproductions (visual or nonvisual) embodying such recordings, to lease, license, convey, or otherwise use or dispose of the recordings by any method now or hereafter known, to release records under any trademarks, trade names, or labels, to perform the records or other reproductions publicly and to permit the public performance thereof by radio broadcast, television, or any other method now or hereafter known, all upon such terms and conditions as we may approve, and to permit others to do any or all of the foregoing.

11. You expressly acknowledge that your services hereunder are of a special, unique, and intellectual character which gives them peculiar value, and that in the event of a breach by you of any term, condition, or covenant hereof we will be caused irreparable injury. You expressly agree that in the event that you shall breach any provision of this Contract we shall be entitled to injunctive and other equitable relief and/or damages, and in addition to any other rights or remedies available to us we shall have the right to recoup any damages from any sums which may thereafter become due and payable to you hereunder, including sums otherwise payable to you after the expiration or termination of this Contract.

12. You warrant and represent that you are under no disability, restriction, or prohibition, whether contractual or otherwise, with respect to your right to execute this Contract and perform its terms and conditions. You agree to and do hereby indemnify, save, and hold us harmless from any and all loss and damage (including attorneys' fees) arising out of or connected with any claim whatsoever by a third party which is inconsistent with any of the warranties, representations, or agreements made by you in this Contract, and you agree to reimburse us, on demand, for any payment made by us at any time after the date hereof with respect to any liability or claim to which the foregoing indemnity applies. Pending the determination of any such claim, we may withhold payment of royalties or other monies hereunder in an amount reasonably related to such claim and our estimated attorney's fees in connection therewith. In the event of any action, suit, or proceeding by either of us against the other under this Contract, the prevailing party shall be entitled to recover its reasonable attorneys' fees in addition to the costs of said action, suit, or proceeding. We agree to give you prompt written notice of any claim to which the foregoing indemnity applies and the opportunity to assist in the defense thereof with counsel of your choice at your expense.

13. Notwithstanding anything to the contrary provided herein, we shall have the right, at our election, to designate other producers for recording sessions with us, in which event you shall have no rights hereunder with respect to recordings produced at such sessions. You shall have the right during the term hereof, subject to your obligations hereunder, to produce recordings for any other person, firm, or corporation. You shall not during the term hereof nor during the three (3) year period commencing after the expiration or termination of this Contract produce any recording for any person, firm, or corporation embodying the same arrangement of any selection as recorded hereunder.

14. We may, at our election, and upon written notice to you, assign this contract to any person, firm, or corporation.

15. Except as otherwise provided herein, the term "records" and "phonograph records" shall include all forms of recordings (both visual and nonvisual) including, without limitation, discs of any speed or size, prerecorded tapes, cartridges, and any other recorded devices now known or which may hereafter become known.

16. This Contract sets forth the entire agreement between you and us with respect to the subject matter hereof. No modification, amendment, waiver, termination, or discharge of this Contract or any provisions hereof shall be binding upon us unless confirmed by a written instrument signed by all of us. No waiver by us of any provision of this Contract or of any default hereunder shall affect our rights thereafter to enforce such provision or to exercise any right or remedy in the event of any other default, whether or not similar.

17. This Contract shall not become effective until signed by you and countersigned by each of us. This contract shall be deemed to have been made in the State of (applicable state) and its validity, construction and effect shall be governed by the laws of the State of (applicable state), applicable to agreements wholly performed therein.

18. All notices to be given to you hereunder and all statements and payments to be submitted or given to you hereunder shall be addressed to you at the address set forth on page 1 hereof or at such other address as you shall designate in writing from time to time. All notices to be given to us hereunder shall be addressed to us at the address set forth in page 1 hereof or at such other address as we shall designate in writing from time to time. All notices shall be in writing and shall either be served personally or by registered or certified mail or telegraph, all charges prepaid. The date of making personal service or of mailing or of deposit in a telegraph office, whichever shall be first, shall be deemed the date of service.

19. Conditioned upon your full and faithful performance of all of the terms hereof, we shall pay, as a nonreturnable advance recoupable from your royalties hereunder, the sum of Ten Thousand Dollars ($10,000) upon your delivery to us of the LP.

20. Nothing herein contained shall constitute a partnership between or joint venture by you and us. Neither party hereto shall hold itself out contrary to the terms of this paragraph, and neither you nor we shall become liable for any representation, act, or omission of the other contrary to the provisions hereof. This contract shall not be deemed to give any right or remedy to any third party whatsoever unless said right or remedy is specifically granted by us in writing to such third party. If the foregoing correctly reflects your understanding and agreement with us, please so indicate by signing below.

Very truly yours,
XYZ RECORDS, INC.

By:_____

Agreed and accepted:

_____
(Mr. Producer)

FOREIGN SUBPUBLISHING CONTRACT*

AGREEMENT made as of this_____day of_____19_____, by and between

_____
(hereinafter called "Owner") and_____
(hereinafter called "Publisher").

*Deals with licensing of musical compositions outside the United States.

W I T N E S S E T H :

WHEREAS, the Owner is engaged in the business of music publishing within the territory designated as the United States of America and owns or controls the copyrights of certain musical compositions; and

WHEREAS, the Publisher is engaged in the business of music publishing within the territory of_____

_____

(herein the "Territory");

NOW, THEREFORE, in consideration of the mutual promises and agreements hereinbefore and hereinafter contained, and other good and valuable consideration, the receipt of which is hereby acknowledged the parties hereto agree as follows:

1. The Owner hereby transfers and assigns to the Publisher the following rights in and to each and every musical composition uncommitted for the Territory, and owned or controlled by the Owner, or any of its subsidiary companies, or here-after acquired in the ordinary course of business (excluding catalog acquisitions) by the Owner during the term of this Agreement and at the time of acquisitions uncommitted for the Territory) hereinafter collectively referred to as the "Compositions").

(a) The exclusive right to print, publish, vend, and cause to be printed, published, and vended printed copies of the Compositions in the Territory; provided, how-ever, that Owner reserves to itself all rights with respect to the importing or licensing of importation into the Territory of printed music manufactured by Owner or its subsidiaries, affiliates or licensees in the United States, and Publisher shall have no right to receive any sums received by Owner on account of such impor-tation or licensing;

(b) The exclusive right, but only for sale within the Territory, to license the manufacture of parts serving to reproduce the Compositions, including, but not limited to, the making of mechanical and electrical reproductions for piano rolls, phonograph records, tapes (cartridges or reel-to-reel), transcriptions, and for any other method as yet known or unknown, and to grant nonexclusive licenses for such rights in and for the Territory, and to collect all royalties and fees payable therefor, but the foregoing shall not include any license for the use of the Composi-tions in connection with commercial or merchandising tie-ups;

(c) The exclusive right of public performance for profit or otherwise (including broadcasting and television), and of licensing such rights and of collecting all royalties and fees payable by reason thereof in the Territory;

(d) Upon securing the prior written consent of Owner, the nonexclusive right to grant nonexclusive licenses for the recording of the Compositions in and with motion pictures and television productions produced in the Territory, and of making copies of the recordings thereof, and exporting such copies into all countries of the world. It is specifically understood and agreed that Publisher shall not share in any fees derived from the public performance outside of the Territory of any Composition contained in a motion picture or television production produced in the Territory, and that all such fees shall be payable to and collected by Owner or its designees. The Owner hereby reserves for itself the exclusive right to grant licenses for the entire world, including the Territory, for the synchronization of the Compositions with sound motion pictures, together with the right to publicly perform for profit the Compositions as contained in such sound motion pictures, if such motion pictures are produced and originated outside the Territory, and the Publisher shall not be entitled to share in any fees received by Owner in respect of such worldwide use;

(e) The right, exercisable only upon the written consent of Owner in each instance (i) to make and publish new adaptations and arrangements of the Compositions; (ii) to procure any new or translated lyric thereof; and (iii) to do every other act and thing in respect of the Compositions to make the same suitable and proper in Publisher's opinion for publication, sale or use in the various countries of the Territories. All such new matter shall be obtained at the sole cost and expense of Publisher, but shall remain the sole property of and be copyrighted in the name of Owner.

(f) The right to collect on behalf of Owner sums now payable in the Territory with respect to the exploitation of rights enumerated in Subparagraphs 1 (a)-(e) occurring prior to the date hereof, except to the extent such rights of collection have heretofore been granted by Owner to others.

2. Owner does not warrant or represent that in the case of each and every Composition it will have the right to transfer and assign to Publisher the rights hereinabove set forth, but Owner shall grant to the Publisher all of the aforesaid rights which it has the right to grant, subject to any restrictions which may have been imposed upon Owner's use or exploitation of any Composition, and subject to the terms of this agreement.

3. Owner hereby reserves unto itself:

(a) All rights in and to the worldwide copyrights in the Compositions and all rights other than as are specifically herein granted to the Publisher;

(b) The exclusive right to dramatize, worldwide, the Compositions, and to license the use and performance of such dramatic versions throughout the world;

(c) The exclusive right to license worldwide uses of the titles of the Compositions; and,

(d) The exclusive right to make literary versions of the Compositions throughout the world, and to print, publish, and vend such literary versions (as well as the dramatic versions aforementioned) throughout the world.

4. All sums payable to Publisher with respect to the exploitation of rights granted hereunder shall be herein "Publishing Income." Publisher agrees that it shall have the duty to collect and to be responsible for the collection of all Publishing Income payable within the Territory. Publisher shall pay to Owner the following royalties in respect of the Compositions:

(a) An amount equal to fifteen percent (15%) of the suggested retail selling price in the country of sale of each printed edition (except folios or similar editions) of the Compositions sold by Publisher and paid for and not returned;

(b) An amount equal to that proportion of fifteen percent (15%) of the suggested retail selling price in the country of sale of each album, folio, or similar edition sold by Publisher and paid for and not returned which the number of Compositions, included in such album, folio, or similar edition shall bear to the total number of Compositions contained therein, for which a royalty is payable.

(c) An amount equal to eighty-five percent (85%) of all gross monies paid by licensees of Publisher to Publisher as royalties for the mechanical reproduction of the Compositions in the Territory; provided, however that if Publisher procures the recording and manufacturing in the Territory of an original recording of a Composition (hereinafter called a "cover recording"), Publisher shall pay to Owner only sixty percent (60%) of all gross monies paid by licensees of Publisher to Publisher as royalties for the mechanical reproduction of such Composition on such cover recording only, from and after such time as said cover recording shall have been released in the Territory;

(d) An amount equal to eighty-five percent (85%) of the Publisher's share of all gross broadcasting and other performing fees and synchronization fees with respect to the Compositions, it being understood and agreed that Publisher shall authorize and direct the appropriate performance-rights society to pay to it one hundred percent (100%) of said Publisher's share,

(e) An amount equal to eighty-five percent (85%) of all gross monies paid by licensees of Publisher from any other rights assigned hereunder in and to the Compositions;

(f) Provided Publisher performs each and all of its covenants, warranties, and agreements hereunder, it shall be entitled to deduct and retain the remainder of Publishing Income.

(g) Publisher shall pay over an amount equal to one hundred percent (100%) of all Publishing Income received by Publisher from any exploitation of rights in and to the Compositions other than those rights expressly set forth in Paragraph 1 hereof. Nothing herein contained shall in any way increase or enlarge the rights granted Publisher hereunder, which are solely as set forth in Paragraph 1. hereto.

(h) Publisher agrees that it shall not license the mechanical reproduction of the Compositions for phonograph records at a rate less than the prevailing rates in the Territory, nor shall it refuse to grant a license at the prevailing rates in the Territory to any authorized manufacturer of recordings embodying the performances of artists recorded by Owner's record-company affiliate, if any.

(i) Notwithstanding the foregoing, with respect to those Compositions, if any, for which Owner does not own or control the copyright but for which Owner only has collection rights, Publisher shall pay to Owner one hundred percent (100%) of the gross monies [less an amount equal to one-half (½) of the percentage collection fee to which Owner is entitled] paid to Publisher by its licensees from any sources whatsoever in connection with said Compositions, if any, are covered by this subparagraph and of the percentage collection fee to which Owner is entitled.

(j) Notwithstanding anything to the contrary herein, all royalties payable to Owner pursuant to this Paragraph are to be computed at the source from which the payments giving rise to such royalties are originally made.

5. The Publisher shall forward to the Owner at its address two (2) copies of each edition of the Compositions published by the Publisher or its licensees and two (2) copies of each cover recording obtained by Publisher, all within two (2) months after such publication and/or cover recording is secured.

Publisher shall be responsible for and shall pay to the local adapter(s), arranger(s), or lyricist(s) any royalties or fees for such services rendered, out of the Publisher's individual share of mechanical royalties paid by licensees of Publisher with respect to the Composition for which the local adapter(s), arranger(s), or lyricist(s) rendered such services without deduction from Owner's share of royalties payable hereunder.

6. In the event that Publisher is prevented from paying monies payable under Paragraph 4 in the United States in United States dollars due to currency restrictions, Owner shall have the right to elect to accept payment in foreign currency in a depository selected by Owner, and Publisher shall deposit all payable sums to the credit of Owner in such foreign currency, and payment so received shall fulfill Publisher's obligations hereunder as to monies payable to Owner pursuant to Paragraph 4 hereof.

7. True and correct accounts shall be kept by the Publisher on a semiannual basis, and a detailed statement of such accounts shall be delivered within ninety (90) days after June 30 and December 31 of each year to the Owner at the address stated herein, including, with respect to each of the Compositions, the following information: its title, the number of printed copies sold, the nature and amount of the Publishing Income received with respect thereto, and the Owner's share thereof. Without limiting the generality of the foregoing, each statement shall account for and be accompanied by payment of all Owner's share of all Publishing Income received by Publisher's affiliated or subsidiary companies during the preceding semiannual period, whether or not such sums have been received by Publisher. All monies shown to be due thereunder shall be paid by the Publisher in United States currency (except as hereinabove provided) to Owner, together with each such statement. This shall be of the essence of the Agreement and failure to make timely payments shall entitle owner to cancel this Agreement and cause an immediate reversion of all rights assigned hereunder.

Publisher shall permit Owner, or its representatives, to inspect at the place of business of Publisher, during usual business hours, all books, records, and other documents and to make copies of excerpts therefrom, to the extent that they relate to Compositions for the purpose of verifying royalty statements rendered by Publisher or which are delinquent under the terms hereof. All costs of Owner's audit of Publisher's books or records shall be borne by Owner; provided, however, that if it shall be determined that a shortage of Five Hundred Dollars ($500.00) or more has occurred, all costs of such audit shall be paid by Publisher.

8. As a condition precedent to the grant of rights herein contained, all editions of the Compositions published in the Territory must bear appropriate copyright notice in Owner's name, and same must be printed at the bottom of the title page or first page of music of each such edition. Such edition must be in accordance with applicable copyright laws, including the Berne Convention and the Universal Copyright Convention. Any editions of the Compositions published in the Territory which do not conform to the aforesaid requirements shall be deemed to have been published without the authority of Owner. In addition, all such copies shall bear the following legend at the bottom of the title page in easily readable type: "Authorized for sale only in [appropriate country(ies) of the Territory]".

9. Owner hereby appoints Publisher its attorney-in-fact to institute in its name any suit, action, or proceeding in the Territory which Publisher shall deem necessary to enforce and protect Publisher's rights in the Compositions in the Territory, all at the expense of Publisher. In the event of any recovery, eighty-five percent (85%) of the net proceeds resulting after deduction of expenses of litigation, including attorneys' fees and court costs, shall be paid by Publisher to Owner. Provided, however, that if Publisher has not instituted suit within thirty (30) days after Owner's request therefor, Owner shall have the right, exercisable any time thereafter, to institute suit in its own name in which case one hundred percent (100%) of the recovery shall be retained by Owner.

10. Any notice required or desired to be given to either party hereunder shall be written, and shall be mailed (certified or registered mail), telegraphed or wired to either party at the following addresses:

Publisher:

Owner:

or to such other address as either party may hereafter designate in writing to the other. Notice hereunder shall be deemed given upon the deposit by either party of such written notice properly addressed, with all charges prepaid, at an official post office or at a wire, telegraph, or cable office.

11. If either party fails to perform any obligation required of it hereunder, or in the event that either party shall go into compulsory liquidation, or shall go into bankruptcy, or make an assignment for the benefit of creditors, or make any composition with creditors, or any insolvency or composition proceedings shall be commenced by or against either party and shall not be dismissed in forty-five (45) days (said party being hereinafter referred to as the "defaulting party"), then and in any of such events, the other party (hereinafter referred to as the "nondefaulting party"), in addition to such other rights or remedies which it may have at law, or otherwise, under this agreement, may elect to cancel or terminate this agreement upon giving written notice to the defaulting party, as hereinafter provided, without prejudice to any rights or claims the nondefaulting party may have. The nondefaulting party's right to terminate as hereinabove provided shall be conditioned upon the giving of written notice to the defaulting party setting forth in detail the cause of said termination and indicating the nondefaulting party's intent to so terminate. The defaulting party shall have twenty (20) days from the giving of said notice within which to cure said default before the notice of termination shall become effective.

12. No third party shall be deemed to be or is intended by the parties hereto to be a third-party beneficiary of this Agreement.

13. Each party hereto warrants and represents to the other that it has the right to enter into this Agreement and to grant the rights herein granted.

14. If either party hereto institutes any action or proceeding under or in connection with this Agreement, the prevailing party in such action shall be entitled to reasonable attorneys' fees and court costs.

15. The parties shall execute any further documents and do all acts necessary to fully effectuate the terms and provisions of this Agreement.

16. Publisher agrees to defend, indemnify, and hold Owner harmless against any and all liability, loss, damage, cost, or expense, including reasonable attorneys'

fees paid or incurred by reason of any breach or alleged breach by Publisher of any covenants, warranties, or representations hereunder.

This Agreement shall inure to the benefit of and be binding upon the parties hereto, and all of their respective successors and assigns; provided that Publisher shall not assign this Agreement to any person, firm, or corporation other than to Publisher's affiliated companies without the prior written consent of Owner. No assignment shall relieve the assignor from his obligations hereunder.

17. The term of this agreement shall commence as of the date hereof and shall continue for a period of one year. At the expiration or termination of this Agreement, all rights of any kind or nature granted to Publisher hereunder shall automatically revert to and be the sole and exclusive property of Owner without formality or execution of any documents, and Publisher shall have no further rights and shall have no right to collect any further income hereunder regardless of when said income was earned or is payable or for what periods it is payable.

18. This Agreement constitutes the entire agreement between the parties with regard to the subject matter hereof, and cannot be altered, amended, or modified, in part or in full, in any way except by an instrument in writing signed by the party sought to be bound, unless otherwise expressly provided herein.

19. This Agreement shall be governed by and construed under the laws of the State of (applicable state), United States of America, applicable to contracts executed and wholly to be performed therein. The venue for any action, suit, or proceeding brought by either party against the other, respecting this agreement shall be in the County of (applicable county), (applicable state).

20. It is expressly agreed that the Publisher shall not be entitled to deduct or withhold income or other similar tax from sums payable to Owner hereunder pursuant to the laws of the Territory unless Publisher shall furnish to Owner, with each statement, a certificate in the form of an affidavit setting forth the amount of tax which shall have been withheld, the rate of tax, and any other necessary information which shall enable Owner, upon presentation of such certificate, to obtain income tax credit from the United States Internal Revenue Service for the tax so withheld.

21. As used in this agreement, unless the context calls for a contrary interpretation, the masculine gender shall include the feminine, and the term "person" shall include any person, firm or corporation.

IN WITNESS WHEREOF, the parties hereto have caused this instrument to be duly executed the day and year first above written.

_____   _____
            (Publisher)   (Owner)

ARTIST'S GUARANTEE OF PERFORMANCE

Date:_____

XYZ RECORDS, INC.
Beverly Hills, California

Gentlemen:

Pursuant to a personal service contract between the undersigned and Artist's Recording Company (herein "Producer"), said Producer is entitled to my services for the recording of phonograph records. I have been advised that Producer is about to enter into an agreement in writing with you (herein "Agreement"), pursuant to which Producer is to make my services available to you for the purposes and upon terms and conditions as to my services which have been fully explained to me.

I understand and acknowledge that but for my entering into this Artist's Guarantee of Performance with you (herein "Guarantee") you would not enter into said Agreement with Producer, and I further understand and acknowledge that you are relying on the representations, warranties, guarantees, and agreements made by me therein in entering said Agreement with Producer. Therefore, in consideration of your executing said Agreement, and as a material inducement to you to do so, I make, in addition to the acknowledgements and representations set forth above, the following representations, warranties, guarantees, and agreements:

1. I represent and warrant that:

(a) I am over/under the age of twenty-one years, having been born on the date shown beside by signature below.

(b) Producer has the right, insofar as I am concerned, to enter into the Agreement and to assume all of the obligations, warranties, and undertakings to you on the part of Producer therein contained, and that Producer will continue to have such right until the said obligations, warranties, and undertakings have been fully performed and discharged.

(c) All of the warranties and representations on the part of Producer contained in the Agreement, concerning me, are true and correct insofar as I am concerned.

(d) I will duly and to the best of my ability perform and discharge all of the obligations and undertakings of the Agreement insofar as same are required of me and which Producer has undertaken to procure me to do and perform in the Agreement.

(e) I will continue my activities in the field of public entertainment whenever possible.

2. If during the term of the Agreement or any extension thereof, Producer shall cease to be entitled to make my services available to you in accordance with the terms of said Agreement, or fail or refuse to make my services available to you, I shall, at your request, do all such acts and things as shall give to you the same rights, privileges, and benefits as you would have had under the Agreement if Producer had continued to be entitled to my services and/or had made same available to you, and such rights, privileges and benefits shall be enforceable in your behalf against me individually.

3. I hereby consent to your having the exclusive right for phonograph-record purposes during the term thereof and nonexclusively thereafter, to use and publish and permit others to use and publish my photograph and name, including my professional name now used or later adopted, and to write and publish and to permit others to write and publish articles concerning me for advertising and trade purposes in connection with the sale and exploitation of phonograph records recorded under the Agreement and to use as descriptive of me the phrase "XYZ Artist" or any other similar or appropriate phrase in connection with any trade name or label used by you, all as provided in the Agreement, and I agree that I will not, during the term of the Agreement, or any extension or renewal thereof, perform for anyone else for the purpose of making phonograph records, nor will I, for such period of time as is provided in the Agreement, perform for the purpose of making phonograph records for anyone else other than you any musical composition or material recorded under the Agreement.

4. No termination of your Agreement with Producer shall operate to diminish my liability or obligation hereunder without your consent.

5. I hereby consent and agree that you may, in your own name, institute any action or proceeding against me to enforce your rights under the Agreement and/or pursuant to this Artist's Guarantee of Performance and/or pursuant to my recording agreement with Producer.

6. You may, at your option, at any time during the term of the Agreement or any extension thereof, guarantee payment to me in the amount of Six Thousand Dollars ($6,000.00) annually, which amount or such portion thereof as is paid, if you so elect, shall be deemed an advance against royalties and/or other compensation payable to Producer and/or to me under said Agreement.

7. Notwithstanding when this Guarantee is actually executed, it shall be deemed to have been executed concurrently with the execution of said Agreement between you and Producer.

Very truly yours,

_____

(Artist's Signature
and Birthdate)

Agreed and accepted:
XYZ RECORDS, INC.

By_____

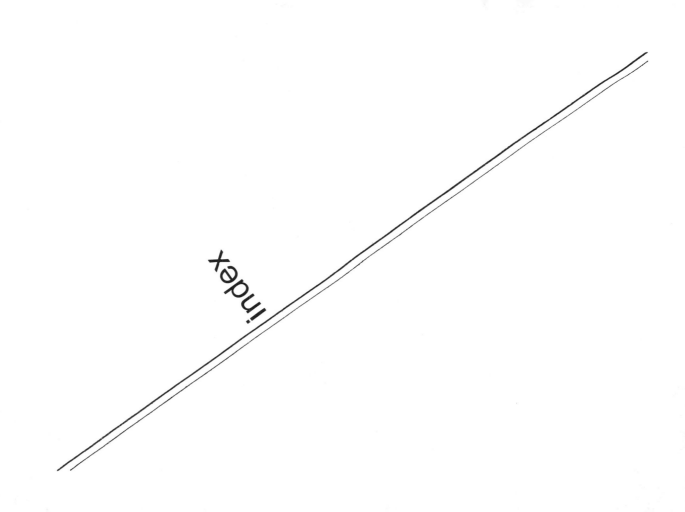